Praise for ~~Son of Man~~

Rarely in the history of theological writing and biblical exegesis has a book emerged that makes its point so clearly, yet one that is most foundational to the content of the gospel: namely, that Jesus wanted His people Israel and the nations of the world to recognize Him as "the Son of Man" as announced in Daniel 7 and repeated some 78 times in the Gospels with an added 53 associated themes that also came from Daniel 7. I was personally enriched and corrected as this title of *The Son of Man* was biblically shown to take precedence over all other titles and functions of our Lord in Scripture, such as *Messiah* or the *Son of God*. Surely, this book will offer one of the richest rewards for all who will carefully follow the truth of this title from Daniel 7 as demonstrated by Jesus. I can hardly find the adequate words to commend this book as highly as I think it should be received and shared broadly in our day and age.

Dr. Walter C. Kaiser, Jr., *President Emeritus*, Gordon-Conwell Theological Seminary, Hamilton, MA

There is absolutely nothing greater in the Christian life than when the Holy Spirit reveals Jesus Christ through the Word of God. One phrase from one verse can open up a door of revelation where all you can say is, "I've never seen this before," "This is absolutely astounding," or "This changes everything." I believe that the revelation of Jesus as T*he Son of Man* changes everything. I watched how the Holy Spirit took this phrase out of Daniel 7 and began to take Samuel on a journey into the ocean of revelation and implication surrounding this phrase. Samuel provoked me because I had never seen it before. He challenged me because the Holy Spirit was calling me to go deeper. And he taught me and gave me insight and understanding into one of the most overlooked, misunderstood, and yet absolutely critical revelations for the end-time church. In 1 Peter 1, we read that the prophets of old inquired and searched carefully of that which was coming, and I believe Samuel is in the same spirit as he has written this book. This book will become one of the central books to the church in the coming days. I cannot overemphasize our need to give ourselves to it today.

Corey Russell, Author and Speaker, Dallas, TX

Contemporary scholarship on the Synoptic Gospels asserts that the book of Daniel was very important for the first century and for the self-understanding of Yeshua and the Synoptic Gospel writers. Daniel 7 is especially emphasized. These texts give us a window into the important Son of Man idea and the Deity of Yeshua. Orthodox writer Daniel Boyarin from the University of California at Berkeley has emphasized this. Now, Samuel Whitefield has written an important book that greatly expands our understanding of Daniel 7 as an interpretive key. I consider this book a must read!

Daniel Juster, Restoration from Zion of Tikkun International

The term *Son of Man* is not new to those who attend church. What is new in this book is what it means. Beyond a passing reference to Jesus, somehow, no one clearly explained the term's meaning or its significance. Learning that of all the available titles to refer to Himself Jesus used this one, *Son of Man*, far and away beyond all others, invites you to ask, "Why?" and then "What does it mean?" You'll find the answers in this book. You will see how it reveals who Jesus is and how it has a direct impact on your life.

Rick Clough, Businessman, Atlanta, GA

For as long as I've known my friend Samuel, he's always been the guy that's looking at things from an angle that you didn't see, but then after he unpacks what he's observing, I always think to myself: *Why didn't I see that? It was sitting right in front of me!* Samuel's new book, *Son of Man: The Gospel of Daniel 7*, read exactly this way when I picked it up—a theological adventure of looking at Daniel, Jesus, and the kingdom of God. At the end of the book, all of these things were clearer and more alive in my mind and my heart than before the reading began. Be prepared to be challenged, stretched, and stirred as God's kingdom comes to light in a fresh way!

Jim Stern, *Lead Pastor*, Destiny Church of St. Louis

Samuel has a God-given grace for breaking down and giving solid, prophetic insight into complex passages. He exegetes them in a way that is biblically sound, easy to grasp, and accompanied by a clear life application for the reader. These two volumes on the Son of Man are very clear representations of that grace. Expect Jesus to challenge, enlarge, and provoke your heart as you see Him in the Gospels and Epistles through the lens of Daniel 7 as you never have before!

Chris Rue, *Senior Pastor*, Word of Life Christian Center, Newark, DE

SON OF MAN
THE GOSPEL OF DANIEL 7

VOLUME 1

SAMUEL WHITEFIELD

Son of Man: The Gospel of Daniel 7, Volume 1
By Samuel Whitefield

Published by OneKing Publishing
PO Box 375
Grandview, MO 64030

Email: contact@oneking.global
Web: https://oneking.global

Copyright © 2019 by OneKing, Inc.
All rights reserved.
ISBN: 978-1-7323380-4-3
eBook ISBN: 978-1-7323380-5-0

This book and the companion volume are dedicated to the man we refer to as the prophet Daniel. The life he lived and the revelation given to him produced an astounding revelation of Jesus and His people.

I pray his life provokes us to live the way he did and the Lord would respond by giving us revelation about the beauty of His Son as He did for Daniel.

May this book provoke you to treasure Daniel's book the way Jesus does.

CONTENTS

FOREWORD

In August 2018, shortly after Singapore's National Day (Day of Independence), we felt a stirring to call for a twenty-one-day fast as a community. It was the fortieth year since the late Billy Graham's Evangelistic stadium crusades were held in Singapore in 1978. That year, our 55,000-seat stadium was packed out for four full days with believers and non-believers. Twenty thousand salvations were recorded in a span of four days. The gospel came to Singapore in a remarkable way. It was a milestone for our nation and played a role in shaping the Singapore we know today.

As we reflected on what God had done in 1978, there was a burning desire to see God move again. Like many others, I long to see the church in Singapore become an "Antioch" like the church in the New Testament that sent the apostle Paul and played a pivotal role in the gospel advancing into the nations of the earth. With this burden, I felt the need to call for a fast to seek the Lord for greater understanding of what it meant to become an Antioch-type church.

I focused on Revelation 4 during my time in our prayer room, and I began to see everything through the lens of the beauty of Jesus and the knowledge of God. I realized that, whenever God gives us revelation, it acts as an invitation for us to draw near to Him to seek understanding, and it opens our eyes to pursue the knowledge of God above anything else. It was then the Lord reminded me of a message I had heard strongly encouraging us to go deep in two books, and Daniel was one of them.

The Lord gave Daniel a series of dreams about Israel's destiny, but he did not fully understand, so Daniel responded to the Lord by consecrating himself and fasting for twenty-one days. In that spirit, we called for the 21-Day Fast as a community to contend for understanding like

Daniel did. For twenty-one days, we met daily and intentionally gave ourselves to prayer as we read and discussed Daniel 7–12. I invited Samuel Whitefield to join us for this fast and to teach the book of Daniel through a weekly Skype call. He agreed. Samuel faithfully joined us, shared his thoughts, and we discussed Daniel together. Those times were like gold.

Needless to say, we had taken a risk to dig into this particular section of Scripture because of the nature of its content, but the Lord surprised us by giving us profound clarity and courage. As we read Daniel's visions about the craziness and chaos of the end of the age, we found ourselves caught up in the revelation and vision of the Son of Man in Daniel 7. That particular vision became our anchor and hope, producing in us an unusual sense of comfort, confidence, and courage.

We found ourselves looking at the "gospel of the kingdom" that Jesus talked about through a new lens because of the vision Daniel had of the Son of Man. Our understanding of the gospel radically shifted when we realized the revelation of the Son of Man could be found everywhere in the New Testament. We discovered it was the lens that the first-century church used when they looked at the gospel.

If the church is to send anointed messengers to proclaim the gospel of the kingdom to all the nations, I believe we need to reinstate the understanding of the gospel that Jesus and the apostles preached.

What you are about to read in these pages will revolutionize your understanding of the gospel of the kingdom. I have personally witnessed the process and the formation of this book. I know Samuel did not write these words through mere academic research and studies, but it was birthed from a place of prayer and fasting for months. He has given himself to this.

I believe God is inviting you to be a person of understanding likened to Daniel. The fact that you are picking up this book reveals the desire you carry to understand what the gospel of the kingdom is. We live in a day and age where the word *gospel* is understood in many ways, but I believe God is raising up a people who will truly understand His redemptive plan for humanity so that we will proclaim the gospel of this kingdom boldly, full of confidence and clarity.

I pray that the Father of Glory will open your eyes to see the beautiful Son of Man. May He fill you with the knowledge of His will in all spiritual wisdom and understanding.

Jason Chua, *Founder*, Burning Hearts, Singapore

INTRODUCTION

Do we know the gospel the way Jesus taught it?

Over the last centuries, the church has faithfully proclaimed who Jesus is, and a great number of people have come into the kingdom as a result. In many cases, we have right conclusions about who Jesus is, but what if I told you that the church as a whole does not fully grasp how Jesus revealed Himself in the Gospels. The fact is we have faithfully declared what we know, but we have missed the way Jesus chose to reveal Himself and present His gospel.

What you are about to read is going to surprise you. You are going to find Jesus chose to unlock the mystery of who He was through one biblical passage more than any other: *Daniel 7*. He used it to declare His identity, His Father, His saints, His kingdom, His suffering, and His judgment.

When you grasp how Jesus used Daniel 7, it changes the way you read the Gospels, and most importantly, it presents Jesus' beauty in a fresh new way. Expect to be stunned. Expect to cry. Expect to worship. You are going to discover Jesus is everything He claimed to be, but we have missed the way He chose to reveal who He is.

You are about to discover a single Old Testament chapter can completely change the way you read the Gospels and speak about Jesus. Furthermore, that one chapter—Daniel 7—provides the biblical framework for the gospel of the kingdom.

If you had told me a year ago Jesus referenced Daniel 7 more than any other passage, I would not have believed it, but it is true. As a result of a year-long study, I will never read the Gospels the same way again, and I pray you have a similar experience.

My journey began when I was asked to join some friends on a twenty-one-day fast, studying the book of Daniel. I knew I would enjoy the focused time in Daniel with good friends, so I joined. I did not anticipate that twenty-one days would radically change the way I read the Gospels. Nor did I know the new facets of Jesus' beauty I would discover in one small chapter. I certainly never expected to discover Daniel 7 is the key to the gospel of the kingdom.

While most people study Daniel to understand the book of Revelation, our study of Daniel led us into the Gospels and the preaching of the apostles. Most of us had seen Daniel as a book mainly about end-time events, but we suddenly saw Daniel 7 is a gospel-centered chapter that reveals the majesty of Jesus and the glory of the gospel message.

What Is the Gospel?

Jesus commissioned the church to carry the "gospel of the kingdom" to all peoples before the end would come:

> *And this gospel of the kingdom will be proclaimed throughout the whole world as a testimony to all nations, and then the end will come. (Matthew 24:14)*

> *This raises a profound question: What is the gospel of the kingdom?*

Even if we are familiar with this verse, we may still struggle to clearly articulate what the gospel of the kingdom is. If we do not know the message we claim to believe, how can we carry it to the nations with confidence? Understanding the gospel of the kingdom is not optional: It is good news, it is our hope, and it is our message to the world.

The fact most Christians cannot clearly articulate the gospel reveals a crisis: We do not know the basis of our hope. The answer to this crisis is fairly simple: We need to recover the way Jesus presented Himself and His gospel. This book will give you complete confidence Jesus is everything He said He was as you discover the answer to many of the debates about Jesus and His kingdom is found in Daniel.

The book of Daniel is an incredible gift to us, and Jesus used it over seventy-eight times to make a stunning statement: "*I am the divine Human, and I will dethrone the beasts and exalt a people to rule with Me.*"

The Gospel Jesus Preached

Jesus did not present Himself the way you probably think He did.

The identity of Jesus is central to the gospel because everything revolves around Him. Matthew, Mark, Luke, and John carefully recorded the words of Jesus. In these words, we find how He consistently presented Himself in a very specific way. We have assumptions about the way Jesus presented Himself, but as we will see, many of our assumptions are wrong.

For example, most people believe Jesus presented Himself as Messiah. Although Jesus confirmed He was Messiah, He did not typically present Himself that way. Jesus never publicly claimed to be Messiah and told the disciples not to spread that message before His resurrection. Nor was He condemned to death for the claim of being Messiah. *We must understand why.* The fact we do not know how Jesus preached the gospel should trouble us and cause us to rediscover the meaning and power of Jesus' words.

As we study Jesus' own words, we will find He referenced Daniel 7 more than any other passage. He used it like a key to unlock the rest of the prophets. He used it to present His divine identity and to support every one of His main teaching themes.

Based on Jesus' words, Daniel 7 is the premier summary of Jesus' majesty.

This one relatively short Old Testament passage is the most concise summary of the gospel of the kingdom in the Bible, and it contains the key to making sense of Jesus' presentation of the gospel. If we do not learn how Jesus used Daniel 7 to preach the gospel, we cannot fully understand His gospel.

Jesus did not quote many of the best known Old Testament prophecies, but He consistently used one passage—Daniel 7—to define His identity, His Father, His kingdom, His suffering, His people, and His return.

While the gospel of the kingdom may be a little mysterious to many, in reality it is relatively simple when we begin to see how Jesus proclaimed it. This is especially critical for the church's witness to Israel. The gentile church has good intentions but often presents Jesus in a way that seems very foreign to a Jewish audience. We tend to present Jesus as Messiah, but that was not the way He spoke to Israel. Jesus came to Israel in His first coming,[1] and His words teach us how He wants to be presented to Israel.

---

[1]Matthew 15:24.

The Gospel the Apostles Preached

We have more information about the Bible than any generation in history, and yet the vast majority of believers cannot understand or communicate the gospel from the Old Testament.

Preaching the gospel from the New Testament is certainly not bad, and the New Testament did add significant revelation. However, the early church was able to present the beauty of Jesus and the glory of the gospel using Old Testament passages, and we are unable to do the same.

While the gospel can certainly be known from the New Testament, our inability to read and preach the Old Testament the way the early church did means we are missing something. They saw something in these books that we have passed by, and we desperately need to recover it.

Jesus' use of Daniel exposes a key issue: We need to learn how to preach the gospel from the Old Testament.

The Journey Begins Here

What you are about to discover will radically *simplify* many things. As you watch Jesus use Daniel 7 time and again to communicate His message, Jesus' teaching will make much more sense and take on new significance and meaning. You will find the gospel of the kingdom is very straightforward, and you will learn to share it with confidence and clarity.

Please don't let the size of this book intimidate you. You are about to find the gospel is both simple and majestic. We will begin by laying some foundations regarding the way Jesus read the book of Daniel. Then, we will reexamine Jesus' teaching in light of those foundations. Finally, we will see how Jesus presented the gospel through the lens of Daniel 7. In the process, you will discover the beauty of Jesus in a fresh way and learn how He wants us to speak about Him.

This book is the first of two volumes. In this volume, we focus exclusively on how Jesus used Daniel 7 to reveal Himself and present the gospel. The second volume, *Son of Man: The Apostles' Gospel*, examines the preaching of the apostles. Like Jesus, they also used Daniel 7 as a framework for their gospel, and I would encourage you to read the second volume as well. You will discover how the apostles presented the gospel of the kingdom, and it will sharpen your own understanding and sharing of the gospel.

This book is divided into sections, and as we go through each section, it will be similar to bringing a picture into focus. When a camera is out of focus, you can still see the image, but you cannot see the details. When you focus in, you begin to see the image more clearly, and you see things you did not see before. This is what we are about to do with the gospel. Daniel 7 is a lens that is going to bring things into focus. As we move through each section, expect to see things you have not seen as the glorious picture of the gospel becomes more complete.

Before we get going, here is our roadmap—a brief description of what will be addressed in each section:

- *Rediscovering Jesus' Gospel*—We need to rediscover Jesus' gospel. Jesus was not mysterious and did not hide His identity. However, most of us do not understand how He revealed Himself and why He chose to do it the way He did.

- *The Gospel of the Kingdom Introduced*—We will learn to read Daniel 7 as a summary of the gospel of the kingdom to understand why Jesus referenced it so much. We will discover Daniel was not simply given an end-time vision. He was given the most concise and complete summary of the gospel of the kingdom in the Bible.

- *Daniel's Greatest Expositor*—After discovering how much Daniel was shown in Daniel 7, we will turn to Jesus' own words. We will make the surprising discovery that Jesus used Daniel 7 far more than any other chapter. Once we see how He used Daniel, we will notice a new depth in His teaching, and we will see many of the debates about who Jesus was are easily answered by Jesus' use of Daniel.

- *The Son of Man, His Father, and His People*—We will discover Jesus used Daniel's vision to establish His relationship to His Father in the heavens. Then, we will see how Jesus used Daniel to describe His relationship to His people and their future with Him.

- *The Son of Man's Kingdom*—Jesus used Daniel 7 to describe the nature of His kingdom and how He will become King. We will learn how to use Daniel 7 to understand the kingdom the way Daniel presented it.

- *The Son of Man's Judgment*—Judgment is far more central to the biblical story of redemption than most people recognize. Daniel 7 introduces Jesus in a judgment scene, and we will discover why salvation is incomplete without judgment and why the Bible predicts salvation will come through judgment.

- *The Son of Man's Suffering*—We will find Daniel 7 was the main passage referenced in Jesus' prediction of His death and in the accounts of His betrayal, arrest, trial, and execution. We will consider why Jesus pointed to Daniel 7 in each situation instead of referencing better known passages.

- *The Son of Man's Exaltation*—We will discover Jesus' ascension in Acts 1 was a Daniel 7 event and a dramatic demonstration of everything Jesus had taught. Moreover, it demonstrated Jesus will fulfill everything predicted by Daniel.

- *The Gospel of Daniel 7*—We will summarize each aspect of Jesus' gospel and make the surprising discovery that the Gospels in the New Testament rise and fall on Daniel 7.

- *"Who Do You Say that I Am?"*—In the final section, we will examine how Jesus summarized the gospel of the kingdom. We will identify the key themes and see how Jesus used Daniel 7 to present those themes. We will finish by clearly laying out the message Jesus commissioned us to carry to all nations.

Now, let's rediscover the gospel the way Jesus presented it.[2]

---

[2] For readers new to the subject of Daniel, I must note not all scholars hold to the conviction that Daniel is an inspired and authentic book. Therefore, references to other works in this book are not necessarily recommendations of the work being referenced. It is possible for scholars to do helpful and valuable work yet teach incorrect conclusions.

"Who is this 'Son of Man'?" (John 12:34)

Rediscovering Jesus' Gospel

MISREADING JESUS

Jesus told the disciples more than once *not* to tell people who He was.[1] It is one of the oddest things in the New Testament. The men whom Jesus chose to be His close companions, the leaders of the movement, and "fishers of men" could not be trusted to tell people who He was for over three years.

Why would Jesus say something so strange?

Jesus did not want His disciples to speak about Him because they could not yet be trusted to accurately spread the message of who He truly was. The disciples had good intentions, and Jesus sincerely loved them, but because they did not grasp who Jesus was, He asked them not to speak about Him until they understood His message.

If Jesus said this to the disciples, would He say the same thing to us?

Perhaps He would, but the good news is that this was not Jesus' final word to the disciples. Jesus labored with them until they understood the gospel. Then, He commissioned them and anointed them with power to boldly and publicly proclaim it. He will do the same thing for us.

In the pages ahead, we will discover Jesus referenced one Old Testament chapter far more than any other passage. He overwhelmingly used this one chapter to define His identity, and that same chapter served as a primary basis for the main themes of His teaching.

That chapter is Daniel 7.

Missing the Message

The New Testament Gospels, as they are written, depend on Daniel 7.

---

[1]Matthew 16:20; 17:9; Mark 8:30; 9:9; Luke 9:21.

The gospel message does not depend on Daniel, but the record of Jesus' teaching we have *does* depend on Daniel 7. It was the primary Old Testament source Jesus used to define Himself and undergird His teaching. While it is certainly possible to grasp the main conclusions of Jesus' message without understanding His use of the Old Testament, without this understanding we miss a tremendous amount of Jesus' message.

Jesus was a Jewish teacher, and Jewish teachers in the first century used the Old Testament profusely. They expected their audience to be familiar with the passages they referenced. When a teacher referenced a few words from an Old Testament passage, they expected their audience to understand the passage the words came from and use that passage to interpret their message.

When we miss Jesus' use of the Old Testament, we may understand the main points of His conclusion, but we miss a substantial part of His message. Because we have the benefit of the New Testament, we can have the correct conclusions about who Jesus is yet not truly grasp how He revealed Himself. The result is we get the main conclusion right but do not understand His full message. This in turn affects our understanding of who Jesus is, our grasp of the biblical story, and our ability to clearly communicate the gospel. In short, we can be like the apostles.

The church has been given the awesome and holy task of communicating the identity of Jesus to the earth. To fulfill this assignment, we need to carefully study how He presented Himself.

The Myth of Jesus' Secret Identity

We tend to assume Jesus hid His identity through vague and mysterious language. We usually assume Jesus did this to preserve His life until the time for His crucifixion. We also assume Jesus radically redefined many things the prophets had said, particularly their predictions about the Messiah.

These ideas typically come from a lack of familiarity with the Old Testament and the way Jesus used it. As we will see, Jesus revealed a hidden mystery, but He did not hide His identity. He was very clear and very bold about who He was:

Jesus answered him, "I have spoken openly to the world. I have always taught in synagogues and in the temple.... I have said nothing in secret." (John 18:20)

If you study Jesus' words carefully, Jesus did not present Himself publicly as Messiah in His first coming (though He did not deny it either). Instead, He associated His messianic function with His second coming. Some have noticed this and called it the *Messianic Secret* in order to propose Jesus did not want to reveal His full identity. However, we will see Jesus was not trying to keep a secret—He was trying to avoid confusion.

Jesus did not try to hide His identity nor try to preserve His life. He died for the same message He repeatedly, publicly gave throughout His ministry. Jesus faced controversy because of the *implications* of His message, not because people did not understand His message.

Jesus' audience was occasionally confused by His statements, and it is true He used parables to communicate certain truths in a way that was not always immediately obvious. There certainly were some statements hidden from the broader audience, but Jesus did not hide His identity. When Jesus' descriptions of Himself are put in a biblical context, we find He was much more direct than most of us realize, and not nearly as mysterious or secretive as most people assume.

Many who heard Jesus were shocked at His claims, some refused to believe, and others found Jesus' claims impossible to believe. But Jesus' audience understood what He was saying.

Rediscovering Jesus' Gospel

Jesus' identity is at the heart of the gospel, and therefore, we must learn how Jesus presented Himself.

The earth is filled with confusion about the identity of Jesus. The Gospels carefully recorded the teaching of Jesus so we could be confident in His identity. Those teachings were filled with references to the Old Testament, and if we do not understand how those references were used, we will not recognize what the Gospels are trying to tell us.

In the chapters ahead, we are going to learn how Jesus presented Himself and His message. In the process, we will find a major foundation of Jesus' gospel has been almost entirely overlooked by the vast majority of Christians. As we rediscover that foundation, it will make Jesus' presentation of Himself much easier to understand and enable us to proclaim His identity with greater *clarity*. As we grow in clarity, let's also ask God to anoint the message we speak with greater *power*.

JESUS' FAVORITE TITLE

We typically assume Jesus generally identified Himself as Messiah (Christ) or Son of God, but this is not true. *Son of Man was the primary title Jesus used to describe who He was.*

He used it:

- 28 times in the book of Matthew[1]
- 13 times in the book of Mark[2]
- 25 times in the book of Luke[3]
- 12 times in the book of John[4]

Son of Man is the title Jesus used most in all four Gospels. Jesus' use of *Son of Man* becomes even more significant when it is compared to other titles frequently associated with Jesus.

The title *Christ* (the Greek equivalent of *Messiah*) is used 49 times in the Gospels to refer to Jesus, and only 11 of those times was it used by Jesus to refer to Himself.[5]

---

[1]Matthew 8:20; 9:6; 10:23; 11:19; 12:8, 32, 40; 13:37, 41; 16:13, 27, 28; 17:9, 12, 22; 19:28; 20:18, 28; 24:27, 30, 37, 39, 44; 25:31; 26:2, 24, 45, 64. Matthew likely contains the most references because it was written more for a Jewish audience deeply acquainted with Daniel 7.

[2]Mark 2:10, 28; 8:31, 38; 9:9, 12, 31; 10:33, 45; 13:26; 14:21, 41, 62.

[3]Luke 5:24; 6:5, 22; 7:34; 9:22, 26, 44, 58; 11:30; 12:8, 10, 40; 17:22, 24, 26, 30; 18:8, 31; 19:10; 21:27, 36; 22:22, 48, 69; 24:7.

[4]John 1:51; 3:13, 14; 5:27; 6:27, 53, 62; 8:28; 9:35; 12:23, 34; 13:31.

[5]Matthew 1:1, 16, 17, 18; 2:4; 11:2; 16:16, 20; 22:42; 23:10; 24:5; 26:63, 68; 27:17, 22; Mark 1:1; 8:29; 9:41; 12:35; 14:61; 15:32; Luke 2:11, 26; 3:15; 4:41; 9:20; 20:41; 22:67; 23:2, 35, 39; 24:26, 46; John 1:17, 25, 41; 4:25, 29; 7:26, 27, 31, 41, 42; 9:22; 10:24;11:27; 12:34; 17:3; 20:31.

The title *Son of God* is used 25 times in the Gospels, and only 5 of those times was it used by Jesus to refer to Himself.[6]

The title *Son of David* is used 14 times in the Gospels, and only 1 of those times was it used by Jesus to refer to Himself.[7] Furthermore, though *Son of David* was a key messianic phrase, John did not use the term at all in his Gospel.

If we arrange these four titles by the number of times they are used in the Gospels, the most frequently used title is evident:

- Son of Man—78
- Christ—49
- Son of God—25
- Son of David—14

If we arrange these four titles according to the number of times Jesus used each one to speak of Himself, there is no question what His favorite title was:

- Son of Man—78
- Christ—11
- Son of God—5
- Son of David—1

Son of Man was Jesus' favorite title by far—no other title comes close. Moreover, every time Son of Man was used to describe Jesus— all 78 times—it was used by Jesus.[8] As we will see, Jesus used this title in an intentional way, and His audience understood it was a reference to Daniel 7. *This means Jesus referenced Daniel 7 more than any other Old Testament passage.*

------

[6]Matthew 4:3, 6; 8:29; 14:33; 26:63; 27:40, 43, 54; Mark 1:1; 3:11; 15:39; Luke 1:35; 4:3, 9, 41; 22:70; John 1:34, 49; 3:18; 5:25; 10:36; 11:4, 27; 19:7; 20:31. There are also four instances of similar titles being used to refer to Jesus. See Matthew 16:16; Mark 5:7; Luke 1:32; 8:28.

[7]Matthew 1:1; 9:27; 12:23; 15:22; 20:30, 31; 21:9, 15; 22:42; Mark 10:47, 48; 12:35; Luke 18:38, 39.

[8]Mark 8:31 is the only reference that is not a direct quote from Jesus, but the verse describes Mark's summary of Jesus' teaching, so it is a summary of Jesus' using the title about Himself. This count only includes Jesus' use of the exact phrase Son of Man. It does not count any allusions Jesus made to His Son of Man identity without explicitly using the phrase.

Jesus the Son of God

We tend to assume *Son of God* was one of Jesus' favorite titles, but Jesus did not use the title frequently, nor did He use it exclusively to refer to Himself. For example, Jesus used the phrase *sons of God* both of Himself and of others:

> *"Blessed are the peacemakers, for they shall be called sons of God." (Matthew 5:9)*

> *And Jesus said to them, "The sons of this age marry and are given in marriage, but those who are considered worthy to attain to that age and to the resurrection from the dead neither marry nor are given in marriage, for they cannot die anymore, because they are equal to angels and are sons of God, being sons of the resurrection." (Luke 20:34–36)*

> *Jesus answered them, "Is it not written in your Law, 'I said, you are gods'? If he called them gods to whom the word of God came—and Scripture cannot be broken—do you say of him whom the Father consecrated and sent into the world, 'You are blaspheming,' because I said, 'I am the Son of God'?" (John 10:34–36)*

In another example, when Nathanael referred to Jesus as the Son of God, the King of Israel, he was identifying Jesus as Messiah. Notice Jesus' response:

> *Nathanael answered him, "Rabbi, you are the Son of God! You are the King of Israel!" Jesus answered him, "...You will see greater things than these.... you will see heaven opened, and the angels of God ascending and descending on the Son of Man." (John 1:49–51)*

Nathanael referred to Jesus as Son of God, but Jesus corrected Nathanael and referred to Himself as the Son of Man. As we will see, *Son of Man* was a superior title, and the reference to heaven and the angels was a reference to Daniel 7 and Genesis 28.

The Gospels *do* use the title *Son of God* to refer to Jesus in a unique way,[9] but the phrase is not as prominent as most people think because the meaning of the title is determined by the context. It *can* be applied to Jesus in a unique way, but in a different context, it can also be used

---

[9]For example, see John 20:31.

to refer to someone other than Jesus.[10] Some critics have claimed this is evidence Jesus did not see Himself as the unique Son of God, but as we will see, the opposite is true.

Son of God was a title applied to Jesus, but it was not exclusive enough to be His main title.

Jesus the Messiah

The title we typically associate with Jesus is *Christ* which is the Greek equivalent of *Messiah.* This is a significant title, and it was frequently applied to Jesus in the Gospels, but surprisingly, Jesus only used it occasionally to refer to Himself.

Messiah basically means *anointed one,* and it was originally used to describe someone anointed by God to fulfill His purposes. It was initially used to refer to the priests who were anointed to do their duty.[11] A form of the word was used when God had a king anointed for His purposes.[12] The word was applied to David because He was God's anointed.[13] The pagan king Cyrus was even referred to as God's messiah because God anointed him to carry out a specific task.[14]

The prophets predicted a coming Messiah would be a descendant from David, would deliver Israel, and would fulfill God's promises to Israel and the nations. There were hints in the prophecies that this Messiah would be something more than a human king, but most people expected a man who would be a greater version of David.

Jesus acknowledged He was the Messiah but avoided using it as His main title. Most Christians assume Jesus nearly always presented Himself as Messiah, but He did not. On the contrary, He tended to avoid the title *Messiah,* and never used it publicly. *We need to understand why.*

---

[10]For an example in the Old Testament, see Genesis 6:2, 4; Deuteronomy 32:8; Job 1:6; 2:1; 38:7.

[11]Leviticus 4:3, 5, 16.

[12]1 Kings 19:15–16.

[13]2 Samuel 23:1.

[14]Isaiah 45:1.

THE UNDENIABLE LINK TO DANIEL

Jesus obviously preferred the title Son of Man over Messiah, but can we be sure this was a link to Daniel?

In the subsequent chapters, we will find Jesus used Daniel 7 for far more than the title *Son of Man*. To begin, though, we need to establish the fact that Son of Man was a link to Daniel.

Over the centuries, many Christians have come to believe Jesus called Himself *Son of Man* to describe His humanity, but this is simply not true. Jesus never used the title to defend His humanity; instead, He used the title to back up nearly every controversial statement He made about His identity and authority.

Some have taught Jesus was *the Son of Man* because He was the ultimate Human—the "model" Human. Jesus was the perfect man, and the perfection of His humanity did flow from the fact that He was the Son of Man. However, *Son of Man* was a declaration of deity, not humanity, and Jesus' deity is what enabled Him to be the perfect example of humanity.

Jesus expected His audience to connect His claim of being the Son of Man to the book of Daniel, and the Gospels demonstrate His audience understood He was claiming to be the One whom Daniel saw. For example, when Jesus was on trial and identified Himself as the Son of Man, the high priest accused Jesus of blasphemy because he understood Jesus was claiming to be the divine Son of Man whom Daniel had described.[1]

Before we move on, we need to consider briefly a number of reasons we can be confident every time Jesus referred to Himself as the

---

[1]Matthew 26:64; Mark 14:63–64.

Son of Man He was referring to the same *son of man* described in Daniel 7:13—

> *"I saw in the night visions, and behold, with the clouds of heaven there came one like a son of man, and he came to the Ancient of Days and was presented before him."*

When we move into the Gospels, we will find even more reasons why the link to Daniel is undeniable.

The Link to Daniel

The phrase *son of man* can be translated as *human* because that is the essential meaning of the phrase. However, Jesus turned the phrase into a title, so if we read the phrase only as the word *human*, we miss a significant part of Jesus' message. The Gospels clearly indicate Jesus used the title to communicate His uniqueness. Let's consider a few reasons.

Jesus' great challenge was revealing His divinity, not proving His humanity. His humanity was never challenged; in fact, the opposite was true. He was so human that people had difficulty believing He was God.[2] The nature of Jesus' humanity only became a question centuries later when the church became predominantly gentile and had to deal with various heresies.

Jesus used the phrase as a title. Jesus called Himself *the Son of Man* (or we could say *the human*). He was not *a son of man*. He was *the* unique *Son of Man*. While *son of man* was an ancient phrase, it was not used as a title, and Jesus' use of *Son of Man* was unusual.[3]

The use of Son of Man is very unique in the Gospels. Jesus was the only person referred to as *Son of Man* in the Gospels. He was also the only person who called Himself *the Son of Man*, and He did it at least 78 times as we've discovered. When other people referred to Jesus, they

---

[2]Matthew 13:46, 55–58; Mark 6:4–5; Luke 4:22–24; John 12:34.

[3]Because Jesus likely taught in Aramaic, scholars have questioned whether Jesus used a definite or indefinite article and if it was significant. However, the Greek version of Jesus' teaching in the Gospels always included the definite article to make it apparent Jesus used *Son of Man* as a specific title that applied only to Himself.

called him *a man*—not *a Son of Man*—over 50 times in the Gospels.[4] Furthermore, Jesus used *man* to refer to Himself as a man in John,[5] revealing Jesus did not use *Son of Man* to reference His humanity. The Gospel authors made a clear distinction between Son of Man and generic references to humanity. They did not use *Son of Man* and *man* or *human* interchangeably. They expected us to read *Son of Man* as a unique title and not a generic reference to humanity.

Son of Man was an unusual title, but Jesus never had to explain it. Jesus' audiences and His opponents understood *Son of Man* was a title, and it made sense to them. No one ever challenged Jesus to explain what He meant by the title or where it came from.

No one else dared to claim the title Son of Man. Others claimed the title *messiah,* and gentile rulers claimed to be *sons of god,* but no one else claimed *Son of Man.* It was unique.

Jesus repeatedly used Son of Man as the justification for His exalted status. As we will see in the Gospels, Jesus consistently used *Son of Man* to justify His exalted status, establish the authority of His teaching, and present Himself as divine. He also used His identity as Son of Man as the basis for His central teaching themes.

Jesus lived in Galilee, a religious area familiar with the Scriptures. The Jewish Galileans whom Jesus lived among were religious and knew the Bible well enough to recognize Jesus was referring to the book of Daniel. Again, this is demonstrated in the fact that Jesus used the title to make bold claims and did not have to explain it.

Jesus was accused of blasphemy for claiming to be the Son of Man. Three of the four times Jesus was accused of blasphemy were directly related to His claim to be the Son of Man,[6] and a case can be made the fourth instance was also a reference to the Son of Man as we will see in a future chapter.[7]

---

[4]Matthew 9:3; 12:24; 13:54, 56; 26:48, 61, 72, 74; 27:19, 24, 47; Mark 2:7; 6:2; 14:44, 71; Mark 15:12; Luke 7:39; 15:2; 23:2, 4; 23:6, 14, 18, 41, 47; John 1:30; 4:29; 5:11–12; 6:52; 7:15, 25, 27, 31, 35; 9:16, 24, 29, 33; 10:41; 11:37, 50; 18:14, 17, 29–30, 40; 19:5, 12, 21. Jesus was questioned one time, "Who is this Son of Man?" but it was a response to Jesus' teaching. The people did not address Jesus that way (John 12:34).

[5]John 8:40.

[6]Matthew 26:64–65; Mark 14:62–64; Luke 5:21–24.

[7]John 10:24–25, 33.

Jesus' claim to be the Son of Man was the final claim that led to His execution.[8] Jesus did not die for claiming to be human, He did not die for claiming to be Messiah, and He did not die for claiming to be a prophet. Jesus was asked if He was the Messiah and the Son of God, but He answered He was the Son of Man. That answer provoked the high priest to accuse Jesus of blasphemy and demand His death, demonstrating Jesus' opponents knew what He meant when He called Himself the Son of Man.

Jesus was betrayed as the Son of Man. Jesus asked Judas at the time of Jesus' arrest, "Judas, would you betray the Son of Man with a kiss?" (Luke 22:48).

The first Christian martyr died for claiming Jesus was the Son of Man. Stephen was executed when he declared Jesus as the Son of Man in the heavens.[9]

Jesus usually combined Son of Man with other themes from Daniel 7. This indicated He expected His audience to connect Son of Man with Daniel. For example, in the 78 verses where Jesus referred to Himself as Son of Man, He directly referenced other themes from Daniel in 53 of those verses and made allusions to themes in Daniel in another 7 verses. This means 60 out of 78 references to *Son of Man* also include other elements from Daniel. (See "Appendix 1—Son of Man Combined with Daniel Themes in the Gospels" for more details.)

Additionally, we will see that Jesus likely was alluding to Daniel's prediction of suffering when He predicted He must suffer as the Son of Man. (This may seem surprising, but we will examine it in depth when we consider Jesus' use of Daniel.) If we consider suffering as a Daniel theme, it leaves only 6 references to Son of Man in the Gospels that do not also include another reference to a theme from Daniel 7.

Finally, referencing a phrase or excerpt from a passage to make a connection to that passage was a common teaching technique used by Jewish teachers during Jesus' time. When they used a key phrase, their audience understood they were expounding on the larger passage from which the phrase or quotation was pulled. This teaching technique is found throughout the New Testament, but unfortunately our lack of familiarity with the Old Testament often causes us to miss many intentional references to the Old

---

[8]Matthew 26:63–65; Mark 14:61–64.

[9]Acts 7:56.

Testament. And *Son of Man* is a critical Old Testament reference many readers miss.[10]

While there has been considerable debate over the title *Son of Man*, we will find Jesus intentionally referenced Daniel, His audience knew He was referencing Daniel, and the Gospels were written so we could recognize Jesus' use of Daniel.

The Uniqueness of the Phrase *Son of Man*

To grasp how unique the phrase *Son of Man* is, we must also consider it in light of the original languages of the Bible. There is much that has been said about this, but we can summarize a few main points for our purposes.

Nearly the entire Old Testament was written in Hebrew, but Daniel 2:4 through Daniel 7:28 is one of the exceptions because this section was written in Aramaic. While there are other phrases in the Bible which can be translated *son of man* in English, Daniel 7:13 contains the only time in the Bible *son of man* was written in Aramaic (בר אנש, *bar enasha*). Every other instance of *son of man* in the Old Testament was written in Hebrew (בן אדם, *ben adam*).

While Hebrew and Aramaic are related languages, the words are different, which means *son of man* in Daniel 7:13 is completely unique. No other verse in the Bible contains *bar enasha*. This is even true in the book of Daniel. In an English translation, we find *son of man* in Daniel 7:13 and Daniel 8:17, but because Daniel 7 was written in Aramaic and Daniel 8 was written in Hebrew, it is not the same. Daniel 7 contains *bar enasha* and Daniel 8 *ben adam*. The difference in meaning is also obvious when you read the chapters in English. In Daniel 7, *son of man* is used to describe a divine figure in the heavens, and in Daniel 8, *son of man* is used to address Daniel. They are obviously not the same person.

This may seem to be a small detail, but it is very significant. Jesus was multilingual, but most of His public teaching was probably done in Aramaic. Therefore, when He referred to Himself as the *Son of Man*, He likely spoke the Aramaic phrase (*bar enasha*) found only in Daniel 7 rather than the Hebrew phrase (*ben adam*) found in a few other pas-

---

[10]While many Christians have not been taught the connection to Daniel, scholars have recognized the connection to Daniel for some time and have written quite a bit about Jesus' use of *Son of Man* as a deliberate and intentional reference to Daniel.

sages. Again, Daniel 7 contains the only *bar enasha* phrase in the Old Testament.

With this in mind, we need to briefly consider the way Jesus' words are recorded for us in the Gospels. Once again, Jesus taught in Aramaic, but the Gospels were written in Greek.[11] What we want to notice is the way Jesus' words were translated into Greek emphasized the link between Son of Man and Daniel.

During Jesus' time, *son of man* was used in Aramaic to indicate *human*, which is the way Daniel also used the phrase:

> *"I saw in the night visions, and behold, with the clouds of heaven there came one like a son of man, and he came to the Ancient of Days and was presented before him." (v. 13)*

His description of Jesus could literally be translated as, "I saw one who looked human coming with the clouds in the heavens." While *son of man* meant *human* in Aramaic, *son of man* was not used in Greek. In Greek, you would simply say *man* (ἄνθρωπος, *anthrōpos*). Therefore, if Jesus had used the phrase *Son of Man* to mean *human,* the authors of the Gospels could have translated His words directly to *anthrōpos,* but they did not.

When the Gospel authors recorded Jesus' claim to be *the Son of Man* (ὁ υἱὸς τοῦ ἀνθρώπου, *ho huios ho anthrōpos*), they wrote Jesus' Aramaic literally in the Greek rather than translating what Jesus said into proper Greek. This indicates the authors wanted to make sure we knew exactly what Jesus said in Aramaic. They also included the definite article *the* (ὁ, *ho*) so readers would recognize Jesus used *Son of Man* as a title. He did not say He was *a son of man*. He said He was *the Son of Man*.[12]

---

[11] The Bible is an inspired book which has been miraculously preserved, and God chose to preserve it in Greek. Some have proposed part of all of the Gospels were originally written in Aramaic. For our purposes, we will consider the Gospels that have been preserved as the authentic Gospels.

[12] There has been much debate on the significance of the use of the definite article in Aramaic, but the fact that the Gospel authors used a definite article in Greek is significant because *the Son of Man* is not a Greek phrase, thus indicating they want their readers to connect to the underlying Aramaic.

This becomes even more significant when we remember *Son of Man* was used 78 times in the Gospels, and every time it referred to Jesus, and Jesus was the speaker in every reference but 1.[13] As we have already noted, the word *man* (*anthrōpos*) was used in over 190 verses. People used it to describe Jesus as a human, Jesus used it to describe His humanity, and people used it to describe other humans. *Son of Man* was obviously used very differently from the typical Greek word for *human*.

We've covered a lot in a few pages. Let's summarize the main points as they are foundational for the rest of our study.

The Son of Man was an intentional title in the Gospels. Son of Man was an Aramaic phrase. It made sense in Aramaic and basically meant *human*. However, it was an odd phrase in Greek[14] and not the way to say *human* in Greek. This means the Gospel authors did not translate *Son of Man* into proper Greek because they clearly wanted to communicate the Aramaic phrase Jesus used. Furthermore, every time Jesus used *Son of Man*, the Gospels included the definite article *the* which made the phrase a distinct title. Jesus was not just *a son of man*; He was *the Son of Man*. While the Gospels were written in Greek, they were written in such a way to emphasize the Aramaic Jesus used, and the Aramaic phrase is only found one place in the Old Testament—Daniel 7.

The Gospel authors did not use son of man in a generic sense to refer to humanity. The Gospel authors consistently used the normal Greek word for *man* (*anthrōpos*) when they wanted to refer to humanity. This word was used to describe Jesus' humanity by Jesus and others. So, *the Son of Man* was used by Jesus in an intentional way while *man* was consistently used in a generic way to speak of humanity. Again, this is important because these conversations did not originally happen in Greek. They are translated conversations. When the people in the Gospels spoke about humanity, they may have used the phrase *son of man* because that would have been correct Aramaic. However, when these conversations

---

[13]The one exception is John 12:34. In this verse, the crowd says, "Who is this 'Son of Man'?" The speaker was not Jesus, but the crowd was speaking Jesus' words back to Him.

[14]"The Greek expression ὁ υἱὸς τοῦ ἀνθρώπου is not normal monoglot Greek…" Maurice Casey, *The Solution to the "Son of Man" Problem* (New York: T&T Clark International, 2009), 61.

were recorded in the Greek, they were translated into correct Greek as *man*. The Gospels frequently use the generic Greek word for man, but they never use the phrase *Son of Man* to speak about humanity in a generic way.

The Gospel authors used the Greek phrase for Son of Man found in the Greek translation of Daniel used by the early church. The Septuagint (LXX) was the Greek translation of the Old Testament frequently used by the apostles. In the Septuagint, Daniel 7:13 was translated into Greek as "like a son of man" instead of "like a human." The translators of the Septuagint preserved the Aramaic phrase *Son of Man* in Greek instead of converting it into the proper Greek equivalent. The Gospel authors did the same. They used this translation to demonstrate they were quoting Daniel 7:13 instead of trying to say "human."

The authors of the Gospels translated the conversations in the Gospels in a very intentional way. When Jesus called Himself *the Son of Man,* it was an Aramaic phrase literally written in Greek. However, when speaking of humanity, the Gospel authors used the typical Greek word. Their translation was obviously intentional. They wanted us to know what Jesus said in Aramaic when He called Himself *the Son of Man.* In other cases, they only communicated that someone spoke about *a man.*

The Gospel authors intentionally created a connection between Jesus' words and Daniel 7. We have to remember the Bible was written intentionally so readers could make connections and come to correct conclusions. This was done by using biblical language from other passages to help readers make connections to those passages.

Though they wrote in a different language from the Old Testament, the Gospel authors were clearly trying to communicate a direct connection to Daniel in the language they chose. When we consider their choice of language in light of everything we have already seen, the connection to Daniel is simply undeniable.

Missing the Forest for the Trees

Conservative scholars who believe the Bible is divinely inspired have written extensively on the connection between Daniel and Jesus' use of *Son of Man.* In this book, we will build on their work to show Jesus used Daniel much more extensively than most readers realize, and His use of Daniel went far beyond one phrase.

Even though the connection is clear when the Gospels are viewed in light of their historical context, thousands and thousands of pages have been written debating what Jesus meant to say when He called Himself *the Son of Man*. Every nuance of ancient Aramaic has been carefully and repeatedly examined to try to ascertain the precise meaning. As a result, there have been scholars who question the connection to Daniel. While there are various reasons for this, two common reasons are important to our discussion.

The first reason is lack of basic confidence in the Bible. The concept of the unique and divine Son of Man is a problem for scholars who do not trust the Gospels and do not believe Daniel is an authentic book. These kinds of scholars often come up with very creative theories about the Bible, and this includes Jesus' use of *Son of Man*. While critical scholars can offer helpful insight, lack of confidence in the Bible frequently affects their interpretation. I have not written this book to address these issues. I wrote this book with the conviction that the Bible we have is divinely inspired, authentic, and supernaturally preserved.

The second reason could be summarized as "missing the forest for the trees." This is a colloquial phrase used to describe what happens when we focus in so much on a special tree we lose sight of the forest the tree is in. When you focus in only on a tree and forget the forest, you don't have any context. Without context, the purpose of a tree in the bigger forest can be lost.

This second reason is probably the more common error of the two. Sometimes, details are carefully and endlessly analyzed to the point the broader context is ignored. For example, when we get into the Gospels, we will find *Son of Man* is not the only thing that links to Daniel. The context and content of Jesus' teaching and the reaction of Jesus' audience *combined* with His use of *Son of Man* establish a robust link to Daniel. If we isolate the phrase *Son of Man* and study it in a vacuum, we can end up with creative interpretations. If, on the other hand, we consider it in light of the broader context of Jesus' ministry, we become even more certain Jesus intended to link the phrase to Daniel.

Reading the Bible in Context

The fact that Jesus spoke an exact phrase written nearly five hundred years before which occurs only in one place in the Bible must be significant.

The Bible is the preserved Word of God, even small details are inspired for God's purposes.

If Jesus had chosen to use any other unique phrase found in only one Old Testament passage to describe a vision of God in human form, we would automatically consider every use of the title to be a reference to that passage. For example, if Jesus had called Himself *the Suffering Servant*, we would not need to study Roman culture or dissect the meaning of *servant* to understand what He meant. Studies like that could add meaning, but the biblical context alone would be enough to know Jesus was referencing Isaiah's prophecies, not describing His social status.

Some have proposed *Son of Man* is a reference to Daniel when it is specifically included with other language from Daniel 7:13 (such as "coming with the clouds"), but in other cases, the title is used in a generic sense. However, Jesus used the word *man* when He wanted to speak of His humanity, and the vast majority of *Son of Man* references include other themes also found in Daniel. Because *the Son of Man* was an unusual title, there is no reason to think Jesus meant it as a reference to Daniel in some cases but not in others.

A lot of the confusion over Jesus' use of *Son of Man* comes from reading the phrase out of context. For example, the idea that it was a statement of Jesus' humanity emerged from well-intentioned commentators who, nonetheless, read backwards from a Christian perspective and assumed Jesus needed to repeatedly state His humanity, which simply was not true.

While Jesus did not need to prove His humanity, He did need to declare His divinity. While we tend to assume Jesus did this by claiming to be Messiah and Son of God, we will find Jesus' use of *Son of Man* was the primary way He declared His divine identity.

We cannot read the Gospels through the lens of two thousand years of predominantly Western Christian interpretation. We have to read the Bible in context as a divine, unfolding revelation, and seek to understand it the way the original audience did. We must do our best to read the Gospels through the lens of a first-century Jewish audience who was familiar with the Old Testament and considered Daniel Scripture.

Unfortunately, the Christian world lost a lot of historical context as Christianity grew in the centuries after Jesus' first coming. Compounding the problem, what we now call *Judaism* also shifted in substantial ways after the first century. Both Christian and Jewish histories add complexity to the challenge of interpreting the Bible correctly. The good news is that, over the last century or so, there has been a tremendous increase in the depth of scholarship relating to the first century. Through the discovery of information and the faithful, rigorous work of Bible-loving scholars, the Lord is helping us recover important first-century foundations.

Ezekiel and Enoch

Because the question of Ezekiel and Enoch often comes up in relationship to the phrase *son of man,* we need to mention both briefly. The vast majority of the uses of *son of man* outside the book of Daniel are found in Ezekiel because he was addressed as *son of man* over 90 times in the book bearing his name. Studying this phrase in Ezekiel is out of the scope of this book, but a few things should be noted.

First, based on the context in the Gospels we have already summarized, it is clear Jesus was not claiming to be Ezekiel or comparing Himself to Ezekiel. Second, though the translation of *son of man* in Ezekiel and Daniel 7:13 is the same in English, it was different in the original language. Ezekiel was written in Hebrew, and as we've already discussed, Daniel 7:13 was written in Aramaic.

There are scholars who believe Ezekiel's use of *son of man* could have inspired Daniel to use the same phrase because there is an extent to which Ezekiel was a prototype of Jesus. (For example, Ezekiel was a prophet like Moses, who symbolically bore the punishment of Israel and Judah with the people even though he was innocent.[15]) Even if Daniel chose language to remind the reader of Ezekiel's suffering, it is a secondary point and out of the scope of this book. For our purposes,

---

[15]James M. Hamilton, Jr. *With the Clouds of Heaven: The Book of Daniel in Biblical Theology, New Studies in Biblical Theology* (Downers Grove: IL, InterVarsity Press, 2014), Kindle edition, 150–51.

Jesus used *Son of Man* to identify Himself with Daniel 7, not with Ezekiel.

The *Similitudes of Enoch* is another collection of writings that describes the Son of Man. Because they contain an account virtually identical to Daniel 7—with a divine Person referred to as *the Son of Man*—some have proposed it is substantial evidence that *Son of Man* was a well-known title understood to refer to a divine Person in human form.[16] However, a discussion of the *Similitudes* is also out of the scope for this book. Because the *Similitudes* are not Scripture, they should not be used as a basis for theology, and we will limit our interpretation of Jesus' words to Scripture.

Rediscovering the Son of Man

Jesus called Himself the Son of Man *nearly 80 times, and on that basis alone, we can say He referenced Daniel 7 more than any other passage.* This may sound surprising or even unbelievable, but it will become increasingly obvious as we examine Jesus' own words in light of Daniel.

When we view Jesus' teaching through the lens of Daniel 7, it opens up a new depth of meaning for many passages because Jesus used Daniel 7 more than any other passage to undergird His teaching on His identity, His Father, His kingdom, His people, His judgments, and His coming. It also greatly simplifies the gospel when we recognize Jesus' main teachings were not entirely new but built on foundations already laid in the Old Testament.

---

[16]Daniel Boyarin, *The Jewish Gospels: The Story of the Jewish Christ* (New York: The New Press, 2013), Kindle edition, Location 1111.

WHY JESUS AVOIDED BEING CALLED THE CHRIST

Understanding why Jesus tended to avoid being called Christ is critical to grasping how Jesus presented Himself.

Jesus told the disciples not to tell anyone He was the Christ,[1] and Jesus' tendency to avoid the title *Christ* is sometimes referred to as the *Messianic Secret* by commentators. The phrase *Messianic Secret* tends to give the impression that Jesus hid His identity during His ministry in order to confront people's concept of Messiah or because He wanted to preserve His life until the time came for His death.

However, neither are true. As we will see, Jesus was very open about His identity, and He embraced His death and suffering. Besides, He was not executed for His claim of being Messiah but rather His claim of being the Son of Man—a claim He made openly and publicly throughout His ministry.

When Jesus avoided referring to Himself as Messiah and asked His disciples not to speak about Him as Messiah, He was not trying to preserve His life—He was trying to preserve His message. He was not trying to hide His identity—He was trying to reveal it.

Jesus did not want the disciples to speak about Him as Messiah because they did not yet have clarity on who He truly was. Their preconceived notions of Messiah would have caused confusion.

When we read Jesus' constant use of *Son of Man* in the Gospels, we should hear Him saying:

Don't confuse Me with the other so called "messiahs." I am not like them. I am in a completely different category. I am the divine Human—the only One who has descended from heaven. I am not only your King, I am your God in the flesh

---

[1]Matthew 16:20; Mark 8:29–30.

and standing before you. I'm not only the One who will rule from Jerusalem, I am the One who shook Sinai.

Avoiding Confusion

When Jesus came, there was a lot of messianic expectation fueled by prophetic expectation, Jewish nationalism, and a passionate desire for freedom from the domination of Rome. The Messiah was seen chiefly as a political Deliverer, and as a result, many would-be political deliverers tried to mobilize a revolt against Rome by claiming to be *the Messiah*.

Though Jesus is the true Messiah, the claim to be Messiah was not an exclusive claim in the first century—there were many who claimed to be Messiah. Messianic expectation was running high, and Jesus did not want to be identified as yet another potential liberator.

If Jesus' followers had aggressively spread the word that He was Messiah, He would have immediately been caught in a political conflict. Jewish nationalists would have looked to Him to organize resistance against Rome, and Rome would have seen Him as yet another political nationalist trying to incite a revolt. However, Jesus knew it was not time for the kingdoms of this age to be judged and the kingdom to be established on the earth. Therefore, He did not present Himself as Messiah then, though that day will come.

Jesus' decision to avoid using *Christ* as His main title did not preserve His life or avoid controversy. If Jesus had chosen to primarily use the term *Christ,* He would have had a much better reception from many of the Jews. When Jesus revealed Himself as the *Son of Man*, He chose a much more controversial title that ultimately led to His execution.

The title *Messiah* essentially describes a political Deliverer who will restore Israel and bring the nations under God's leadership. It is a functional title that describes one of Jesus' assignments. The title *Son of Man* is altogether different. It is not an *assignment*; it is an *identity*.

Identity over Function

When people asked Jesus if He was the Christ, they were not so much asking *who* He was but rather *what* He would do. Jesus avoided the title *Messiah* because He wanted to be known for who He was and not only for what He would do. We tend to relate to people *functionally* based on how they may or may not benefit us, but this is a utilitarian way of relating.

Messiah would have communicated what Jesus will do. Son of Man communicated who He is and what He will do.

Jesus' presented Himself as the Son of Man because He wants us to relate to Him on the basis of who He is. He wants to be known first for who He is as a Person and secondarily for what He will do. He wants us to know Him *first* as God and *then* as King.

Malachi was the last prophet of the Old Testament, and his book opened with YHWH's complaint against Israel. Israel was doing everything He had asked them to do, but they were relating to Him in a functional way. They served Him so they could receive blessing. However, God wanted deeper relationship. He wanted relationship so badly He told them their obedience was worthless and He wished someone was brave enough to shut down Israel's worship:

> *"Oh that there were one among you who would shut the doors, that you might not kindle fire on my altar in vain! I have no pleasure in you, says the LORD of hosts, and I will not accept an offering from your hand." (Malachi 1:10)*

Because Malachi was the last prophet, this complaint set the stage for the arrival of the Son of Man, and when He came, He refused a functional relationship with His people. Instead, He required them to relate to Him for who He was.

Jesus wanted to be known, received, and loved as the divine Son of Man who had descended from heaven—YHWH in a human form. He will joyfully deliver the nations as Messiah, but He wants to be received and loved first as God in the flesh.

During the Exodus, YHWH revealed Himself to Israel in the wilderness before He gave them the inheritance of the land. They wanted to go directly to the land, but He wanted to reveal Himself in the desert before He established the kingdom and brought the nation into the land.

God's desire for communion in the desert came into conflict with Israel's desire to enter the land immediately and establish the land, and it was the basis for much of the conflict in the wilderness. God wanted to bring Israel into the land, but He wanted relationship first.

In the same way, YHWH wants to reveal Himself in the Person of Jesus before liberating Israel and the nations. Therefore, as a title, *Son of Man* served Jesus' purposes better than the title of *Christ*. He was not another political deliverer competing with other "christs" for the loyalty of Israel—He was YHWH in the flesh, and He wanted to be known for who He was.

The claim to be Christ was a claim to *do* something—namely, liberate Israel. The claim to be the Son of Man was a claim to *be* the divine Man who had descended from heaven and would descend again in the day of judgment. The claim to be the Son of Man forced people to grapple with His true identity.[2]

Jesus' claim to be the Son of Man was much bigger than the claim to be the Christ.

The One Who Will Be Messiah

Jesus also avoided the title Christ because He knew He would not fulfill the prophecies of Messiah in His first coming. He did not want to create the expectation He was going to politically liberate Israel at that time. Jesus *is* the Christ, and the day will come when He liberates Israel and the nations, but Israel's deliverance will come at His second coming, not His first.[3]

According to Daniel, Messiah will descend from the heavens as a divine Man to fulfill the promise of the kingdom. Before Jesus' ascension, there was not a divine Man in the heavens who could descend to judge and deliver. Because it was impossible for Jesus to come as Messiah until His ascension into the heavens, He could not fulfill the messianic prophecies in His first coming.

We must understand this to properly interpret the prophets and speak to Israel about Jesus. For the last two thousand years, many Christians have essentially reinterpreted much of what the prophets said about Messiah because Jesus did not seem to fulfill what the prophets predicted. In an attempt to prove Jesus is Messiah, prophecies have been "spiritualized" and interpreted in ways that would not have made any sense to the prophets.

While God's plan of redemption contains mystery, and there is no question the messianic prophecies will be fulfilled in ways the prophets

---

[2]While the apostles did not use *Son of Man* as often as Jesus did, they followed this same pattern by presenting Jesus as "Lord Jesus Christ." This title was a formula which meant YHWH (divine), Jesus (a human), Messiah (king). The order was significant because it presented Jesus as He was. This is covered in more depth in *Son of Man: The Apostles' Gospel*, Volume 2.

[3]Acts 1:6–7; 3:19–21.

could not anticipate, neither Jesus nor the apostles completely reinterpreted these prophecies. They expanded them, but they maintained the expectation of the prophets that Jesus would fulfill the messianic prophecies in His second coming. Daniel 7 is key to understanding how the messianic prophecies will unfold.

Recovering the Identity of Jesus

Jesus was the Son of David (the promised King). He was the Son of God (with a divine nature and uniquely born of a virgin). He was the Messiah (Israel's political Deliverer). Other passages give Him even more titles,[4] and He deserves them all because each one describes an aspect of His Person.

According to Jesus, Daniel 7 was the Old Testament passage that best summarized His unique identity. The vast majority of believers do not realize Daniel 7 was the main prophetic vision to which Jesus referred. Because we do not recognize how Jesus presented Himself, we have lost something of who He is, and we have lost clarity on the gospel of the kingdom.

We need to know how Jesus used Daniel because we want to better understand Jesus and His gospel.

---

[4]Isaiah 9:6 is one example.

OUR MESSAGE TO ISRAEL AND THE NATIONS

Jesus used the phrase "gospel of the kingdom" to communicate the message He wanted proclaimed throughout the earth before the end would come:

> *And this gospel of the kingdom will be proclaimed throughout the whole world as a testimony to all nations, and then the end will come. (Matthew 24:14)[1]*

If the end will not come until this message is proclaimed, we desperately need to know what this message is. However, if you asked the vast majority of Christians, "What is the gospel of the kingdom?" they would either be unable to answer the question or give incomplete answers.

Beloved, this is a crisis. The church as a whole does not currently have clarity on the foundation of the message Jesus wants carried to the nations before the end will come. We have some understanding of the message of individual salvation—which is glorious—but that message is not enough to fulfill the commission Jesus gave us.

We stand at a critical juncture in history. We live in the first generation in history with the possibility of carrying the gospel to every people group. However, we do not know the full message that Jesus asked us to carry before the end will come. This means, if we carry a message of personal salvation to all people groups but do not proclaim the gospel of the kingdom, the task will not be completed.

Gaining clarity on the gospel of the kingdom must be a priority for every believer, every church, and every laborer who wants to carry this message to people who have not yet heard it.

---

[1]See also Matthew 4:23; 9:35; Acts 20:25.

The gospel of the kingdom is not a confusing message. After all, it must be carried to every people, language, and culture. It is not overly complex or mysterious. It only seems complex because we do not grasp the biblical foundations of that gospel.

We assume the New Testament was the beginning of a new message. *However, it was not.* It was the unfolding of a mystery already proclaimed. The New Testament reveals a mystery; it does not invent a new theology. To properly understand the gospel, we must grasp the foundations of that gospel.

You cannot form a comprehensive theology from the New Testament. We know this, but practically we continue to teach our people the gospel nearly entirely from the New Testament. If you read the final book in a trilogy but never read the first two books, you will be confused about the story. This is what we have done with the Old Testament, and as a result, our gospel is often unnecessarily confusing, particularly to Israel.

If we want to know what Jesus meant by the gospel of the kingdom, we must begin with the Old Testament passage He referenced far more than any other passage. The fact that Jesus referenced Daniel 7 more than any other passage means this passage should be carefully studied.

If Daniel 7 was this important to Jesus, it should be just as important to us.

It should trouble us that the chapter Jesus referenced more than any other is barely studied in the church. It is virtually ignored, often treated as impossible to grasp, and typically studied only for insight into the nature of the antichrist and the end-time drama. However, Jesus' use of Daniel indicates it was the foundational passage He used to open up the mystery of God's plan and to present His gospel.

We are about to discover Daniel 7 is the most concise and complete summary of the gospel of the kingdom in the Bible.

It is critical we rediscover the foundations of our gospel. In many cases, we continue to send missionaries who do not fully grasp the message they are supposed to carry. We cannot train or send missionaries to carry the gospel of the kingdom to all people without teaching them Daniel 7.[2] It must become part of our core training in the gospel for pastors, missionaries, and every believer.

Part of preaching the gospel is proclaiming Jesus the way He wants to be proclaimed. We tend to preach concepts about the gospel that are true, but we do not carefully study Jesus and proclaim the gospel the way He did.

The word *proclaimed* in Matthew 24:14 refers to the task of a herald. Heralds were used in the ancient world to carry messages for kings. When a king wanted to visit a city, he would send a herald ahead of him. That herald would carry a message from the king to be given before the king arrived. Heralds were also used in large meetings where the voice of the king could not be heard. A herald would use his large voice to deliver the king's message so everyone could hear. Heralds did not carry their own message—they carefully learned the message of their king.

We are *heralds* of King Jesus, proclaiming His message in the earth to prepare the nations for His return. We carry *His* message which is intended to reveal who He is; therefore, we should carefully study how He revealed Himself. We do not get to decide what the gospel is—we simply have the privilege of "heralding" that gospel.

Jesus Is the Heart of the Gospel

The gospel is often presented as a message of forgiveness that is very man-centered. The gospel, however, does not revolve around us—the gospel revolves around Jesus. Paul was the most visible missionary in the New Testament, and he summarized the gospel this way:

> *For I decided to know nothing among you except Jesus Christ and him crucified.*
> *(1 Corinthians 2:2)*

> *Paul had a brilliant intellect, and he decided to limit himself to the subject of Jesus.*

Right now, there is relatively little preaching of the Person of Jesus. Most preaching focuses on practical applications of biblical principles to daily life. While these kinds of messages are important, and the New

---

[2]Daniel 7 is not the only neglected passage. People desperately need solid foundations in the Old Testament, so this principle applies to the whole of Scripture.

Testament is full of them, they must flow from the preaching of Jesus. We should be able to say with Paul that we have "decided" (determined) above all to know Jesus and Him crucified.

Many of our worship songs end up focused on ourselves when they should overwhelmingly be poetic and musical proclamations of the Person of Jesus. He must be preeminent in our preaching, our speaking, and our singing. Every aspect of theology is important, but the Person of Jesus must be central in the church.

The True Finish Line

Not only is Daniel 7 a key to the gospel of the kingdom, it is essential to the true finish line of missions in this age.

Reaching every people group with the gospel is often presumed to be the final finish line, but this is not true. Reaching every people group is a critical milestone, but not the finish line. The finish line for missions in this age is returning the gospel to Israel.

The gospel must be returned to the people where it began. God's expansive plan to bring the gospel to the gentiles must end with the salvation of Israel,[3] and the nations play a significant part in the witness that will lead to that salvation.[4] God is already stirring the nations, and they are being awakened to God's purposes for Israel. The global church needs to embrace God's burden for Israel and give them the witness God wants.

The challenge is, for nearly two thousand years now, the gospel has often been proclaimed to Israel in a way that seemed very foreign because the church lost the Jewish roots of the faith as it became predominantly gentile.

The gentiles have a weighty responsibility to return the gospel to Israel, but how should the gospel be presented to Israel?

Returning the gospel to Israel is a holy thing, and speaking to Israel about their God is a sobering endeavor. It is different from taking the

---

[3]Deuteronomy 30:1–6; Isaiah 4:3; 45:17, 25; 54:13; 59:21; 60:4, 21; 61:8–9; 66:22; Jeremiah 31:31–34; 32:40; Ezekiel 20:40; 36:10, 27–36; 39:22, 28–29; Joel 2:26, 32; Zephaniah 3:9, 12–13; Zechariah 12:10–13; Matthew 23:39; 24:30; Acts 1:6–7; 2:21; Romans 10:13; 11:26–27; Revelation 1:7.

[4]Acts 1:6–8; Romans 1:16; 9:1–3; 10:15; 11:11, 25–26.

gospel to the gentiles because Israel has a story with God that is at least four thousand years old.

Jesus' gives us the answer:

> *He answered, "I was sent only to the lost sheep of the house of Israel." (Matthew 15:24)*

Jesus' ministry in the Gospels was intentionally directed to Israel; therefore, through His teaching, Jesus instructs us on how He wants to be presented to Israel. Jesus has given us the message He wants returned to Israel. It is plainly recorded for us in the Gospels, and that message is surprising. For nearly two thousand years, we have assumed Jesus wants to be presented to Israel as Messiah, but in His own words, He wants to be presented to Israel first as *the Son of Man.*

This presentation of Jesus to Israel is not less controversial, but it is more clear. Jesus wants Israel to hear a proclamation of His identity, and He chose Son of Man as the way to summarize His identity. For Christians who have heard Jesus nearly always described as the Jewish Messiah, this is surprising, which is precisely why we need to carefully study how Jesus presented Himself.

Returning the gospel to Jesus' family is far too precious a task to be approached casually. We must do it precisely the way Jesus wants it done. We must follow His example. Jesus used Daniel 7 to present Himself to Israel, and we must learn to do the same.

A Small Book with a Big Message

We cannot fully grasp the way Jesus preached the gospel without recognizing how He used Daniel to do it.

If you ask Christians to identify the Old Testament passages Jesus quoted most, you will likely hear well-known messianic prophecies about Jesus such as Isaiah 53 or Psalm 110. Surprisingly, Jesus referenced Daniel 7 far more than He referenced either of these passages. The fact that the vast majority of Christians do not realize how Jesus used Daniel demonstrates how detached we are from the way Jesus presented Himself.

The *gospel* does not depend on Daniel because an accurate picture of who Jesus is can be put together without Daniel. However, the *Gospels*—Matthew, Mark, Luke, and John—as they were written rise and fall on their interpretation of Daniel.

The New Testament only contains a small amount of the teaching Jesus did.[1] Given the amount of material that was available to the Gospel authors, it is incredibly significant all four Gospels chose to present Jesus' identity through His use of Daniel. Jesus' use of Daniel 7 establishes it as one of the premier visions of the beauty of Jesus. If we don't read Daniel 7 this way, we do not read it the way Jesus did, and we have missed the main message of the vision.

The gospel is a *revealed* mystery but not a new message. When Jesus came, He opened up what the Bible already said about Him. The mystery of who Jesus is was not knowable until He came, but when He came, it was revealed from the Scriptures.

---

[1]John 21:25.

A Gospel-Centered Chapter

In our time, the book of Daniel has been almost entirely relegated to the subject of apocalyptic, end-time prophecy. Typically, Daniel is studied for end-time information, particularly about the antichrist. This is a valuable and important aspect of Daniel, but a careful reading of the New Testament reveals there is more to Daniel's book. While Daniel does contain a few profound apocalyptic visions,[2] we need to recover the significance of the book related to the gospel.

We have learned to read the book of Daniel as an end-time book, but we must learn to read it as a book of Christology, which declares the majesty and Person of Jesus in a unique way.

Daniel's main message did not center around the antichrist; it centered around Jesus. When we read Daniel the way Jesus did, we discover the book is primarily a book about the gospel. In many ways, the church has been robbed of the main message of Daniel for the last two thousand years. It is time to recover that message and rediscover the essence of the gospel of the kingdom.

Daniel's central message was a call to fascination with the beauty, majesty, and mystery of Jesus.

The Controversy of Daniel

A case can be made for Daniel's being the most controversial Bible book in the scholarly world. Not only is the interpretation of Daniel endlessly debated, the validity of the book itself has been relentlessly attacked by some scholars. Even though Daniel has been accepted as Scripture for over two thousand years,[3] there are scholars who continue to question every aspect of the integrity of the book.

Jesus had a high view of Daniel, and for the purposes of this book, we will accept Jesus' view of the book. Defending the book of Daniel is not the purpose of this book, but the controversy over the book ultimately raises these two important questions: (1) Do we accept

---

[2]Only two chapters in Daniel, chapters 7 and 8, contain apocalyptic visions. If you include Nebuchadnezzar's vision in Daniel 2, that is still only three chapters out of twelve.

[3]For an excellent and succinct defense of Daniel's authenticity see pages 33–39 of James Hamilton's excellent work, *With the Clouds of Heaven: The Book of Daniel in Biblical Theology.*

the Bible as it was written? (2) Are we willing to let Jesus be the supreme interpreter of the Bible?[4]

Jesus clearly spoke about Daniel as a real person, and He affirmed Daniel's book as being authentic and prophetic. Jesus used Daniel to reveal His identity and taught the key prophecies in the book had not yet been fulfilled.

Jesus is the most authoritative interpreter of Scripture; therefore, to question the integrity or validity of Daniel's book is to question Jesus' evaluation of Daniel.

As we will see the undermining of Daniel, in turn, undermines the Gospels, which then undermines the biblical revelation of Jesus. If Daniel's book is not reliable, the message of the Gospels is on shaky ground. With this in mind, perhaps the ultimate reason for the intense controversy around Daniel is the fact that Jesus chose to present and establish His identity on the basis of Daniel.

Daniel the Prototype

The book of Daniel is much more significant than it appears at first glance. The book consists of historical stories and prophetic encounters, but the entire book is telling a prophetic story. To recognize that story, you have to understand the role of Daniel in his book.

Daniel is very unusual because he is completely flawless in the book. He never shows any kind of weakness and never makes any kind of mistake. It is extremely unusual for an individual to be presented this way in the Bible. Daniel is presented this way because in the context of his book he represents something. He is a prototype—a picture.

Daniel lived through a prototype of the end times. Nebuchadnezzar was an antichrist figure. He was proud and arrogant. He commanded people to worship a statue at the point of death. He destroyed Jerusalem and took the Jews as slaves. It is a real historical story, but it is also a prototype of something to come.

Joseph is one of the premier prototypes of Jesus in the Bible, and Daniel is often considered a Joseph figure because there are a number of similarities. For example, both were carried away as slaves, both served gentile kings, both interpreted dreams, both suffered unjustly,

---

[4]If you would like a brief defense of Daniel's integrity, I highly recommend chapter one of James Hamilton's book, *With the Clouds of Heaven: The Book of Daniel in Biblical Theology.*

and both ended up in a prominent position. However, Daniel is also different from Joseph. Joseph has power and authority that Daniel never had. For the most part, Daniel exerted authority through obedience, faithfulness, endurance, and intercession.

Joseph and Daniel have differences because Joseph is a prototype of Jesus, but Daniel is a prototype of the mature, end-time church. He is perhaps the leading biblical prototype of the church in the end times. In his book, Daniel consistently faces the tests that the end-time church will face, and he passes them all. For example, Daniel lives through an antichrist figure, great compromise, suffering, and the seduction of Babylon. God strengthens him with supernatural revelation and insight. Daniel is a prophetic picture of where the church is going, so all his stories are prophetic.

Daniel's life is a key part of the message of his book, which means Daniel's message cost him his life. Because Daniel is a prototype of the mature, end-time church, quite a bit is at stake in the reading of Daniel, and because he is a prototype of the end-time church, it makes sense he was given a summary of the message that the end-time church must proclaim.

Approaching Prophecy Correctly

Many believers neglect a serious study of Bible prophecy for a number of reasons. Some believe it is too difficult to understand. Others are fixated on their lives now and are disconnected from the biblical hope of Jesus' return. Many want to wisely avoid unbiblical extremes. In spite of the recent neglect of biblical prophecy, across different parts of the church, there is a renewed desire to examine and understand the main message of biblical prophecy.

There are a number of important reasons to study biblical prophecy,[5] but there is one in particular we will focus on in this book:

> For the testimony of Jesus is the spirit of prophecy. (Revelation 19:10)

> One of the ways we avoid unbiblical approaches to prophecy is by realizing prophecy is first and foremost a testimony about Jesus.

---

[5] For more on this, see my book *It Must Be Finished: Making Sense of the Return of Jesus.*

The Bible does give insight into future events, but even those events are ultimately designed by God to make the beauty and majesty of His Son known. Far too many people approach prophecy like a riddle to be solved, and focus mainly on the interpretation of secret information.

When we study prophecy, we should be on a search for the revelation of the beauty of Jesus. When we prioritize the study of events over discovering the beauty of Jesus, we quickly get off track in our study of prophecy. The events the prophets spoke about are important, but they are secondary to the revelation of the beauty of Jesus.

Sealed for the End-Time Church's Witness to Israel

Daniel was told his book was to be sealed up in order to preserve it for the time of the end:

> *He said, "Go your way, Daniel, for the words are shut up and sealed until the time of the end." (Daniel 12:9)*

The book of Daniel had to be sealed because it would be foundational to the revelation of Jesus contained in the Gospels. Daniel 7 was the central prophecy Jesus used to reveal Himself, and it had to be preserved so the church could give an accurate, biblical witness of Jesus to Israel and the nations.

The apostle John taught the "spirit of antichrist" is the attempt to redefine or reject the biblical identity of Jesus.[6] This has happened throughout history, but as we approach the time of *the* antichrist, the identity of Jesus will come under assault like no other time in human history.[7] Jesus used Daniel 7 more than any other passage to summarize His identity, and the end-time church will as well.

The Lord has preserved Daniel 7 as a gift to the end-time church because it is a concise, straightforward, biblical witness to the identity of Jesus.

---

[6] 1 John 2:22; 4:2–3; 2 John 7.

[7] 1 John 2:18.

The Gospel of the
Kingdom Introduced

THE MYSTERIOUS PROPHECY OF DANIEL 7

Our main goal for this section is to see how Daniel 7 became a foundation for the New Testament gospel of the kingdom, so we will examine it through this lens. Many aspects of the prophecy were shrouded in mystery until Jesus came to unveil the mystery of God,[1] but the prophecy laid a clear foundation for the gospel.

Before we move to the New Testament, we need to look a little more closely and see just how much of the gospel was given to Daniel over five hundred years before Jesus came. In this section, we will consider what Daniel (and his readers) could have understood about the vision *before* Jesus came. This will help us set the stage for the next section, where we will examine how Jesus interpreted Daniel and opened up the mystery of the chapter.

We have access to more information about the Bible than we have had at any time in history, and yet most of us remain unaware of how the gospel developed from the Old Testament.

We know Jesus fulfilled a number of Old Testament predictions, but we tend to believe the gospel was a radical new development. Tragically, some of us even treat the Old Testament as if it is at odds with the New Testament, but the essential elements of the gospel were in the Old Testament. Once Jesus revealed the mystery of the gospel, the early church preached the gospel powerfully from the Old Testament.[2]

If we learn to read the Old Testament the way the apostles did, we can learn to preach the gospel the way they did.

We also must remember the gospel is more than the message of individual salvation. The gospel is a cosmic message focused on the

---

[1]Romans 16:25; Ephesians 1:9; 3:3–9; 6:19; Colossians 1:26–27; 2:2; 4:3; 1 Timothy 3:16.

[2]Acts 18:24–28; 2 Timothy 3:16.

beautiful Son of Man who is going to take dominion over the cosmos, restore it, and form a people like Himself in the process.

The Main Themes of the Vision

Before we continue, we need to take a minute and summarize the main characters and events found in Daniel 7.

The Beasts

Daniel 7 begins with a vision of four beasts:

> *"And four great beasts came up out of the sea, different from one another." (v. 3)*

There were three beasts who were similar and then a fourth beast completely different from all the rest. The first three beasts all resembled natural creatures that were either distorted or had unusual abilities. For example, there was a lion with wings, a bear with ribs in its teeth, and a leopard with four wings and four heads. Daniel concluded the description of each beast with an unusual statement:

- The first beast was made to stand like a man and given a man's mind.[3]
- The second beast was told to devour much flesh.[4]
- The third beast was given dominion.[5]

The fourth beast Daniel saw was dreadful and terrible in comparison to the other three beasts. It was so terrible Daniel was unable to find words to give a complete description of the beast. Unlike the other three beasts, it did not have any resemblance to a natural creature. The main word Daniel used to describe this beast was *different*.[6] Though it was a beast, it also had the appearance of a man speaking boastful things.[7]

Daniel's description of the vision focused on a "little horn" that came out from this beast. Daniel was told this "little horn" represented

---

[3]Daniel 7:4.

[4]Daniel 7:5.

[5]Daniel 7:6.

[6]Daniel 7:7, 19, 23–24.

[7]Daniel 7:8.

a terrible king who will come.[8] There is a similarity between all the beasts, but a significant distinction between the final beast and the rest of the beasts. The little horn or king who comes from the fourth beast will be incredibly arrogant and bring immense suffering to God's people.[9]

The Ancient of Days

After Daniel had seen the beasts, he suddenly saw the Ancient of Days respond to the beasts:

> *"As I looked, thrones were placed, and the Ancient of Days took his seat; his clothing was white as snow, and the hair of his head like pure wool; his throne was fiery flames; its wheels were burning fire. A stream of fire issued and came out from before him; a thousand thousands served him, and ten thousand times ten thousand stood before him; the court sat in judgment, and the books were opened." (Daniel 7:9–10)*

When Daniel saw the Ancient of Days, He was awe-inspiring and terrifying. He was surrounded by burning fire and ready to judge the beasts and bring an end to the devouring, dominion, and crushing they had inflicted. Daniel described the Ancient of Days in human terms (He took a seat, had clothing, and had hair), but this was clearly YHWH. YHWH was not the only one enthroned. Multiple thrones were set, which indicated YHWH was going to exalt at least one person alongside Himself. It raised a significant question: Who is going to sit on those thrones?

The End of the Beasts

In verses 11 through 12 of the chapter, we read:

> *"I looked then because of the sound of the great words that the horn was speaking. And as I looked, the beast was killed, and its body destroyed and given over to be burned with fire. As for the rest of the beasts, their dominion was taken away, but their lives were prolonged for a season and a time."*

As Daniel saw the Ancient of Days seated in judgment, the scene was interrupted by the loud words of the little horn from the fourth

---

[8]Daniel 7:17, 23–25.

[9]Daniel 7:8, 20–21, 25.

beast. This set up a great contrast in the scene. God was making His majesty known in judgment, and yet the little horn continued to arrogantly challenge Him. As Daniel watched, the beast was killed. His dead body destroyed and burned by fire. God's judgment caused the rest of the beasts to lose their dominion as well.

The Glory of the Son of Man

The destruction of the beasts was followed by another staggering vision.

> *"I saw in the night visions, and behold, with the clouds of heaven there came one like a son of man, and he came to the Ancient of Days and was presented before him." (Daniel 7:13)*

This time Daniel saw the most spectacular part of the vision yet. Suddenly in the clouds of heaven, Daniel saw a Person who was like *a son of man*. This Person boldly approached the Ancient of Days, and He is obviously going to sit on one of the empty thrones.

As we discussed in an earlier chapter, the meaning of *son of man* can be translated simply as *human*. He was coming with the clouds of heaven—meaning He was divine—but He had the appearance of a man. He is the image of God, but in human form. He's God, but He is also presented as a perfect Human and the complete fulfillment of man's calling in Genesis 1 to be the visible image of God.[10] Because He is the perfect Human, He is the ideal whom humans should resemble.

The vision of the Son of Man occurred in the center of chapter 7, and this placement established the Son of Man as the central theme of the chapter. Everything before and after this section of the vision ultimately exists in relation to the central revelation of the Son of Man.

The scene was an echo of Psalm 2:

> *I will tell of the decree: The LORD said to me, "You are my Son; today I have begotten you. Ask of me, and I will make the nations your heritage, and the ends of the earth your possession." (vv. 7–8)*

The Ancient of Days responded to this *Son of Man* in an stunning way:

---

[10]Genesis 1:26.

"And to him was given dominion and glory and a kingdom, that all peoples, nations, and languages should serve him; his dominion is an everlasting dominion, which shall not pass away, and his kingdom one that shall not be destroyed." (Daniel 7:14)

This is by far the most majestic part of Daniel's vision. This Person looked like a man, but He was clearly divine. In a future chapter, we will consider a number of reasons why He was clearly divine. He came from heaven with the clouds rather than from the earth. He boldly approached the Ancient of Days in a courtroom scene, and the Ancient of Days responded by giving all authority to this Son of Man. He was given dominion, glory, and a kingdom. His dominion and rule were and are permanent, and His kingdom will never be destroyed. All peoples, nations, and languages will serve Him forever.

A Global Deliverer

The vision of Daniel 7 occurred approximately thirty years after Nebuchadnezzar completely destroyed the city of Jerusalem and finally put an end to the kingdom of Israel. Before Nebuchadnezzar destroyed the city, the prophets predicted a time would come when God would restore Israel under a leader known as the *son of David*. This prediction was based on God's promise to David in 2 Samuel 7:12–16 that one of his descendants would rule forever. This *son of David* was the hope of Daniel and his people.

The expectation for this deliverer was so profound that the first verse of Matthew's gospel identified Jesus as the long hoped for Son of David:

The book of the genealogy of Jesus Christ, the son of David....

The son of David was the hope of Israel, but Daniel saw someone "like" a son of man, who was much greater than the promised son of David. *He was not just given authority over Israel—He was given global dominion over all peoples.* Other prophets predicted the nations would be given to God's designated king,[11] but this king was usually presented as the king of Israel. Most Jews expected a king of Israel who would also cause the nations to worship YHWH, but this Person was given a kingdom

---

[11]For example, see Psalm 2:6–9; Isaiah 42:6; 49:6; 51:4.

of all nations that seemed to transcend Israel. But the most shocking aspect of the vision was this global King was also divine.

The Interpretation of the Vision

Daniel was so alarmed by the vision that he asked an individual in the encounter to interpret it for him.[12] The interpreter gave Daniel several keys to understanding the vision. The beasts were interpreted as kings who arise from the earth.[13] They will rule for a period of time before "'the saints of the Most High shall receive the kingdom and possess the kingdom forever.'"[14]

Daniel was also given significant details about the fourth best, which was more terrible than all the other beasts. This beast will be "exceedingly terrifying."[15] He will make war on the saints and appear to be successful until the the Ancient of Days comes. This beast will form a kingdom like no other kingdom. He will speak arrogant words against the Most High. He will wear out the saints. He will try to change the "times and the law"[16] to extend his rule, but his time will be limited by the Ancient of Days.

When the time of the beast is up, the Ancient of Days will sit in judgment, take away his dominion, and destroy him. When the beast is destroyed, the government, dominion, and majesty of all kingdoms will be given to the saints of the Most High who will rule with Him in His eternal, sovereign kingdom.[17]

Alarmed by the Vision

Daniel's response to the encounter reveals the intensity of the prophecy:

> "Here is the end of the matter. As for me, Daniel, my thoughts greatly alarmed me, and my color changed, but I kept the matter in my heart." (Daniel 7:28)

---

[12]This interpreter was likely the angel Gabriel based on Daniel 9:21.

[13]Daniel 7:17.

[14]Daniel 7:18.

[15]Daniel 7:19.

[16]Daniel 7:25.

[17]Daniel 7:27.

By this time in his life, Daniel was a mature man who had lived through the trauma of the Babylonian vision and experienced spiritual conflict with the sorcerers and magicians in Babylon. His reaction demonstrates this dream was much more than it seems at first glance. When we react casually to this dream, it demonstrates we have not grasped what Daniel tried to communicate to us.

This dream was so significant that Daniel organized his book to help readers recognize this dream was the main message of the book. Many readers do not recognize how important the structure of Daniel is, so that is what we need to examine next.

THE PIVOTAL CHAPTER IN DANIEL'S VISION

Because Daniel recorded multiple prophetic encounters, it is easy to read his book and not recognize the centrality of Daniel 7.

Daniel carefully organized his book to present Daniel 7 as the most significant chapter in the book of Daniel. It has been called "the single most important chapter"[1] and "the heart of the book of Daniel."[2] Old Testament Scholar Eric Heaton commented, "It would be no exaggeration to say that this chapter is one of the most important passages of the OT."[3]

Andrew Steinmann explains:

> Daniel 7 is the pivot around which the entire book turns, the interlocking device that unites historical narratives (chapters 1–6) and eschatological visions (chapters 7–12). It simultaneously closes out the Aramaic chiasm while introducing the visions that continue in subsequent chapters in Hebrew. This careful arrangement of the divinely inspired book points to this chapter as the book's most important section. It is no accident, then, that more scholarly papers, essays, and discussions have been produced about Daniel 7 than about any other major section of the book.... Therefore, Daniel 7 is the key to understanding the major themes that run throughout the book: God's governance of history, the eschatological kingdom of God, the promise of the Messiah, the protection God affords his people even during the darkest hours of persecution, and eternal

---

[1]W. S. Towner, *Daniel*, INT (Atlanta: John Knox, 1984), 91.

[2]N. W. Porteous, *Daniel*, OTL (Philadelphia: Westminster, 1965), 95.

[3]E. W. Heaton, *The Book of Daniel*, TBC (London: SCM Press, 1956), 169.

salvation he promises to all who are members of his kingdom already now through faith.[4]

The literary structure of the book of Daniel was very intentional, and we have to recognize the structure to interpret the book properly. The book is separated into two parts. The first is Daniel 1–6, which uses historical accounts to present a prophetic message. The second is Daniel 7–12, which uses Daniel's prophetic dreams, visions, and encounters to finish the message.

This arrangement is significant. If Daniel had only wanted to leave an account of his life, he would have mixed the visions and the prophetic encounters together, and ordered them chronologically. Instead, he chose to form two unique sections. Daniel 7 is the glue that holds the entire book together because it is connected to both parts of the book.

It is connected to the first half of the book linguistically. Daniel is unusual because it is the only Old Testament book written in two different languages. The introduction to the book (Daniel 1) and conclusion to the book (Daniel 8–12) were written in Hebrew, but Daniel 2–7 were written in Aramaic.[5] Because Daniel 7 is the final chapter in Aramaic, it concludes the Aramaic section in the first part of the book.

The four kingdoms in Daniel 7 also connect it to the first part of the book. Daniel's relationship to King Nebuchadnezzar was established in Daniel 2 when Daniel interpreted Nebuchadnezzar's dream of four kingdoms, which is the first prophetic dream mentioned in the book. Daniel's interpretation established him as a prophetic man of "understanding"[6] and introduced the key end-time themes of the book. Daniel 2 and 7 are connected because both are dreams involving four kingdoms.

Chronologically, Daniel 7 is also connected to the first part of the book because it happened between the events of chapters 4 and 5. Though Daniel 7 is a prophetic encounter, because of these links to

---

[4]Andrew E. Steinmann, *Daniel*, Concordia Commentary (Saint Louis, MO: Concordia Publishing House, 2008), 332.

[5]To be precise, the shift to Aramaic happens in Daniel 2:4.

[6]Daniel 2:21–23.

the beginning of the book, it provides a conclusion to the first part of the book and a transition to the second part.

Daniel 7 is linked to the first part of the book, but obviously also a part of the second book. There is a literary connection because the second part of the book consists of dreams, visions, and angelic encounters. As the first vision in the second section, Daniel 7 is the foundational vision for the visions that follow and is the most comprehensive vision in the book. In many ways, Daniel 8–12 are a commentary on chapter 7 because each subsequent chapter adds details to the prophetic themes introduced in Daniel 7.

Because Daniel 7 has connections to both parts of the book, Steinmann calls Daniel 7 "the pivot around which the entire book turns"[7] and the "key to understanding the major themes that run throughout the book."[8]

The Main Message Is in the Middle

To understand why a chapter in the middle of a book contains the main message, we need to know a little bit about the ancient literary structure Daniel used.

Present-day authors tend to make their most significant point either at the beginning or end of their writing. They either introduce their conclusion and then support it with their subsequent writing, or they use a sequence of arguments to build up to a grand conclusion. Ancient authors did not always write this way. They frequently used a literary structure called a *chiasm* that put the most profound point in the center. This structure is very common in the Bible, and biblical authors used it to emphasize their main point.

To understand what Daniel was trying to communicate, we have to recognize his book is a "carefully constructed chiasm."[9]

A chiasm places the main subject of a discourse in the center. Any subjects before and after the center subject are secondary subjects that emphasize the main subject. Reading a chiasm is like walking over a mountain. You begin at the bottom and then climb up to the peak, and

---

[7]Steinmann, *Daniel*, 332.

[8]Ibid.

[9]Hamilton, *With the Clouds of Heaven*, 49.

after reaching the peak, you continue on down the back side of the mountain.

In a chiasm, the center peak is the main subject. As you "ascend" to the peak, you progress through subjects that are all secondary to the main subject of the discourse. After you reach the "peak," you "descend," covering secondary subjects again before ending the discourse. Each secondary subject in the "ascent" and "descent" of the discourse serve to support the presentation of the main subject which is like the "mountain peak."

The subjects covered on the "ascent" and "descent" typically correspond to each other. A chiasm can be represented visually this way:

Secondary Point 1

Secondary Point 2

Secondary Point 3

Main Point

Secondary Point 4 (corresponds to Secondary Point 3)

Secondary Point 5 (corresponds to Secondary Point 2)

Secondary Point 6 (corresponds to Secondary Point 1)

In the book of Daniel, Daniel 7 is the peak of the mountain—the main point of his book. The first part of the book builds to that point using Daniel's story. The story begins by presenting Daniel as a man of understanding who is faithful to God through numerous tests.[10] The story also includes three antichrist prototypes—Nebuchadnezzar, Belshazzar, and Darius. The second half of the book corresponds to Daniel's life by giving us information about future "beasts" (kings) and the final wicked king (typically known as the antichrist), and ends with the prediction of a people of understanding who will be faithful to God during the most difficult test.

---

[10]Daniel 1–3.

By summarizing a few chapters, it is easy to see this structure in Daniel:

Daniel is presented as a faithful man of understanding (Daniel 1).

Nebuchadnezzar is described as an arrogant king who demands worship (Daniel 2, 3).

The Son of Man is God's answer to the crisis of this age (Daniel 7).

Daniel predicts an antichrist will come as the most arrogant king in history. Nebuchadnezzar was a prototype of this man (Daniel 8, 11).

Daniel predicts there will be a faithful people of understanding at the end of the age. Daniel was a prototype of this people (Daniel 11, 12).

This illustration is incomplete, but it demonstrates the point. The stories of Daniel 1–6 all carry a prophetic message. Daniel lived through a national crisis when it seemed like the promises of God had failed. Israel had fallen into apostasy, so the nation was handed over to a military adversary and destroyed. Daniel endured tremendous suffering and was carried away as a slave. He was forced to serve the pagan king Nebuchadnezzar who tried to seduce him to Babylon's ways. Daniel's life is a picture of the people of God remaining faithful during the reign of an antichrist (typified by Nebuchadnezzar).

Daniel was faithful throughout his ordeal, but the story of his life in Babylon raises significant questions—What is the end of suffering on the earth? Who will deliver us from the crisis of our own sin and the suffering that follows? How will God finally fulfill His promises? Does suffering mean the promises of God have failed?

Daniel 7 is the answer to all these questions.

The visions that follow in Daniel 8–12 correspond to Daniel 1–6. In these visions, Daniel is given the message that his suffering in Babylon is a picture of a much bigger crisis that will come. A man and a kingdom much worse than Nebuchadnezzar and Babylon will come and bring tremendous suffering. At that time, God will have a faithful people, and God will ultimately deliver His people after an appointed time. Daniel 1–6 and Daniel 8–12 carry a similar message. The opening chapters communicate the message through Daniel's story, and the closing chapters enforce the message with the prediction of a much greater crisis and resolution than what Daniel endured.

Daniel put this vision in the middle of his book as the resolution to the first and second parts of the book. Everything before and after it is secondary and supports it as the main theme. Secondary subjects in a chiasm are like the gold in a diamond ring. The gold in a ring is beautiful and valuable. It is often shaped into an artistic design, and it beautifully complements the diamond. However, the gold is not the main focus of the ring. The gold merely forms a shape to present the diamond.

Daniel 7 is like the diamond in a gold ring. The entire ring is important, valuable, and beautiful, but the ring supports and presents the diamond as the focal point of the ring. Each of Daniel's other eleven chapters are beautiful and valuable in and of themselves, but they also serve a supporting function in the context of the entire book.

When Daniel put chapter 7 in the center, he established it as the central message—the "diamond"—of the entire book. The location of Daniel 7 in the book is a key to unlocking Daniel's message. Because chiastic structure was in common use in the ancient world, the apostles would have easily recognized it in the book of Daniel and interpreted Daniel accordingly.

The Pivotal Person in the Pivotal Vision

It was very common to put a chiasm within another chiasm. As a result, Daniel also structured Daniel 7 as a chiasm so readers could easily recognize the key Person in the key vision in the book: *the Son of Man.*

Because Daniel 7 begins and ends with a prophecy about the terrible "little horn," we usually assume that is the main theme of the chapter. But, when we view the vision according to its chiastic structure, we realize the coming terrible beast and "little horn" are *secondary* subjects who set the context for the *primary* subject.

Daniel 7 follows the symmetry typical of an ancient chiasm:

Beasts who represent the kingdoms of this age are introduced.

The prediction of a little horn who will be arrogant is given.

The Ancient of Days will come in judgment.

The Son of Man (a human) is given the authority of the Ancient of Days.

The interpretation of the little horn is given.

The end of the kingdoms of the age is described.

The "peak" of Daniel 7 includes both the Ancient of Days and the Son of Man. They are together at the center of the message because they are both divine. Though they are at the center together, the coming of the Ancient of Days sets the stage for the Son of Man. When the Son of Man appears, the Ancient of Days gives the kingdom and the right to judge to Him, and this makes Him the unique emphasis of Daniel's prophecy.

Daniel 7 begins and ends with the little horn because of the symmetry involved in a chiastic structure. Daniel introduced the little horn in the first part of the chapter and gave the interpretation of the little horn in the second half of the chapter, but he positioned the Son of Man in the center of the vision as the focal point of the entire vision. The antichrist is significant, but he is secondary—Jesus is the main theme.

Daniel's structure summarizes the end times the same way John did:

The revelation of Jesus Christ…. (Revelation 1:1)

This structure demonstrates the purpose of the antichrist. Though he will be dreadful and terrible, he will set the stage for the glory of Jesus. We cannot properly understand the end-time drama—or the conflict of this age—without grasping the centrality of Jesus to the story. The main theme of the end of the age is not the antichrist, Satan, suffering, the Great Tribulation, or calamity.

The main theme of the end of the age is the revelation of Jesus in His glory.

Strength for the Most Difficult Hour in History

Though all the other themes in Daniel are subject to the revelation of Jesus in His glory, the immensity of these other themes should not be minimized. Jesus warned the end-time trouble would go far beyond anything in history,[11] because the earth has never seen Satan make his last stand against God's purposes. The world, even the church, is completely unprepared for the intensity of what is going to come on the earth. Even the prophets had trouble describing the full extent of the crisis.

The intensity of what is coming is far beyond what we can imagine, and that is precisely why we must know the main theme of the end of the age. In order to survive, we must know the drama of the end of the age is not meaningless. We must know the antichrist and the Great Tribulation that will come with him is not ultimate. We must know God will bring meaning out of the end-time crisis. There is something greater. *Someone* who is supreme.

Knowing the revelation of Jesus is the central purpose of the end of the age will give the church strength to endure the most difficult hour of history.

Suffering, death, and evil were the only things visible when Jesus died. But the crucifixion quickly became the unanticipated victory of God. What seemed for a moment like a terrible defeat became the greatest triumph in history.[12] In many ways, the end of the age resembles the hour of Jesus' crucifixion. It will seem for a moment like darkness has won, and it will be difficult to imagine any good can come out of such darkness and suffering.

Jesus was able to endure the moment of His suffering for the joy set before Him. The same will be true for the end-time church. He knew His suffering would bring about redemption and the exaltation of the church. Jesus endured suffering for the joy set before Him.[13] That joy was His people. *As His people, we will endure end-time suffering for the joy set before us—the return of the Son of Man.*

The crucifixion set the stage for the glory of Jesus to be revealed in His resurrection and subsequent ascension. The end of the age will

---

[11] Matthew 24:21; Mark 13:19.

[12] 1 Corinthians 2:8; Colossians 2:14–15.

[13] Hebrews 12:2.

create a stage for Jesus' glory to be revealed in a way we have not yet known when He descends with the clouds of heaven.

The Interpretive Key to Bible Prophecy

In the book of Revelation, an angel gave John the interpretive key to Bible prophecy:

> *For the testimony of Jesus is the spirit of prophecy. (Revelation 19:10)*

Prophecy exists to give a witness about Jesus because He is the point of prophecy. Prophecies of salvation are descriptions of Jesus and His zeal to restore creation. Prophecies of judgment are also descriptions of Jesus which demonstrate His zeal for justice and righteousness.

If we read Daniel quickly, it is easy to assume the book is mostly about the antichrist and his end-time rage. On the other hand, when we apply the interpretative key John was given, it shifts the way we understand Daniel. It is not all about the antichrist. This key enables us to begin to notice how things like the structure of Daniel's book serve to emphasize Jesus as the main point of the prophecy.

The central message of Daniel and every other message that gives insight into the end times is the supremacy of Jesus. God is using all of history, including the wickedness of the nations and the most wicked man in history, to set a stage He can use to reveal the majesty of His Son in an unprecedented way.

The Message of the Structure

When we interpret Daniel 7 through the literary structure Daniel used, we discover his chief message:

- The Son of Man is the central Person of history. He is the central revelation of all Daniel's revelations.

- The Son of Man is at the very center of God's plan to liberate the planet from darkness. He is God's solution to the wickedness and oppression of this age—past, present, and future.

- The exaltation of the Son of Man is the answer to the crisis of this age. When He is exalted, the evil in this age will be judged, the kingdom of God will be given to Him, and the righteous will be rewarded.

Though Daniel only wrote a few words about the Son of Man, he organized the chapter so we would know the Son of Man was the main point of his book. As we interpret Daniel 7 through this lens, we begin to see why the chapter served as a basis for the gospel in the New Testament.

Daniel Did Not Tell Us Everything

There is an important detail in Daniel's introduction:

> *In the first year of Belshazzar king of Babylon Daniel saw a dream and visions in his mind as he lay on his bed; then he wrote the dream down and related the following summary of it. (Daniel 7:1 NASB95)*

Daniel's prophetic experience in Daniel 7 consisted of a dream *and* visions, meaning this dream was more than a normal prophetic dream. Furthermore, Daniel only communicated *a summary* of the dream. The word Daniel used here means he only wrote down the main facts.

The brevity of Daniel's description of the Son of Man can lead us to think the vision was not as significant as it was, but Daniel did not tell us everything he saw. This means there were parts of the vision so precious to Daniel that he chose not to include them in his public account. *Because of this, we do not know the full extent of what Daniel saw when he saw the Son of Man.*

There are times when God reveals something, and it is not to be written down. This typically happens for two reasons. The first is because there are details the Lord does not want communicated at that time. For example, John's vision in Revelation was similar to Daniel's visions, and John was told not to write down certain parts of his vision for this reason:

> *And when the seven thunders had sounded, I was about to write, but I heard a voice from heaven saying, "Seal up what the seven thunders have said, and do not write it down." ... but that in the days of the trumpet call to be sounded by the seventh angel, the mystery of God would be fulfilled, just as he announced to his servants the prophets. (Revelation 10:4–7)*

There were things revealed to John because the Lord wanted to share them with him, but the Lord did not want John to record those things at that point in time. They were to be revealed later when the mystery of God would be fulfilled.

The second reason something is not written down is because it is too precious to be written. When the apostle Paul described a heavenly vision he had, there were things he did not write down:

> *I know a man in Christ who fourteen years ago was caught up to the third heaven.... and he heard things that cannot be told, which man may not utter. (2 Corinthians 12:2, 4)*

Either of these reasons could cause a biblical author to not write something down. In Daniel's case, it is likely both reasons led him to summarize the vision for the future.

This dream left Daniel alarmed:

> *"Here is the end of the matter. As for me, Daniel, my thoughts greatly alarmed me, and my color changed, but I kept the matter in my heart." (Daniel 7:28)*

Considering everything Daniel had lived through, this reaction also helps explain what Daniel meant when he said he only told the summary of the vision. Daniel's words clearly could not convey the full intensity of the dream.

The significance of Daniel 7 in the New Testament indicates Daniel's vision of Jesus was probably much more majestic than what he recorded in Daniel 7. For example, when Jesus displayed His glory on the Mount of Transfiguration, He appeared as the Son of Man, and His glory was described by terms used in Daniel 7.[14] When the disciples saw Him this way, they were terrified.[15] John the apostle knew Jesus very well, but when he saw Jesus as the Son of Man, he also fell at Jesus' feet as a dead man.[16]

---

[14]Daniel 7:9–10; Matthew 17:2; Luke 9:29.

[15]Mark 9:6.

[16]Revelation 1:12–17.

The Centrality of the Son of Man

Many Bible teachers have looked for an overarching theme that unifies the Bible and helps readers make sense of the diverse books of the Bible. Many theologians have proposed reading the Bible as a story. This is helpful because the Bible was captured as an unfolding story, but the story is not the main point of the Bible.

The ultimate message of the Bible is the revelation of God.

This entire age only serves two purposes in the end. The first is the revelation of God to His creation, and the second is the formation of a people to be God's eternal companion. The story of redemption is not the ultimate point of the Bible. The story of redemption serves the ultimate point: the revelation of God to His creation.

There are a number of ways we can read the Bible that helps us better grasp it, but everything in it—creation, the story, the covenants, etc.—is part of an elaborate stage God has built to reveal Himself. We need to understand the stage, but the main actor on the stage—God Himself—must remain the central focus.

If the story of the Bible is not read with this in mind way, we tend to think the story is all about the rescue of humanity, and we inadvertently develop a man-centered gospel that revolves around God's rescue of man as the central theme of the story.

The knowledge of God—not the rescue of humanity—is the main point of the story, and it is expressed in two ways. First, God reveals Himself in a unique and unprecedented way through His activity in the story of redemption. Second, God's revelation of Himself in the work of redemption also transforms a people into His own likeness. As God makes Himself known, it reveals the image He wants us to be formed into. God deeply desires and enjoys us, but the story is not all about us.

Daniel 7 was structured according to this paradigm. The vision in Daniel 7 unfolded according to a well-known ancient structure that was obvious to Daniel. Daniel wrote the vision down according to this structure so we would recognize the Son of Man—and not the beasts—as the central message of his book.

Daniel's structure communicated a profound message: *The knowledge and nature of God must be the preeminent focus of biblical preaching and singing.*

THE DIVINE SON OF MAN

The gospel given to us in the Scripture is a God-centered message that answers the deepest desires of the human heart by giving us access to the revelation of the Person of God.

The gospel is often communicated as a man-centered message, but it was not given that way. When we emphasize human needs and human fulfillment above the knowledge of God, we withhold the thing the human heart desires the most—an encounter with the knowledge of God.

When we become man-centered, we choose lesser pleasures over the true pleasure of the gospel: *God.* Many preachers try to make the gospel appealing by communicating it in a man-centered way as if God exists solely for our sakes and our success. While that carries a measure of appeal, that is not the way the human heart was designed.

Fallen humans are self-centered, but they still deeply crave an encounter with something bigger and more majestic than themselves. We may search for this in a number of different ways, but this craving is meant to be satisfied in God Himself.

God chose to answer this craving by coming to us like a Son of Man:

"I saw in the night visions, and behold, with the clouds of heaven there came one like a son of man, and he came to the Ancient of Days and was presented before him. And to him was given dominion and glory and a kingdom, that all peoples, nations, and languages should serve him; his dominion is an everlasting dominion, which shall not pass away, and his kingdom one that shall not be destroyed." (Daniel 7:13–14)

Daniel's description of the Son of Man clearly presented Him as a divine Person in human form. Because we read the Bible with very little foundation in the Old Testament, we can easily miss important details. With that in mind, we need to review Daniel's description of the Son of Man to see how Daniel presented Him as divine.

He Came with the Clouds

The Son of Man "came with the clouds" (v. 13). The Old Testament contains four other references to a figure riding the clouds (the heavens), and each time YHWH is the one who rides the clouds:

> *"There is none like God, O Jeshurun, who rides through the heavens to your help, through the skies in his majesty." (Deuteronomy 33:26)*

> *O kingdoms of the earth, sing to God; sing praises to the Lord, Selah to him who rides in the heavens, the ancient heavens; behold, he sends out his voice, his mighty voice. (Psalm 68:32–33)*

> *Bless the LORD, O my soul! O LORD my God, you are very great! You are clothed with splendor and majesty, covering yourself with light as with a garment, stretching out the heavens like a tent. He lays the beams of his chambers on the waters; he makes the clouds his chariot; he rides on the wings of the wind; he makes his messengers winds, his ministers a flaming fire. (Psalm 104:1–4)*

> *An oracle concerning Egypt. Behold, the LORD is riding on a swift cloud and comes to Egypt; and the idols of Egypt will tremble at his presence, and the heart of the Egyptians will melt within them. (Isaiah 19:1)*

Moses wrote there was "none like God" who rides the heavens because the ancient Israelites believed anyone who came riding clouds was divine. As scholar Peter Gentry notes, this alone reveals the Son of Man is divine:

> *The coming on clouds suggests an appearance or theophany of Yahweh himself. If Daniel 7:13 does not refer to an appearance of deity, it is the only exception in about seventy instances in the Old Testament.[1]*

Not only was *riding* the clouds an exclusively divine activity, God repeatedly descended in a cloud or appeared to His people in a cloud,

---

[1]Peter J. Gentry, "The Son of Man in Daniel 7: Individual or Corporate?" in *Acorns to Oaks: The Primacy and Practice of Biblical Theology*, ed. Michael A. G. Haykin, (Toronto: Joshua, 2003), 73.

and a person appearing in clouds would immediately bring to mind God on Mount Sinai:[2]

> *The LORD descended in the cloud and stood with him there, and proclaimed the name of the LORD. (Exodus 34:5)*

The real shock of the passage is the Ancient of Days—the One who came descended on Mount Sinai—had already appeared in the scene before a second Person came in the clouds like YHWH had done on Mount Sinai. The God of Mount Sinai appeared to Daniel in two Persons. God had periodically appeared in human form in the Old Testament, but two distinct manifestations of YHWH in the same moment are very rare.

One Like a Son of Man

Daniel described this person as one *"like* a son of man" (v. 13, emphasis added). This was a real Person, not an entity representing something else, because He interacted with the Ancient of Days as a Person.[3] If this Person was only a man, Daniel would have plainly said it. Instead, Daniel compared this Person to a man just as he had compared kingdoms to beasts. Each of the beasts that Daniel saw in the beginning of the chapter were both *like* a beast and at the same time completely *different* from those beasts. They looked *like* a beast but were in reality something else.[4]

As Daniel Boyarin wrote:

> *We cannot see this coming with the clouds of heaven as a "gift" to a human, for then he would not be One like a Son of Man, but simply a son of man. In the simile lies the divinity....*[5]

This Person was clearly divine, so He was not an ordinary human. However, He looked *like* a human—so much so Daniel did not explain

---

[2]Exodus 13:21; 16:10; 20:21; 24:16; 33:9, 10; 34:5; 40:34, 38; 2 Chronicles 5:13; 1 Kings 8:10–13; Psalm 18:9–11; 68:32–33; 104:3.

[3]Daniel Boyarin, "Intertextuality, and the History of Israel's Cult," *Harvard Theological Review* 105 (March 2012): 147.

[4]John E. Goldingay, *Daniel*, vol. 30, Word Biblical Commentary (Dallas: Word, Incorporated, 1998), 167–68.

[5]Boyarin, "Intertextuality, and the History of Israel's Cult," 155.

why this Person could not be human. Daniel could have described the Son of Man as YHWH in the *appearance* of a man as Ezekiel did,[6] but instead He saw YHWH *like* a human. YHWH had appeared before in the appearance of a man, but this was something different. This time YHWH really looked human but was still divine.

He Came to the Ancient of Days

The Son of Man "came to the Ancient of Days and was presented before Him" (v. 13). No human being could directly approach the Ancient of Days, nor would they even dare.[7] Even Moses was only permitted to see limited expressions of God's glory. The Son of Man not only rode the clouds, He approached the throne of God directly, something else only a divine Person could do.

Also, if the Ancient of Days' throne was set for judgment on the earth, which is likely, it means the Son of Man *descended* from the heavens to approach the Ancient of Days. John Goldingay explains:

> *A number of descriptions of God on his throne of fire surrounded by numerous attendants locate the scene in heaven…. Where it is specifically a matter of God judging, however, the scene is normally on earth: see Jer 49:38; Joel 4 [3]:1–2, 12; Zech 14:1–5; Ps 50; 96:10–13; 1 Enoch 1.3–9; 25.3; 90.20–27. In Dan 7, there is no reason to suppose that the scene on earth that Daniel has been watching (vv 2–8) has changed. Indeed, the opening phrase of v 9 implies a continuity of perspective: Daniel continues to look in the direction he had been looking. That the scene takes place on earth is presupposed by v 22….[8]*

Jesus seemed to read Daniel this way because He used verse 13 to predict He would descend from heaven to the earth in His second coming to judge the nations.

The One Who Judges

Daniel 7:9–10 and verse 13 depict the Son of Man in judgment:

---

[6]Ezekiel 1:26.

[7]Exodus 33:18, 20; Deuteronomy 4:12; John 1:18; 6:46.

[8]Goldingay, *Daniel*, 164–65.

"Thrones were placed, and the Ancient of Days took his seat…. the court sat in judgment, and the books were opened…. and he came to the Ancient of Days and was presented before him."

The appearance of the Son of Man in a judgment scene was very significant. In the ancient Jewish world, one of the markers of deity was the ability to create and the ability to judge creation. (For example, when the New Testament presents Jesus as involved in creation and judgment, it is a statement of His deity.[9])

When the Son of Man approached the Ancient of Days to receive the right to judge, the Son of Man further established Himself as a divine figure. This demonstrated He was in a different category from men like Moses or David who had favor with God. *This Son of Man was essentially put in the place of God.*

Other prophets also predicted YHWH would judge the nations:[10]

"I will gather all the nations and bring them down to the Valley of Jehoshaphat. And I will enter into judgment with them there, on behalf of my people and my heritage Israel, because they have scattered them among the nations and have divided up my land." (Joel 3:2)

"Therefore wait for me," declares the LORD, "for the day when I rise up to seize the prey. For my decision is to gather nations, to assemble kingdoms, to pour out upon them my indignation, all my burning anger; for in the fire of my jealousy all the earth shall be consumed." (Zephaniah 3:8)

However, Daniel added a distinction not clear in other prophecies: God would descend from heaven in the appearance of a man to execute the Ancient of Days' judgment.

He Was Given Everlasting Dominion

When the Son of Man approached the Ancient of Days, He was given three things: dominion, glory, and a kingdom.

---

[9]Matthew 16:27; 25:31–46; 28:18; John 1:1–4; 5:22–23; 17:2; Acts 10:42–43; 17:31; Romans 2:16; 2 Corinthians 5:10; Colossians 1:15–16; 2 Thessalonians 1:7–10; 2 Timothy 4:1; Hebrews 1:1–6; 1 Peter 4:5; Revelation 19:11–16; 20:11–12.

[10]See also Isaiah 34:1–3, 42:14–15; 63:1–9; Jeremiah 25:15–38; Joel 3:9–14; Zephaniah 1:14–15; 3:8; Zechariah 14:1–5.

> *"And to him was given dominion and glory and a kingdom, that all peoples, nations, and languages should serve him; his dominion is an everlasting dominion, which shall not pass away, and his kingdom one that shall not be destroyed." (Daniel 7:14)*

Dominion is a significant word in Daniel. It was used to compare the temporary rule of proud kings to God's eternal rule.[11] Rulers like Nebuchadnezzar and the other beasts would be given *temporary* dominion, but God alone had and has *everlasting* dominion:

> *At the end of the days I, Nebuchadnezzar, lifted my eyes to heaven, and my reason returned to me, and I blessed the Most High, and praised and honored him who lives forever, for his dominion is an everlasting dominion, and his kingdom endures from generation to generation. (Daniel 4:34)*

Nebuchadnezzar acknowledged the dominion and supremacy of the Most High (YHWH) when he was profoundly humbled. Nebuchadnezzar's statement about the dominion of the Most High in Daniel 4 was applied to the Son of Man in Daniel 7, which means the dominion of the Son of Man is equivalent to the dominion of YHWH.

The Son of Man is not just an agent of YHWH; He is the One who has everlasting dominion. The Son of Man was given glory with His dominion because, if He shared YHWH's dominion, He shared YHWH's glory as well. As a result, both His dominion *and* His glory were everlasting.[12]

He Was Given a Kingdom

Dominion, glory, and kingdoms are connected to kings in the book of Daniel.[13] Other kings in Daniel were given limited time and limited dominion, but only the Son of Man will have everlasting dominion. The characteristics of the kingdom indicate certain things about the Son of Man:

- His dominion is everlasting, so He must be everlasting.

---

[11] Daniel 4:3, 22, 34; 6:26; 7:6, 12, 14, 26.

[12] *Everlasting* is an Old Testament equivalent of *eternal* in the New Testament.

[13] Daniel 2:6, 37, 39–42, 44; 4:3, 17–18, 22, 25–26, 29–32, 34, 36; 5:7, 11, 16, 18, 20–21, 26–29, 31; 6:1, 3–4, 7, 26, 28; 7:6, 12, 14, 18, 22–24, 26–27.

- His kingdom will not pass away; therefore, He will never pass away.

- His kingdom cannot be destroyed; therefore, He cannot be destroyed.

The implications are obvious: These are characteristics only God has, and the Son of Man shares these characteristics. Other prophets predicted YHWH would become king over the earth, but they did not know how:[14]

Clap your hands, all peoples! Shout to God with loud songs of joy! For the LORD, the Most High, is to be feared, a great king over all the earth…. For God is the King of all the earth; sing praises with a psalm! (Psalm 47:1–2, 7)

"As I live, declares the Lord GOD, surely with a mighty hand and an outstretched arm and with wrath poured out I will be king over you." (Ezekiel 20:33)

And the LORD will be king over all the earth. On that day the LORD will be one and his name one. (Zechariah 14:9)

Daniel was shown YHWH will become the king over the earth through One like a Son of Man.

The kingdom in Daniel 7 was connected to the dream given to Nebuchadnezzar in Daniel 2. In Nebuchadnezzar's dream, God revealed He would destroy all the kingdoms of this age and set up a kingdom which would never be destroyed:

"And in the days of those kings the God of heaven will set up a kingdom that shall never be destroyed, nor shall the kingdom be left to another people. It shall break in pieces all these kingdoms and bring them to an end, and it shall stand forever." (Daniel 2:44)

The kingdom of the Son of Man is the Daniel 2 kingdom that never ends and will never be destroyed. There will never be "another people" who will replace this kingdom because the King is everlasting.

---

[14]See also Isaiah 2:2–4; 49:7; Ezekiel 20:33; Daniel 2:44; Micah 4:1–3; Zechariah 8:20–23; 14:17; Revelation 11:15.

King over All People

Daniel 7:14 predicted the kingdoms of the earth would be given to the Son of Man when God judged the beast empires of this age. Other prophets also predicted YHWH would rule the nations as King when He came to judge the nations:[15]

> For the LORD, the Most High, is to be feared, a great king over all the earth. (Psalm 47:2)

> For God is the King of all the earth; sing praises with a psalm! (Psalm 47:7)

> "As I live, declares the Lord GOD, surely with a mighty hand and an outstretched arm and with wrath poured out I will be king over you." (Ezekiel 20:33)

> And the LORD will be king over all the earth. On that day the LORD will be one and his name one. (Zechariah 14:9)

The Son of Man will be given a kingdom of all "peoples, nations, and languages." This was a profound detail because prophecies of Messiah's rule usually focused on Israel and then expanded their scope to include the nations of the earth:

> "As for me, I have set my King on Zion, my holy hill." ...Ask of me, and I will make the nations your heritage, and the ends of the earth your possession. (Psalm 2:6, 8)

> "It is too light a thing that you should be my servant to raise up the tribes of Jacob and to bring back the preserved of Israel; I will make you as a light for the nations, that my salvation may reach to the end of the earth." (Isaiah 49:6)

Daniel's prediction was very different from most messianic prophecies. The Messiah was typically expected to be a political deliverer who would be king over Israel and then lead the nations to worship YHWH. The Son of Man was presented as the ruler over all na-

---

[15]See also Isaiah 2:2–4; Daniel 2:44; Micah 4:1–3; Zechariah 8:20–23; Revelation 11:15.

tions and all peoples, a description usually applied to YHWH.[16] Daniel was not trying to discard the clear prophecies of Israel's future salvation.[17] He still expected the salvation of Israel, but he now understood the coming King and His kingdom would be much more than a restored Israel.

The Most High and the Highest One

Daniel frequently referred to God as *the Most High*, and he did something very interesting with the title in Daniel 7.[18] Daniel referred to the Ancient of Days and the Son of Man with two different terms that both mean *Most High*. Because the two terms mean the same thing, some English Bibles translate both terms using the same English phrase, but Daniel's decision to use two different but similar words was very significant.

The NASB translates these terms differently so English readers can recognize what Daniel did. The NASB translated the term typically used by Daniel as *Most High* and the term Daniel added in Daniel 7 as *Highest One*.

Daniel used this new term in four verses in chapter 7:

> *"But the saints of the Highest One will receive the kingdom and possess the kingdom forever, for all ages to come.'" (v. 18 NASB95)*

> *"Until the Ancient of Days came and judgment was passed in favor of the saints of the Highest One, and the time arrived when the saints took possession of the kingdom." (v. 22 NASB95)*

> *"He will speak out against the Most High and wear down the saints of the Highest One, and he will intend to make alterations in times and in law; and they will be given into his hand for a time, times, and half a time." (v. 25 NASB95)*

---

[16]Psalm 10:16; 29:10; 45; 47:2, 7; 74:12; 93; 96; 97–99; 103; Isaiah 2:2–4; 49:7; Jeremiah 10:10; Ezekiel 20:33; Daniel 2:44; Micah 4:1–3; Zechariah 8:3, 20–23; 14:9, 17.

[17]Deuteronomy 30:1–6; Isaiah 4:3; 45:17, 25; 54:13; 59:21; 60:4, 21; 61:8–9; 66:22; Jeremiah 31:31–34; 32:40; Ezekiel 20:40; 36:10, 27–36; 39:22, 28–29; Joel 2:26, 32; Zephaniah 3:9, 12–13; Zechariah 12:10–13; Matthew 23:39; 24:30; Acts 1:6–7; 2:21; Romans 10:13; 11:26–27; Revelation 1:7.

[18]Daniel 3:26; 4:2, 17, 24, 25, 32, 34; 5:18, 21; 7:18, 22, 25, 27.

"Then the sovereignty, the dominion and the greatness of all the kingdoms under the whole heaven will be given to the people of the saints of the Highest One; His kingdom will be an everlasting kingdom, and all the dominions will serve and obey Him."" (v. 27 NASB95)

Because both terms for *Most High* mean the same thing, it raises important questions. *First, why did Daniel introduce a new term for the Most High?* He already had a term he used consistently. *Second, why did Daniel use two different terms that mean the same thing in the same chapter?*

The answer is found in Daniel 7:25 where both terms are used in the same verse:

"He will speak out against the Most High and wear down the saints of the Highest One, and he will intend to make alterations in times and in law; and they will be given into his hand for a time, times, and half a time."" (NASB95)

The verse predicts the "little horn" will speak out against the Most High and also wear down the saints of the Most High (*Highest One* in the NASB). The first *Most High* is the *Ancient of Days*. The saints belong to the *Son of Man*, so He is the second *Most High*. Daniel used two different terms for Most High to communicate an incredible message:

Both the Ancient of Days and the Son of Man can be referred to as the Most High.

James Hamilton explains this unusual use of language:

Daniel uses the two terms side by side in 7: 25 'He shall speak words against the Most High עילא, *'illāyā', / and shall wear out the saints of the Most High* וינוילע, *'elyônîn', prompting Gentry to ask: Why does the author use a Hebrew expression (with Aramaic ending) for the Most High in the Aramaic section and side by side with the expression standard in Aramaic? It seems a deliberate attempt to draw some distinction between a divine figure associated with the saints and yet perhaps distinguished from Yahweh in some way. Because of the similarity of the statements in Daniel 7:14 and 7:27, we can be certain that the Most High referred to with* וינוילע *('elyônîn) and associated with the saints in the phrase 'saints of the Most High' is the 'one like a son of man.'[19]*

Let's summarize Hamilton's observation: *Most High* was a term used for YHWH, whom Daniel referred to as the *Ancient of Days* in

---

[19]Hamilton, *With the Clouds of Heaven,*151–52.

Daniel 7. However, Daniel also described the *Son of Man* as the *Most High*. Yet, Daniel used a second term for *Most High*. By using a second term with the same meaning, Daniel presented the Ancient of Days and Son of Man as distinct from each other, yet both can be called the *Most High*, which means *both* are YHWH.

Daniel also provided another connection between the Most High and the Son of Man. Compare Daniel 7:14 to Daniel 7:27:

> *"And to him was given dominion and glory and a kingdom, that all peoples, nations, and languages should serve him; his dominion is an everlasting dominion, which shall not pass away, and his kingdom one that shall not be destroyed." (v. 14)*

> *"And the kingdom and the dominion and the greatness of the kingdoms under the whole heaven shall be given to the people of the saints of the Most High; his kingdom shall be an everlasting kingdom, and all dominions shall serve and obey him.'" (v. 27)*

In Daniel 7:14, the dominion and the kingdom are given to the Son of Man, and all people, nations, and languages serve Him. In Daniel 7:27, the dominion and the kingdom are given to the saints of the Most High, and all dominions serve and obey Him. In one verse, all dominions serve the Son of Man, and in the other, they serve the Most High. *Both will be served by every lesser power.* This "service" is religious service, which means the Son of Man will be worshipped:

> *Daniel's reference to the Son of Man being "served" implies a divine status for the Son of Man, not merely because of the use of that one word, but because of the context in which it is used. The universal sovereignty attributed to the Son of Man is earlier attributed to Daniel's God by the Babylonian and Persian kings.*[20]

---

[20]Robert Bowman and J. Ed Komoszewski, *Putting Jesus in His Place: The Case for the Deity of Christ* (Grand Rapids, MI: Kregel Publications, 2007), Kindle edition, Locations 649–51.

Again, Hamilton explains what is going on here:[21]

Finally the reuse of a phrase from Daniel 7:13 in 7:27 identifies the 'one like a son of man' with the 'Most High'. Daniel 7:14 states that peoples, nations and languages will 'serve' the son of man, and the same Hebrew phrase is used in 7:27 וְחַלְפִי הַל, lēh yiplĕḥûn) to state that all dominions will serve the Most High. This is language used elsewhere in Daniel to refer to the kind of service one renders to what one worships (cf. the use of the verb in 3:12, 14, 17–18, 28; 6:17, 21 MT), and it is more probable that such service would be rendered to the Most High than to the people. Here again, Daniel used the Hebrew adjective with the Aramaic plural ending (וְינוּלַע, 'elyônîn) to refer to the 'one like a son of man' as Most High, distinguishing him from the Ancient of Days, for whom he used the normal Aramaic expression (אִילַע, 'illāyā') when designating him as Most High.[22]

Once more, Hamilton gives an excellent summary of Daniel's message about the Son of Man:

By using these distinct forms for 'Most High' consistently Daniel identified both the Ancient of Days and the one like a son of man as the Most High, even as he distinguished them from one another. In this passage, Daniel communicates that the one like a son of man will be enthroned alongside the Ancient of Days, that he comes with the clouds as Yahweh does elsewhere (e.g. Pss 18:10; 97: 2; 104:3, etc.), that he receives service and worship—described with terms only elsewhere used for describing obeisance done for deity (Gentry 2003: 72–73), and that he will receive the everlasting kingdom which shall not pass away, which is exactly how God's kingdom is described. The Ancient of Days is described as Most High with one term, while the one like a son of man is described as Most High with another. And the term used to describe the one like a son of man as Most High is always used in the phrase 'saints of the Most High', apparently because the Psalm 8:5 son of man who receives dominion over the beasts, the Psalm 110:1 Lord of David who sits at Yahweh's right hand, will be king over the saints, their representative who is somehow both identified with and

---

[21]See also Stephen R. Miller, *Daniel*, vol. 18, The New American Commentary (Nashville: Broadman & Holman Publishers, 1994), 208–9 and André Lacocque, *The Book of Daniel: Commentary*, trans. David Pellauer (Eugene, OR: Wipf & Stock, 2014), 147–48.

[22]Hamilton, *With the Clouds of Heaven: The Book of Daniel in Biblical Theology*, 162.

distinguished from the Ancient of Days, even as he is both a descendant of David and a divine figure.[23]

The Big Question

Daniel repeatedly took phrases, predictions, and attributes that belonged to YHWH and applied them to the Son of Man. In context, the One like a Son of Man is unquestionably divine. Consequently, when Jesus claimed to be the Son of Man, He was accused of blasphemy and sentenced to execution for making Himself equal to God, demonstrating Jesus' audience knew the Son of Man was divine.[24]

The vision raised some very significant questions: *Who was this Son of Man? Why did YHWH appear as two distinct individuals in the same vision? Why did Daniel present a divine, heavenly Person as both YHWH and "like a son of man"?* The Son of Man was God, but He also seemed to be genuinely human. Daniel's description of the Son of Man created a mystery which would not be solved until the Son of Man took centerstage in history.

---

[23]Hamilton, *With the Clouds of Heaven: The Book of Daniel in Biblical Theology*, 152–53.

[24]Matthew 26:64–66; John 5:18–29.

DANIEL'S FRAMEWORK

Daniel's vision of the Son of Man was remarkable, but he saw much more than a divine Human. He was given a basic framework that would become the foundation of the gospel of the kingdom.

Before we move to the New Testament, we need to briefly summarize what Daniel knew about the gospel of the kingdom as a result of his vision. We will identify the key gospel-related themes of the vision, and this will enable us to better appreciate the way Jesus used Daniel to proclaim His gospel.

Salvation through Judgment

The Son of Man was introduced to Daniel in a dramatic judgment scene. YHWH was seated in judgment with a river of fire in front of Him, bringing absolute judgment on the beasts who had destroyed His creation. In this setting, the Son of Man approached the Ancient of Days and was given absolute dominion, implying the Son of Man was given the right to judge.

The Son of Man's participation in the Ancient of Days' judgments communicated three profound messages: (1) The glory of the Son of Man will be revealed in judgment; (2) the Son of Man will come through judgment; and (3) mercy will be given in judgment.

The Glory of the Son of Man Will Be Revealed in Judgment

The glory of the Ancient of Days and the Son of Man was revealed to Daniel in a judgment scene, indicating God intends to reveal the glory of the Son of Man through His judgments at the end of the age.

God could have revealed the glory of the Son of Man to Daniel in a number of ways, but He chose to reveal the Son of Man in a judgment scene as He came with the clouds to render judgment and take dominion. This indicates the Son of Man will be fully unveiled when

He comes in judgment, and there are dimensions of His glory only revealed in judgment.

The rule of the beasts and the suffering they bring serve a purpose in God's sovereign plan, but God will decisively and permanently judge the beasts at His appointed time. Though God's judgment may seem to be delayed, it will come.

Salvation Will Come through Judgment

The Son of Man was given absolute dominion and an everlasting kingdom. This kingdom will bring salvation to the earth, and it will be established in the context of judgment. This kingdom itself is a judgment because it removes and ends every other "beast" kingdom. We tend to think of salvation as a rescue *from* judgment, but Daniel saw the Son of Man bring salvation *through* judgment.

Judgment is necessary because it brings an end to evil. It punishes and removes every individual and system that perpetuates destruction and evil. We tend to think of judgment as the opposite of salvation, but without judgment, there is no salvation. If evil is never punished, good never triumphs. If the instruments and systems of evil are never removed, true salvation never comes.

Salvation must come through judgment.

We tend to think of salvation as the gift of mercy, but it goes far beyond that. Salvation includes deliverance from evil and the destruction of every evil system. The need for judgment is only shocking to us because we are familiar with the presence of evil in this age and do not realize how pervasive it is in our world. Evil has affected and penetrated all the systems of this age, even the ones we do not see as overtly evil. Therefore, true salvation requires a judgment of every structure of evil—humans, spiritual powers, and systems.

God's plan to bring salvation through judgment is often overlooked, but it is so central to the Bible that James Hamilton has proposed it is the unifying theme of the biblical narrative:

> *I am putting forth the theory that the glory of God in salvation through judgment is the center of biblical theology.*[1]

---

[1]James M. Hamilton, Jr., *God's Glory in Salvation through Judgment: A Biblical Theology* (Wheaton, IL: Crossway, 2010), Kindle edition, Location 565.

Regardless of whether Hamilton's proposal is correct, the fact a scholar of his caliber would propose salvation through judgment as the central unifying theme of the Bible indicates how prominent this theme is.

Mercy Will Be Given in Judgment

Daniel saw the Ancient of Days judge the beast kingdoms of this age (Daniel 7:9–12), but then he saw something surprising—when YHWH judges the beast kingdoms of this age, the Son of Man will be given a people from every nation and language (Daniel 7:14). This prediction was significant because it occurred in the middle of a judgment scene. YHWH destroyed the "beasts" (nations) but also delivered a people out of those nations to be given to the Son of Man as an inheritance. This revealed something profound: Though salvation will come through judgment, mercy will also be given in judgment.

Without judgment, there is no salvation. However, *if judgment removes everyone, then salvation cannot be enjoyed by anyone other than God.* YHWH's mercy will deliver a people to enjoy the salvation that comes through His judgments. The fact that the people come from all nations indicates mercy will be shown to people who were part of the beast kingdoms that YHWH will destroy in judgment.

This mysterious prophecy highlighted both judgment *and* mercy. In YHWH's judgment, He will display His mercy, and the terror of those judgments will reveal the full beauty of His mercy. YHWH will be glorified in mercy and judgment.

Dominion of the Beasts

Daniel was also shown the world is currently under the dominion of "beasts." This scene was intended to remind us of the Garden of Eden. In the garden, an unusual beast (serpent) gained dominion over man and brought chaos and evil into the earth. As a result, humans who should be the image of God, have instead become like "beasts." The earth should be a garden ruled by men, but instead it's ruled by beasts who take dominion over men.[2]

---

[2]There is a lot of Garden of Eden imagery in Daniel. Daniel and Nebuchadnezzar are two examples. The first test Daniel faces is a test over eating forbidden food. Nebuchadnezzar is a glorious king who exalts himself to become like God and is reduced to a beast, symbolizing the fall of man.

This dominion of the beasts is temporary, and it will climax with one dreadful, terrible beast that will be radically different from every other beast. This beast is described as "different" from the other beasts to identify him with the original strange beast (serpent) who first appeared in the garden. A king will come from this beast who will be arrogant and persecute God's people, but his time will be limited. He will seek to extend his time, but after a brief time God will come in judgment, destroy him, and end the rule of the beasts.

We cannot be completely sure why Daniel used these four beasts to symbolize evil empires, but it was likely a reference to Hosea 13:[3]

So I am to them like a lion; like a leopard I will lurk beside the way. I will fall upon them like a bear robbed of her cubs; I will tear open their breast, and there I will devour them like a lion, as a wild beast would rip them open. (vv. 7–8)

Hosea described God's judgment of Israel by the nations with four images: lion, leopard, bear, and wild beast. This link emphasizes the beasts are evil yet fully under God's sovereignty, accomplishing His purposes in a surprising and shocking way. Just as Hosea warned Israel, Daniel was also told the saints would be given into the hands of the beast for a limited time.[4]

The imagery of the beasts, the Son of Man, and the end of the beasts is a description of the fulfillment of Genesis 3:15. The last beast is the "offspring" of the serpent, and the "Son of Man" is the "offspring" of the woman. He will crush the beasts and take dominion as a man:

"I will put enmity between you and the woman, and between your offspring and her offspring; he shall bruise your head, and you shall bruise his heel." (Genesis 3:15)

These beasts are both spiritual powers and kings because evil spiritual powers rule through the evil empires of this age until the Son of Man takes dominion, judges the powers, and replaces them with His

---

[3]John Joseph Collins and Adela Yarbro Collins, *Daniel: A Commentary on the Book of Daniel*, Hermeneia—A Critical and Historical Commentary on the Bible, ed. Frank Moore Cross (Minneapolis, MN: Fortress Press, 1993), 295.

[4]Daniel 7:21, 25.

kingdom.[5] The ancient world assumed a deep connection between spiritual powers and empires. For example, Babylon assumed its victories came from its god Marduk, and the Assyrians warned Judah that YHWH could not protect Jerusalem from the god of the Assyrians.[6] Daniel's vision confirmed this view of the world.

The New Adam

The central figure in God's redemptive plan is a Person known as the Son of Man. He will appear in the heavens when the time comes for judgment. He will be given the right to judge and rule the nations.

Though the Son of Man was divine, He was presented as a human, a new Adam, exercising dominion over the beasts as Adam was commissioned to do.[7] This heavenly Man will fulfill the mandate Adam was given.

This was a profound act of divine poetry. In Genesis, Adam was made in the image of God to rule the beasts, but Adam failed. In Daniel 7, God appears in the image of Adam to rule over the beasts, and God succeeds.

Though the beasts in Daniel 7 are kings and powers of darkness, the vision of a man who would subdue the beasts reminded readers of Genesis 1–3 and likely also brought Psalm 8 to mind:[8]

> *O LORD, our Lord, how majestic is your name in all the earth! You have set your glory above the heavens…. what is man that you are mindful of him, and the son of man that you care for him? Yet you have made him a little lower than the heavenly beings and crowned him with glory and honor. You have given him dominion over the works of your hands; you have put all things under his feet, all sheep and oxen, and also the beasts of the field, the birds of the heavens, and the fish of the sea, whatever passes along the paths of the seas. (vv. 1, 4–8)*

The Kingdom

The Son of Man will be given a permanent, indestructible kingdom, and He will rule forever. This kingdom will be given to Him as an inheritance and reward. It will be God's kingdom, and He will rule in

---

[5]Daniel 7:17.

[6]Isaiah 36:14–20.

[7]Genesis 1:26–28.

[8]Hamilton, *With the Clouds of Heaven: The Book of Daniel in Biblical Theology*, 90.

God's place. When this kingdom comes, it will replace every other kingdom on the earth permanently, and it will consist of people redeemed out of every people group.

The People

The Son of Man was not only given a kingdom, He was given a people as well:

> *"But the saints of the Most High shall receive the kingdom and possess the kingdom forever, forever and ever.... until the Ancient of Days came, and judgment was given for the saints of the Most High, and the time came when the saints possessed the kingdom.... 'And the kingdom and the dominion and the greatness of the kingdoms under the whole heaven shall be given to the people of the saints of the Most High; his kingdom shall be an everlasting kingdom, and all dominions shall serve and obey him.'"* (Daniel 7:18, 22, 27)

According to verse 27, the kingdom with dominion over all kingdoms is the kingdom of the Most High, but it will also be given to the saints. The conclusion is inescapable: *The Son of Man, as YHWH, will be deeply connected to a people, and He will share His dominion with them.* While these people are not divine, they will be exalted to co-rule with the Son of Man forever.

When the Ancient of Days appeared in Daniel 7, *thrones* were placed. In light of verse 27, it is likely Daniel saw multiple thrones set for the exalted saints to rule alongside the Son of Man:[9]

> *"As I looked, thrones were placed, and the Ancient of Days took his seat."* (v. 9)

The Son of Man was the most significant part of the prophecy, but this people is the second most significant part of the prophecy. They will be raised to near divine status. They will rule forever, implying they are no longer mortals. They are some sort of resurrected, immortal humanity who will come from every nation and every people.

---

[9]Some believe there were only two thrones: one for the Ancient of Days and one for the Son of Man. However, Daniel could have easily indicated there were only two thrones, and he did not do so. Furthermore, the New Testament interprets this as multiple thrones (see *Son of Man: The Apostles' Gospel*, Volume 2).

Daniel was shown God's plan for Israel would result in something much bigger than a saved Israel—it would produce a people gathered from all the nations who resembled the Son of Man. God would continue His unique plan with Israel, but that plan was going to bring the nations into Israel just as He promised Abraham.[10]

Daniel's vision is both a prediction and an invitation. Those who read the prophecy and respond to it could become part of a people out of every people who will be exalted to near-divine status and inherit an everlasting kingdom.

Exaltation through Suffering

Daniel was given a shocking revelation about the exalted people who will rule with the Son of Man:

> *"As I looked, this horn made war with the saints and prevailed over them, until the Ancient of Days came, and judgment was given for the saints of the Most High, and the time came when the saints possessed the kingdom." (Daniel 7:21–22)*

Suffering was not a new subject in the Old Testament, but Daniel's vision challenged some key assumptions about suffering. In the Old Testament, sin and disobedience were assumed to be the main source of suffering. For example, in the story of Job, Job's friends assumed his suffering was a result of his sin. This kind of assumption did have a biblical basis because God's covenant with Israel warned the nation would suffer any time it embraced sin.[11] The righteous could suffer at the hands of the wicked, but this was assumed to be a temporary condition until God granted victory and blessing.

This prediction of the saints' suffering was surprising because there was no mention of sin, unrighteousness, or judgment in relationship to the saints. Nor was there a mention of the need for repentance

---

[10]This does not mean God has "replaced" Israel. For example, Daniel's prayer for Israel in Daniel 9 shows he still expected a unique salvation of Israel even after the Daniel 7 vision. See Genesis 12:1–3. The promise made to Abraham was both specific to Israel and held a promise for the peoples of the earth. For more on this, see my books *It Must Be Finished* and *One King: A Jesus-Centered Answer To The Question Of Zion And The People Of God*.

[11]Leviticus 26:14–46; Deuteronomy 28:15–29; 29.

as there was in Daniel 9.[12] On the contrary, the saints are described as being faithful and loyal.[13]

Though the saints were apparently righteous, Daniel predicted they would be subject to suffering *until* God destroys the beasts and gives the Son of Man the kingdom:

> *"As I looked, this horn made war with the saints and prevailed over them.... He shall speak words against the Most High, and shall wear out the saints of the Most High, and shall think to change the times and the law; and they shall be given into his hand for a time, times, and half a time."* (Daniel 7:21, 25)

The saints will even be given over to the final, most terrible beast. If Daniel had been told the beast would have temporary success, that would have been appalling enough, but Daniel was told the saints would be *given over* to the beast. *In other words, God's sovereign activity was the categorical cause of the saints' suffering.*

Daniel articulated an astonishing paradigm of suffering: The saints will suffer until the Son of Man appears. This suffering is part of God's sovereign leadership over His people, and it is connected to their possession of the kingdom:

> *"Until the Ancient of Days came, and judgment was given for the saints of the Most High, and the time came when the saints possessed the kingdom."* (Daniel 7:22)

While the beasts rule, the saints will endure suffering. This suffering will prepare them to inherit the kingdom.

Daniel was given a radical paradigm of suffering: The saints will be subject to suffering as a part of God's sovereign purpose until God brings an end to the reign of the beasts. This suffering will prepare them to inherit the kingdom and be exalted to immortality.

The Waiting

In this age, the saints must wait for the Son of Man to judge the beasts and establish the kingdom. His coming is the permanent resolution to the crisis of this age. It will feel at times like the beasts have dominion,

---

[12]Daniel 9:3–19.

[13]Daniel 7:18, 21–22, 25, 27.

but the world is fully under God's careful control. He is carefully moving history toward His designed conclusion.

SUMMARIZING DANIEL'S GOSPEL

Daniel's vision was a profound summary of the gospel, and in subsequent chapters we will discover it was even more profound than Daniel realized. Let's summarize the key points of Daniel's gospel:

- The earth is presently under the control of spiritual beasts (rulers and authorities) who lead and have dominion over kings and kingdoms. These spiritual powers act through men, devour, and take dominion.

- The kingdoms of this age are all distortions of what God intended. They do not possess the dignity originally given to man, and they do not function in righteousness because they act like beasts.

- The kingdoms of this age are setting the stage for the ultimate evil kingdom of this age. When the evil kingdom comes, it will be more dark, evil, and cruel than anything in history.

- The evil kingdom will be led by a king who will challenge God with his arrogant words and rebellious actions. He will be different from every other ruler in history.

- God is not going to leave the world under the dominion of the beasts. He is going to come in judgment to deliver the world from the dominion of the beasts. He will bring His final judgment at the time that the most wicked beast emerges.

- This beast will be given a limited time, and then he will be suddenly and finally destroyed by God. When this beast is destroyed, God will bring an end to the dominion of all the beasts, and the earth will never again suffer under oppressive kingdoms.

- God's appointed ruler is one "like a son of man." This ruler is the main focus of Daniel 7 and the most majestic part of the prophecy. He appeared in human form but was divine. He will be given dominion and the right to judge. His glory will be revealed when He comes to carry out God's judgment on the "beasts" of the age.

- When this Ruler comes to judge, deliver, and rule, He does not come from the earth. Instead, He descends and comes with the clouds of heaven. He is God's response to all the beasts and especially the most terrible beast. He is a new Adam—a perfect Human.

- God's judgment through the Son of Man will bring salvation. It will set into motion a transition from this age to the next. The dominion of the beasts will be taken away, they will be judged, and the Son of Man will take dominion over the earth through a kingdom that will never end.

- The kingdom was the ultimate fulfillment of Israel's promises. Daniel would have understood the kingdom as the ultimate kingdom of Israel, and yet it was coming from the heavens, which indicated the messianic kingdom was much more extensive than Israel had anticipated.

- This Son of Man will be given dominion over all the nations. Every tribe and tongue will serve Him and worship Him. This Son of Man is both divine and God's chosen King. He is the Deliverer of Israel, yet He is much more than that. He will be given dominion over the entire earth *and* every other spiritual authority or power.

- There will be a people who belong to the Son of Man, and they will rule with Him. They were referred to as "the saints." Normally, this would have been the righteous remnant of Israel, but Daniel was told the kingdom would encompass "all peoples."

- Until the Ancient of Days sits in judgment and the Son of Man comes with the clouds, it will seem as though the beast kingdoms have authority. The final beast in particular will seem to overcome the saints. However, his time is limited, and the saints should be prepared to endure his rage by knowing he cannot change the times or extend his rule in any way. This final ruler will challenge God in an unprecedented way but only for a limited amount of time.

- When the Son of Man appears with the clouds, He will come in judgment, reward the saints, set up an indestructible kingdom, and elevate the saints to rule with Him. This people will share in the Son of Man's dominion over every power and will rule forever with Him.

- The Son of Man's government on the earth will not be established until the Son of Man comes with the clouds and judges the beasts. Until He comes in judgment, the saints must be patient and endure, knowing the Ancient of Days controls the times and there is an appointed time for judgment.

When we summarize these main points, we can already begin to see the seeds of the gospel. Daniel was shown the current condition of the earth and the reason for that condition. He was also shown God's appointed answer to the crisis of the earth and a summary of God's plan to deliver creation, glorify Himself, and exalt a people into partnership with Him.

Each of these key points are foundational to the message of the gospel of the kingdom. These points are clearly stated in the New Testament, but it is easy to overlook that they came from Daniel 7. As we begin to view Daniel through a gospel-centered lens, we will see just how pervasive Daniel is in the New Testament.

Daniel 7 received a summary of the gospel, but many of the details remained hidden in mystery. Daniel would have wondered who this Son of Man was and how this divine Person in human form related to the Ancient of Days. This mystery would remain hidden until Jesus' first coming.

Conclusion

The concept of Daniel 7 as the gospel of the kingdom may seem strange, but as we work through the next section, we will begin to see how foundational this chapter is to the New Testament. Even when Daniel was not directly quoted, Jesus and the apostles viewed the gospel of the kingdom through the lens of Daniel 7.

This does not mean Daniel 7 is the only passage that describes the gospel of the kingdom. There are many other passages which describe this gospel, and numerous passages expound on details of the kingdom Daniel only briefly mentions or alludes to. To say Daniel 7 contains the gospel of the kingdom does not mean it is the only biblical description of this gospel, but no other passage includes as many aspects of the gospel of the kingdom as Daniel 7 does.

The amount of insight Daniel communicated in a small number of words is simply breathtaking. Daniel 7 contained the most complete summary of the gospel of the kingdom in the prophets, but there was more that needed to be made known. (For example, the suffering and death of the Son of Man are central to the gospel but not immediately apparent in Daniel's vision.) Revealing the true depth of Daniel 7 would require an interpreter who knew the full message—the Son of Man Daniel had seen.

THE DEPTH OF DANIEL

Much of what is revealed in the New Testament likely was not fully understood by Daniel. It was a mystery until the Son of Man was revealed because *Jesus' coming unlocked the mystery of Daniel 7.* The depth of Daniel is demonstrated by just how much of the New Testament gospel can be undergirded by the book.

Not everything described in Daniel is unique to Daniel. Many things in Daniel 7 can also be found in other Old Testament passages, and other passages expound much more than Daniel on very important biblical themes. Some prophets devote entire chapters to things Daniel barely mentions.

The miracle of Daniel 7 is how many different aspects of the gospel can be found in that one chapter. *If you could only choose one Old Testament passage to summarize the gospel, Daniel 7 could be the most important chapter.* This depth caused the apostles to use it as a framework to preach the gospel, but like many Old Testament prophecies, Daniel 7 could only be fully understood in hindsight, which is a key feature of biblical prophecy.

The Glory of Biblical Prophecy

Part of the glory of the Bible is that it is self-authenticating. That means the Bible proves it is true and divinely inspired without outside evidence. Outside evidence can be interesting and helpful, but ultimately the Bible contains proof of its own validity. One of the primary ways the Bible proves its divine origin is through the way it uses prophecy.

We frequently assume the evidence of prophecy's divine origin is found in the fulfillment of the prophecy, but the Bible uses prophecy in a much more miraculous way. Biblical authors recorded prophecies they did not fully comprehend. No one could fulfill these prophecies because they could not be fully understood until after they were fulfilled in intricate detail in ways that could never be anticipated ahead of time. *This is the glory of biblical prophecy.* It can only be fully understood and appreciated *after* it has happened and not before.

For example, consider Isaiah 53. Isaiah's prophecy contains a poetic prediction of Messiah's death:

> *But he was pierced for our transgressions; he was crushed for our iniquities; upon him was the chastisement that brought us peace, and with his wounds we are healed. All we like sheep have gone astray; we have turned—every one—to his own way; and the LORD has laid on him the iniquity of us all. He was oppressed, and he was afflicted, yet he opened not his mouth; like a lamb that is led to the slaughter, and like a sheep that before its shearers is silent, so he opened not his mouth. (Isaiah 53:5–7)*

This prophecy was vividly fulfilled in the crucifixion of Jesus, yet neither Isaiah nor anyone who read his prophecy ever anticipated this would be fulfilled as literally as it was. When the prophecy was fulfilled, however, it was a profound and precise fulfillment of everything Isaiah had prophesied.

If the prophecy had been plainly understood by Isaiah, perhaps someone would have attempted to manipulate events to fulfill the prophecy. But Isaiah did not even know how to fulfill this prophecy, and no one after Isaiah's time would ever have imagined the prophecy would be fulfilled in the way it was. Only after the prophecy was fulfilled, and we look at it in hindsight, we find it to be a precise prediction of what would happen. This demonstrates the unique nature of Scripture, and it is part of the glory of Scripture.

In our time, for instance, scholars heavily debate the book of Isaiah. Some claim there were multiple authors and the book was heavily edited after Isaiah recorded it. But there is a much, much bigger question than whether Isaiah's prophecies were edited by later compilers of the Scripture. *How did Isaiah get prophecies like Isaiah 53?* How did Isaiah predict the death of Messiah—even the way He would die—without understanding what he was predicting? Even if there were edits made to his prophecies after the fact, the book of Isaiah we have demonstrates divine inspiration in the text handed down to us.

The Bible contains prophecies the authors did not fully grasp that are fulfilled centuries later in ways no one could have anticipated, and when they are fulfilled, we discover the details were in the prophecy all along. All of this demonstrates biblical prophecy came from a divine origin.

Only God can give a prediction no man understands and then lead history to fulfill that prediction precisely.

Daniel 7 follows this pattern. Daniel understood quite a bit about the foundation of the gospel, but we will find the chapter contained much more than Daniel understood.

Recovering Gospel Foundations

The gospel is the good news of God's plan to redeem creation through Jesus. Human language is incapable of presenting the majesty of Jesus in a *full* way, but it is capable of portraying His majesty in a *true* way. The Scriptures, particularly the prophetic Scriptures,[1] were given to provide us with a true witness of who Jesus is.

Though the mystery of the gospel is revealed in the New Testament, the foundations of the gospel are not in the New Testament. The apostles and messengers in the New Testament used the Old Testament as the basis for their claims about Jesus. Tragically, we no longer know how to preach the gospel this way. While the content of our gospel is true, we lack the ability to reveal the majesty of Jesus' using Old Testament texts.

It is certainly not wrong to preach from the New Testament. It is Scripture, it is a true witness about Jesus, and it makes known a mystery hidden in the Old Testament.[2] Yet, if we are not able to reveal the beauty of Jesus from the Old Testament, we have lost something precious, and we need to recover the way the apostles preached the gospel using Old Testament texts. These passages give us fresh insight into the Person of Jesus and the miraculous nature of the Scripture.

In the next section, we will begin to discover how Jesus used the Old Testament to reveal His unique identity and lay the foundations for His gospel.

---

[1]Revelation 19:10.

[2]Romans 16:25; Ephesians 3:9; Colossians 1:26.

Daniel's Greatest Expositor

THE MYSTERY REVEALED

We need to rediscover the gospel by seeing how Jesus revealed it. As you see how Jesus used Daniel 7 to present His gospel, the gospel itself will become much more straightforward.

Daniel's prophecy seemed relatively straightforward, but the center of the prophecy created a mystery: *Who was this figure Daniel referred to as the Son of Man?* This mystery remained for nearly five centuries until the Son of Man appeared:

> *Jesus answered him, "Are you the teacher of Israel and yet you do not understand these things? ...No one has ascended into heaven except he who descended from heaven, the Son of Man." (John 3:10, 13)*

When Jesus revealed Himself as the Son of Man, He quickly became the greatest expositor of Daniel 7. He opened up the mystery of the prophecy and revealed just how much Daniel had been shown. In Jesus' hands, Daniel's prophecy took on a completely new dimension.

Gabriel Returns

Even before He was born, Jesus was intricately connected to Daniel's prophecy.

The angel Gabriel only appears a few times in the Bible. Perhaps his best known appearances are to Zechariah, predicting the birth of John the Baptist, and to Mary, predicting the birth of Jesus.[1] As the angel chosen to announce the birth of Jesus and John, Gabriel obviously has an unusual status. Gabriel emphasized this status when he introduced himself to Zechariah:

> *And the angel answered him, "I am Gabriel. I stand in the presence of God." (Luke 1:19)*

---

[1]Luke 1:13–20, 26–38.

Gabriel only appears in one other place in Scripture: the book of Daniel. Daniel named Gabriel as his interpreting angel in Daniel 8:15–19 and Daniel 9:21–23, and he was probably the interpreter from whom Daniel solicited help in Daniel 7:

"I approached one of those who stood there and asked him the truth concerning all this. So he told me and made known to me the interpretation of the things." (v. 16)

This angelic interpreter was not named but is most likely Gabriel because Daniel identified Gabriel as the one he had seen in the first vision.[2] More than likely, that was a reference to the angelic interpreter in Daniel 7.[3]

If Gabriel was the interpreting angel in Daniel 7, this makes his appearance to announce the birth of John the Baptist even more significant. It means the angelic messenger who first spoke about the Son of Man in Daniel 7 also came to commission a human messenger to prepare a people for the the Son of Man.

After announcing John's birth, Gabriel appeared to Mary to announce Jesus' birth, and he used language from Daniel:

He will be great and will be called the Son of the Most High. And the Lord God will give to him the throne of his father David, and he will reign over the house of Jacob forever, and of his kingdom there will be no end. (Luke 1:32–33)

The one who first interpreted Daniel 7 to Daniel gave Mary a prophecy that was also an interpretation of Daniel 7. As we saw in a previous chapter, Daniel knew the Ancient of Days and Son of Man were both divine, and he referred to both of them as the *Most High*. Daniel saw them as a heavenly Father and Son; consequently, Gabriel announced Jesus would be known as the Son of the Most High.[4] Gabriel also repeated Daniel's prediction that Jesus will reign forever and receive the everlasting kingdom.

---

[2]Daniel 9:21.

[3]Collins and Collins, *Daniel: A Commentary on the Book of Daniel*, 311. See also Hamilton, *With the Clouds of Heaven: The Book of Daniel in Biblical Theology*, 142.

[4]See also Luke 1:35.

PREPARING THE WAY OF THE LORD

Gabriel only announced two births—those of Jesus and John the Baptist. This is a profound indication of the significance of John's ministry. John was commissioned to prepare the people for the coming of the Son of Man. If God prepared the earth for the first coming of the Son of Man, how much more will He prepare the earth for the time the Son of Man comes with the clouds to dethrone the beasts, reward the saints, and establish an everlasting kingdom on the earth?

John's ministry should be viewed as something more than a historical event. It is also a foreshadowing of what will come before the return of Jesus. Through the church, God will prepare the earth for the Son of Man to come with the clouds in judgment just as He prepared the earth for the Son of Man to come quietly in a manger. In fact, one definition of missions is partnering with God to fulfill the tasks necessary to prepare the nations for the return of Jesus.

Because John is a foreshadowing of the church's end-time witness, his witness of Jesus is especially important for us.

When we consider John's words carefully, we notice something surprising: John did not predominantly present Jesus as Messiah. He only referred to Jesus as Messiah one time near the end of his ministry, and he did so to encourage people to follow Jesus.[1]

The people were longing for a messiah, but they were not prepared to receive God in the flesh. We tend to assume John was sent to prepare Israel to receive Jesus as Messiah which is true, but John's ministry and his message were unique because he prepared Israel to receive Jesus *as God.*

John absolutely knew Jesus was Messiah, but he principally presented Jesus as the God of Israel.

---

[1] John 3:28.

Preparing Israel for Their God

If we consider the different ways John described Jesus, John nearly always emphasized His divinity and did not use the title *Messiah*. Messiah is clearly implied, but John chose other titles to establish Jesus' superior identity.

Though John was born before Jesus, he referred to Jesus as the One "mightier" than him and the "one before him":[2]

And he preached, saying, "After me comes he who is mightier than I, the strap of whose sandals I am not worthy to stoop down and untie." (Mark 1:7)

"This is he of whom I said, 'After me comes a man who ranks before me, because he was before me.'" (John 1:30)

John described his mission as preparing the way of the Lord. This was a quote of Isaiah 40:3, and the Lord is YHWH. By preparing a path for Jesus, John was preparing YHWH's path:

He said, "I am the voice of one crying out in the wilderness, 'Make straight the way of the Lord,' as the prophet Isaiah said." (John 1:23)

John's favorite description of Jesus was the One who would "baptize with the Holy Spirit and fire." YHWH was the One who promised to pour out the Spirit,[3] and this baptism of fire was a prediction of YHWH's judgment,[4] which meant John was describing Jesus as divine:[5]

I baptize you with water for repentance, but he who is coming after me is mightier than I, whose sandals I am not worthy to carry. He will baptize you with the Holy Spirit and fire. His winnowing fork is in his hand, and he will clear his threshing floor and gather his wheat into the barn, but the chaff he will burn with unquenchable fire. (Matthew 3:11–12)

John followed this description with a clear witness that Jesus was the Son of God:

---

[2]See also John 1:15, 26–27.

[3]Isaiah 44:3; 59:21; Ezekiel 36:27; 37:14; 39:29; Joel 2:28.

[4]Isaiah 4:4; 29:6; 66:16; Jeremiah 15:14; Ezekiel 28:18; 30:8; Amos 1:14; Zechariah 13:9.

[5]See also Mark 1:8; Luke 3:16–17.

This is he who baptizes with the Holy Spirit. And I have seen and have borne witness that this is the Son of God. (John 1:33–34)

John also referred to Jesus as the *Lamb of God*. This was a profound statement because it was Passover language. John understood in some way that Jesus was the Lamb whom God had provided and the One to whom the Passover pointed:[6]

The next day he saw Jesus coming toward him, and said, "Behold, the Lamb of God, who takes away the sin of the world!" (John 1:29)

John referred to Jesus as the Bridegroom and himself as the "friend of the bridegroom." This is likely the main way John thought about Jesus because John used this analogy to describe his relationship to Jesus:

The one who has the bride is the bridegroom. The friend of the bridegroom, who stands and hears him, rejoices greatly at the bridegroom's voice. Therefore this joy of mine is now complete. (John 3:29)

Throughout the Old Testament, YHWH compared His relationship with Israel to the relationship between a husband and wife.[7] When John announced to Israel that Jesus was the Bridegroom, he was presenting Jesus as YHWH—the Bridegroom of Israel. This meant Jesus was the One who had come down on Sinai to enter into covenant with Israel, an event God referred to as a "betrothal":

"Thus says the LORD, 'I remember the devotion of your youth, your love as a bride, how you followed me in the wilderness….'" (Jeremiah 2:2)

John's description of himself was significant as well. "Friend of the bridegroom" was a cultural reference to the function of a *shoshbin* who served the bridegroom by helping to administrate the wedding and prepare the bride to be presented to the bridegroom. By preparing the way for Jesus, John was preparing the people to be joined in covenant to YHWH.

John could have simply prepared the people to meet Jesus as Messiah, but instead he chose to present the coming of Jesus as the coming of YHWH.

---

[6]See also John 1:36.

[7]Jeremiah 2:2; Ezekiel 16; 23; Hosea 2.

The Man Who Came from Heaven

John had so much power resting on him that people asked if he was the Messiah, but he refused to be considered as the Messiah.[8] Instead, he used Daniel 7 to make a profound claim Jesus was much more than a messiah:

> *And they came to John and said to him, "Rabbi, he who was with you across the Jordan, to whom you bore witness—look, he is baptizing, and all are going to him." John answered, "A person cannot receive even one thing unless it is given him from heaven. You yourselves bear me witness, that I said, 'I am not the Christ, but I have been sent before him.' ...He who comes from above is above all. He who is of the earth belongs to the earth and speaks in an earthly way. He who comes from heaven is above all." (John 3:26–28, 31)*

John's argument was simple. Jesus was in a different category from every other man because *He was a divine Man who had descended from heaven.* We know this was a reference to Daniel 7 because it was the second time in John 3 that Jesus had been described as the One coming from heaven. Earlier in the chapter, Jesus had used the same claim to establish His authority:

> *No one has ascended into heaven except he who descended from heaven, the Son of Man. (v. 13)*

Preparing the Nations for God

We tend to assume John prepared Israel to receive Jesus as Messiah, but it is more precise to say John prepared the nation to encounter the God of Israel as a man.

Jesus' reaction to John was in stark contrast to His reaction to His own disciples: Jesus encouraged, celebrated, and submitted to John's bold proclamation of His identity, but He asked His own disciples not to proclaim who He was.[9] *What was the difference?*

The most notable difference is John proclaimed Jesus as the God of Israel while the disciples wanted to proclaim Jesus as Messiah. John saw Jesus as Messiah, but he also had a larger vision of Jesus as

---

[8]John 1:20.

[9]Matthew 16:20; 17:9; Mark 8:30; 9:9.

YHWH. In contrast, it seems the disciples did not grasp the full implications of Jesus' identity until the resurrection.

It is critical we understand John's ministry and message because the church has been given the same task.

We have been commissioned to prepare the nations for Jesus' return by proclaiming the gospel. Jesus will return as Messiah, but more importantly, He will return as God descending from the heavens. John did more than prepare the way for the Messiah—he prepared the way for the Son of Man, and so must we.

The prophets predicted the arrival of God would usher in unprecedented shaking, judgments, and salvation,[10] and these prophecies will be fulfilled when God descends from the heavens and comes to the earth in the Person of Jesus.

John could have been the only man in his generation who grasped this. Even Jesus' own disciples struggled to understand. However, the mystery has now been revealed. In our generation, there is no excuse. We must know who Jesus is and proclaim Him with clarity.

---

[10]Isaiah 34:1–3; 42:14–15; 63:1–9; Jeremiah 25:15–38; Joel 3:9–14; Zephaniah 1:14–15; 3:8, Zechariah 12–14.

THE DIVINE MAN

Daniel described the divine Person he saw as One who was *like* a Son of Man, indicating this Person had a human appearance but an identity that was more than human. Based on his language, it is likely Daniel did not expect the Son of Man to be an actual human but God in the appearance of a human.

Jesus never had to prove His humanity. His appearance was so ordinary many people struggled to believe He was anything more than a good teacher.[1] When Jesus adopted *Son of Man* as His primary title, it communicated a surprising message: *The Son of Man is divine and fully human.*

Jesus' claim to be the Son of Man seemed outrageous because Jesus was obviously human, but the Son of Man was obviously divine. Jesus' audience was not shocked by the idea that the Son of Man was divine. They were shocked because Jesus was a human claiming to be a divine figure. When Jesus, as a man, claimed to be *the* Son of Man, He was claiming God had become a human being.

Using Daniel to Prove Divinity

Jesus used Son of Man to be a bold claim to divinity. This was obvious to Jesus' audience, but if we do not understand this, we will misunderstand why Jesus described Himself the way He did.

As we saw in the previous section, Daniel recorded a number of details about the Son of Man that clearly identified Him as divine. Jesus not only identified Himself as the Son of Man, He repeatedly identified with each of these descriptions to establish His divine status.

---

[1]Matthew 13:54–58; Mark 6:4–5; Luke 4:22–24; John 12:34.

He Will Come with the Clouds

Jesus repeatedly promised He would return on the clouds—something only a divine Person could do. This promise is found in the Gospels and repeated in the New Testament Epistles.[2] Some scholars have proposed Jesus' claim to come with the clouds could be symbolic language, but Jesus' ascension removes any doubt Jesus' prediction was to be taken literally:

> *And when he had said these things, as they were looking on, he was lifted up, and a cloud took him out of their sight. And while they were gazing into heaven as he went, behold, two men stood by them in white robes, and said, "Men of Galilee, why do you stand looking into heaven? This Jesus, who was taken up from you into heaven, will come in the same way as you saw him go into heaven." (Acts 1:9–11)*

The angels told the disciples that Jesus would return in the same way He left. He was taken up in a cloud, and He will *physically* return in a cloud—something only God can do.

He Is Like a Son of Man

Daniel referred to Jesus as a divine Person who was "like" a Son of Man, thus blurring the line between His divinity and humanity. Jesus blurred that line throughout the Gospels. He was a man but much greater than a man.

Jesus claimed to be the "I am" who existed before Abraham:

> *Jesus said to them, "Truly, truly, I say to you, before Abraham was, I am." (John 8:58)*

After the resurrection the disciples referred to Jesus as both man *and* God:

> *Thomas answered him, "My Lord and my God!" (John 20:28)*

---

[2]Matthew 24:30; 26:64; Mark 14:62; Luke 21:27; Acts 1:9–11; 1 Thessalonians 4:17; 2 Thessalonians 1:7; Revelation 1:7.

In the transfiguration, Jesus was seen as both human and divine.[3] He was a human and yet in a completely different category than any other human. He was "like" a Son of Man.

Jesus was described as the Son of *the Most High*, a title Daniel applied both to the Ancient of Days and the Son of Man. Jesus is *the* Son of the Most High, *and* He is also the Most High. Therefore, He will receive the everlasting kingdom:[4]

> "He will be great and will be called the Son of the Most High. And the Lord God will give to him the throne of his father David, and he will reign over the house of Jacob forever, and of his kingdom there will be no end." (Luke 1:32–33)

Even demons acknowledged Jesus was the divine Son of the Most High:

> And crying out with a loud voice, he said, "What have you to do with me, Jesus, Son of the Most High God? I adjure you by God, do not torment me." (Mark 5:7)

He Alone Could Approach the Ancient of Days

God drew near to His people in various ways throughout history, but Jesus was the only One who could approach the Ancient of Days:[5]

> "Not that anyone has seen the Father except he who is from God; he has seen the Father." (John 6:46)

Jesus' ascension was just as miraculous as His incarnation. As a human, He left the earth and ascended on a cloud directly to His Father, sitting down at God's right hand.[6] No human could ascend with a cloud to the throne of God. It was inconceivable, and yet Jesus did it, making a statement He could directly approach the Ancient of Days on His own initiative.

---

[3]Matthew 17:1–9; Mark 9:2–9; Luke 9:28–36.

[4]See also Luke 8:28.

[5]See also Exodus 33:20; Deuteronomy 4:12; John 1:18.

[6]Matthew 26:64; Mark 14:62; 16:19; Luke 22:69; 24:51; John 20:17; Acts 2:33–34; 7:55–56; Romans 8:34; Ephesians 1:20; Colossians 3:1; Hebrews 1:3, 13; 8:1; 10:12; 12:2; 1 Peter 3:22.

Jesus also revealed He had come *from* the Ancient of Days. Before He was a man, He had been with His Father in glory. He was the only human who had descended from heaven,[7] and He would return to His Father:[8]

> *"I came forth from the Father and have come into the world; I am leaving the world again and going to the Father." (John 16:28 NASB95)*

He Is the One Who Judges

In the Jewish conception of divinity, only God had the absolute right to judge, which meant the right to execute God's judgment was more than an exalted privilege—it was a claim to divinity. Jesus claimed the right to judge as God, and He based His claim on Daniel 7.

In Luke 12, Jesus described Himself as the Judge who determines men's fate. The judgment scene is similar to Daniel 7 because it is a heavenly court with angels present and the Son of Man presiding in judgment:[9]

> *And I tell you, everyone who acknowledges me before men, the Son of Man also will acknowledge before the angels of God, but the one who denies me before men will be denied before the angels of God. (Luke 12:8–9)*

John 5 recounts Jesus' bold defense of His identity and His right to judge. It begins with a story of Jesus' healing on the Sabbath. This healing created a conflict over whether or not it was right to be healing on the Sabbath because healing was "work." However, the conflict was not really about the Sabbath. The real root of the conflict was Jesus' claim to be God:

> *For this reason therefore the Jews were seeking all the more to kill Him, because He not only was breaking the Sabbath, but also was calling God His own Father, making Himself equal with God. (John 5:18 NASB95)*

The authors of the Gospels arranged their stories to make important points about Jesus. In this case, John arranged the next several verses of John 5 to reveal how Jesus had made Himself equal to God

---

[7]John 1:1–4; 3:13, 31; 6:33, 38, 51, 62; 8:42; 13:3; 16:28–30; 17:5.

[8]See also John 13:3; 16:5, 10.

[9]Collins and Collins, *Daniel: A Commentary on the Book of Daniel,* 99–100.

and provoked this controversy. The conflict in verse 18 follows two different stories of healing, so it would seem logical Jesus had used His miracles to make a claim of divinity. However, Jesus made a different claim:

> *Therefore Jesus answered and was saying to them, "Truly, truly, I say to you, the Son can do nothing of Himself, unless it is something He sees the Father doing; for whatever the Father does, these things the Son also does in like manner. For the Father loves the Son, and shows Him all things that He Himself is doing; and the Father will show Him greater works than these, so that you will marvel. For just as the Father raises the dead and gives them life, even so the Son also gives life to whom He wishes. For not even the Father judges anyone, but He has given all judgment to the Son, so that all will honor the Son even as they honor the Father. He who does not honor the Son does not honor the Father who sent Him. Truly, truly, I say to you, he who hears My word, and believes Him who sent Me, has eternal life, and does not come into judgment, but has passed out of death into life. Truly, truly, I say to you, an hour is coming and now is, when the dead will hear the voice of the Son of God, and those who hear will live. For just as the Father has life in Himself, even so He gave to the Son also to have life in Himself; and He gave Him authority to execute judgment, because He is the Son of Man. Do not marvel at this; for an hour is coming, in which all who are in the tombs will hear His voice, and will come forth; those who did the good deeds to a resurrection of life, those who committed the evil deeds to a resurrection of judgment." (John 5:19–29 NASB95)*

Jesus' answer was filled with allusions to Daniel 7. He claimed divinity by boldly proclaiming God was His Father and had given all judgment to Him:

> *For not even the Father judges anyone, but He has given all judgment to the Son. (John 5:22 NASB95)*

The ability to judge was considered a statement of divinity, so this was a serious claim. Jesus had to back it up with serious evidence. Instead of basing His claim on His miracles, *Jesus based His right to judge as God on His identity as the Son of Man:*

> *And He gave Him authority to execute judgment, because He is the Son of Man. (John 5:27 NASB95)*

When Daniel saw the Son of Man approach the Ancient of Days to receive the right to judge, that action told Daniel the Son of Man was also divine. Other prophets had predicted YHWH would judge the nations,[10] but Daniel revealed the Son of Man would execute that judgment.

Jesus used Daniel 7 and His identity as the Son of Man to establish the radical idea YHWH will judge the nations as a man who had been sent from heaven:

> *I can do nothing on My own initiative. As I hear, I judge; and My judgment is just, because I do not seek My own will, but the will of Him who sent Me. If I alone testify about Myself, My testimony is not true. There is another who testifies of Me, and I know that the testimony which He gives about Me is true.... You search the Scriptures because you think that in them you have eternal life; it is these that testify about Me.... I have come in My Father's name, and you do not receive Me; if another comes in his own name, you will receive him. (John 5:30–32, 39, 43 NASB95)*

Here, Jesus identified the root of His conflict with the Pharisees: They refused to believe He was the One of whom Daniel prophesied.

The right to judge included the right to forgive sin in order to determine who receives mercy rather than judgment. Jesus also claimed this right on the basis of Daniel 7. In Matthew 9, some people sought healing for a paralyzed man, but Jesus gave the man an unusual response:

> *And behold, some people brought to him a paralytic, lying on a bed. And when Jesus saw their faith, he said to the paralytic, "Take heart, my son; your sins are forgiven." (Matthew 9:2)*

Healing could come through a prophet, but forgiveness of sin could only come from God and typically through the temple ordinances. When Jesus addressed the man's sin, He identified Himself as someone much greater than a prophet or a holy man. *He was God.*

Jesus' enemies understood what Jesus was saying:

---

[10]See also Isaiah 34:1–3, 63:1–9; Jeremiah 25:15–38; Joel 3:2, 9–14; Zephaniah 1:14–15; 3:8, Zechariah 14:1–5.

And behold, some of the scribes said to themselves, "This man is blaspheming." (Matthew 9:3)

Jesus knew what they were thinking, so He used His power to heal to demonstrate He was who He claimed to be:

But Jesus, knowing their thoughts, said, "Why do you think evil in your hearts? For which is easier, to say, 'Your sins are forgiven,' or to say, 'Rise and walk'? But that you may know that the Son of Man has authority on earth to forgive sins"—he then said to the paralytic—"Rise, pick up your bed and go home." And he rose and went home. When the crowds saw it, they were afraid, and they glorified God, who had given such authority to men. (Matthew 9:1–8)

Jesus healed the man to demonstrate He had divine authority to forgive sins because He was the Son of Man. The story highlights the mystery of Jesus' divinity. Jesus claimed a divine status which caused the scribes to accuse Him of blasphemy. However, Jesus was obviously human, so the crowd was afraid and glorified God because He had "given such authority to men." They recognized Jesus was human and yet had divine authority.

In Matthew 25, Jesus sat on the Mount of Olives, looked over the Valley of Jehoshaphat, and predicted He would judge the nations in that valley:

When the Son of Man comes in his glory, and all the angels with him, then he will sit on his glorious throne. Before him will be gathered all the nations, and he will separate people one from another as a shepherd separates the sheep from the goats. And he will place the sheep on his right, but the goats on the left. (vv. 31–33)

As in John 5, Jesus predicted He would judge as the Son of Man; however, this was not a new prediction. Jesus was repeating a prophecy Joel had given:

"I will gather all the nations and bring them down to the Valley of Jehoshaphat. And I will enter into judgment with them there." (3:2)

Joel predicted *YHWH* would gather the nations into the Valley of Jehoshaphat and judge them. Jesus predicted *He* would gather the nations into the Valley of Jehoshaphat and judge them as the Son of

Man. Jesus combined Daniel 7 and Joel 3 to reveal He would judge the nations as YHWH.

In Luke 18, Jesus told a parable where He contrasted Himself with an unjust judge and predicted He would be an Advocate for His people when He came, again presenting Himself as the eschatological Judge:

> *He said, "In a certain city there was a judge who neither feared God nor respected man.... Nevertheless, when the Son of Man comes, will he find faith on earth?" (Luke 18:2, 8)*

Jesus did not come with the clouds in His first coming because it was not the time of judgment. However, in His second coming, He will come with the clouds as the Judge.

He Has All Authority (Dominion) over All Realms

Everything that belongs to the Father has been given to Jesus:

> *"All things that the Father has are Mine; therefore I said that He takes of Mine and will disclose it to you." (John 16:15 NASB95)*

The Great Commission was given by Jesus on the basis that He had been given—as God—all authority over heaven and earth:

> *And Jesus came and said to them, "All authority in heaven and on earth has been given to me. Go therefore and make disciples of all nations, baptizing them in the name of the Father and of the Son and of the Holy Spirit, teaching them to observe all that I have commanded you. And behold, I am with you always, to the end of the age." (Matthew 28:18–20)*

Jesus demonstrated He had all authority and dominion over nations,[11] powers,[12] and creation.[13]

The Kingdom of God Is His Kingdom

The inheritance given to the Son of Man was a permanent, indestructible kingdom and a people. Jesus made the kingdom one of the preeminent themes of His teaching. He described the kingdom more than

---

[11]Matthew 28:18–20; John 17:1–2; 19:11.

[12]Mark 9:25; Luke 4:40–41.

[13]Matthew 8:23–27; Mark 4:35–41; Luke 8:22–25.

any other subject.[14] The kingdom was the subject of His first and last messages.[15]

Jesus identified the kingdom of God as *His* kingdom:

The Son of Man will send his angels, and they will gather out of his kingdom all causes of sin and all law-breakers. (Matthew 13:41)

Truly, I say to you, there are some standing here who will not taste death until they see the Son of Man coming in his kingdom. (Matthew 16:28)

The gospel is the message of His kingdom:

"And this gospel of the kingdom will be proclaimed throughout the whole world as a testimony to all nations, and then the end will come." (Matthew 24:14)

Jesus' kingdom is not of this world because it comes from a higher realm. This was a reference to Daniel 2 and Daniel 7. It is the indestructible kingdom that comes from heaven to replace all the kingdoms of men and will never end:

Jesus answered, "My kingdom is not of this world. If my kingdom were of this world, my servants would have been fighting, that I might not be delivered over to the Jews. But my kingdom is not from the world." (John 18:36)

"And he will reign over the house of Jacob forever, and of his kingdom there will be no end." (Luke 1:33)

All People Will Worship Him

The Son of Man was given glory and a kingdom so all people would serve Him. This is what we saw in a previous section, and it was a reference to worship. Jesus received worship as the Son of Man:[16]

---

[14]Matthew 3:2; 4:17; 5:3, 10, 19–20; 6:33; 7:21; 8:11; 10:7; 11:11–12; 12:28; 13:11, 24, 31, 33, 44–45, 47, 52; 16:19; 18:1, 3–4, 23; 19:12, 14, 23–24; 20:1; 21:31, 43; 22:2; 23:13; 25:1; Mark 1:15; 4:11, 26, 30; 9:1, 47; 10:14–15, 23–25; 12:34; 14:25; 15:43; Luke 4:43; 6:20; 7:28; 8:1, 10; 9:2, 11, 27, 60, 62; 10:9, 11; 11:20; 13:18, 20, 28–29; 14:15; 16:16; 17:20–21; 18:16–17; 18:24–25, 29; 19:11; 21:31; 22:16, 18; 23:51; John 3:3, 5.

[15]Matthew 4:17; Acts 1:3.

[16]See also Matthew 2:11; 14:33; 28:9, 17; Luke 24:52.

Jesus heard that they had cast him out, and having found him he said, "Do you believe in the Son of Man?" He answered, "And who is he, sir, that I may believe in him?" Jesus said to him, "You have seen him, and it is he who is speaking to you." He said, "Lord, I believe," and he worshiped him. (John 9:35–38)

He Is the Lord of the Sabbath

Jesus also used Daniel 7 to make additional claims to divinity. One example is Jesus' claim to be "Lord of the Sabbath" because He was the Son of Man:[17]

For the Son of Man is lord of the Sabbath. (Matthew 12:8)

As Ben Witherington notes, this was another statement of deity:

Since God had created the Sabbath, only God was the Lord thereof. Yet here, Jesus claims, as Son of man, to be Lord over the Sabbath, and claims that He can reinterpret the Sabbath....[18]

Only YHWH was the "Lord of the Sabbath," yet Jesus claimed He was Lord of the Sabbath *because* He was the Son of Man. Once again, Jesus' identification with Daniel 7 allowed Him to claim full equality with YHWH.

The Charge of Blasphemy

The charge of blasphemy was the basis of Jesus' execution, and the evidence for the charge was Jesus' claim to be the Son of Man. Jesus was accused of blasphemy four times. Three of those charges were directly related to Daniel 7:

Jesus said to him, "You have said so. But I tell you, from now on you will see the Son of Man seated at the right hand of Power and coming on the clouds of heaven." Then the high priest tore his robes and said, "He has uttered blasphemy. What further witnesses do we need? You have now heard his blasphemy." (Matthew 26:64–65)

---

[17]See also Mark 2:28; Luke 6:5.

[18]Ben Witherington, III, "Did Jesus Believe He Was the Son of Man?" *NAMB Blog*, 20 Mar. 2016, https://www.namb.net/apologetics-blog/did-jesus-believe-he-was-the-son-of-man/.

And Jesus said, "I am, and you will see the Son of Man seated at the right hand of Power, and coming with the clouds of heaven." And the high priest tore his garments and said, "What further witnesses do we need? You have heard his blasphemy. What is your decision?" And they all condemned him as deserving death. (Mark 14:62–64)

And the scribes and the Pharisees began to question, saying, "Who is this who speaks blasphemies? Who can forgive sins but God alone?" When Jesus perceived their thoughts, he answered them, "Why do you question in your hearts? Which is easier, to say, 'Your sins are forgiven you,' or to say, 'Rise and walk'? But that you may know that the Son of Man has authority on earth to forgive sins"—he said to the man who was paralyzed—"I say to you, rise, pick up your bed and go home." (Luke 5:21–24)

The fourth instance is found in John 10 and could also be a reference to Daniel:

So the Jews gathered around him and said to him, "How long will you keep us in suspense? If you are the Christ, tell us plainly." Jesus answered them, "I told you, and you do not believe...." The Jews answered him, "It is not for a good work that we are going to stone you but for blasphemy, because you, being a man, make yourself God." (vv. 24–25, 33)

This passage does not contain a direct reference to Daniel 7, but there are some interesting connections that lead to Daniel 7. Jesus told His accusers He had already told them who He was but they refused to believe Him. There is not a clear statement of identity in this chapter, but there are a few clues to indicate Jesus may have been referring to the conversation about His identity in John 5.

In both chapters, Jesus used Father and Son language to refer to His relationship with the Father, and in both chapters, He was accused of making Himself equal to God:

For this reason therefore the Jews were seeking all the more to kill Him, because He not only was breaking the Sabbath, but also was calling God His own Father, making Himself equal with God. (John 5:18 NASB95)

"I and the Father are one." ...The Jews answered him, "It is not for a good work that we are going to stone you but for blasphemy, because you, being a man, make yourself God." (John 10:30, 33)

In both chapters, Jesus described His Father's connection with His work:

> *But He answered them, "My Father is working until now, and I Myself am working." (John 5:17 NASB95)*

> *Jesus answered them, "I told you, and you do not believe. The works that I do in my Father's name bear witness about me." (John 10:25)*

The similarities between the two chapters are not accidental. If John intended us to read John 10 with John 5 in mind, which seems likely, then John 5 gives us the reason Jesus was accused of blasphemy in John 10:

> *And He gave Him authority to execute judgment, because He is the Son of Man. (John 5:27 NASB95)*

With this in mind, it is likely every charge of blasphemy made against Jesus was related to Daniel 7. Even if we do not include John 10, every charge except one was clearly related to Daniel 7.

JESUS' BOLD, JEWISH CLAIM TO DIVINITY

As we saw earlier, *Son of Man* was by far Jesus' favorite title. As a quick review, Jesus never referred to Himself as *Messiah* publicly. Instead, He overwhelmingly chose to present Himself as the Son of Man. Again, here are the number of times Jesus used well-known titles:

- Son of Man—78
- Christ—11
- Son of God—5
- Son of David—1

Jesus clearly did not present Himself the way most people assume He did, and we need to understand why He chose the title He did.

The debate over who Jesus is has continued for over two thousand years, and it all basically comes down to one question: Is Jesus divine? Though there have been cults and heresies denying Jesus' full humanity, His humanity has never seriously been in question. No one in the Gospels ever doubted His humanity, and even today most people think Jesus was a historical figure who lived in ancient Israel.

While the Bible clearly presents Jesus as divine throughout history, there have been critics who try to argue Jesus never claimed to be God. They typically do this either by dismissing the reliability of the Bible or by evaluating Jesus' language without considering the full context.

Jesus repeatedly and openly claimed divine status, but He did not do it according to a modern, gentile paradigm. *Jesus made a bold, Jewish claim to divinity.*

The Son of God

When critics make arguments that Jesus never claimed to be divine, it is usually on the basis of what they expect Jesus to say to prove His divinity. They frequently point to Jesus' infrequent use of the title *Son of*

God. Critics note Jesus only referred to Himself as *Son of God* four times, and they all occur in just one Gospel.[1] They also point to Jesus' quote of Psalm 82 which mentions "sons of god":[2]

> *The Jews answered him, "It is not for a good work that we are going to stone you but for blasphemy, because you, being a man, make yourself God." Jesus answered them, "Is it not written in your Law, 'I said, you are gods'? If he called them gods to whom the word of God came—and Scripture cannot be broken— do you say of him whom the Father consecrated and sent into the world, 'You are blaspheming,' because I said, 'I am the Son of God'?" (John 10:33–36)*

Critics also note Jesus predicted His followers could become sons of god:

> *Blessed are the peacemakers, for they shall be called sons of God. (Matthew 5:9)*

> *For they cannot die anymore, because they are equal to angels and are sons of God, being sons of the resurrection. (Luke 20:36)*

Finally, critics point out the concept of a "son of god" was relatively common in the ancient world. Kings in particular (including Roman Caesars) often claimed divine status and presented themselves as a "son of god." Based on this, critics argue the idea that Jesus is divine was either the adaption of an ancient concept of divine kings or the invention of the church in the subsequent centuries.

To a modern, Western thinker, Jesus' use of the title *Son of God* raises a significant question: If Jesus is divine, why didn't He principally identify Himself as the Son of God? The answer is relatively simple: *Jesus was not a modern, Western thinker.*

---

[1]John 3:18; 5:25; 10:36; 11:4.

[2]Jesus' comment in John 10 was not a statement of His own identity. It was a simple rebuke meant to expose His opponents' hypocrisy. They were accusing Him of blasphemy because He had referred to God as *Father.* However, the real issue was not Jesus' use of language. The concept of God as a Father was established in the Old Testament. The real issue was not that it was impossible for God to have a divine Son. The real issue was they did not believe He *was* divine. Jesus followed this statement with a claim to divinity in verses 37–38.

Avoiding Confusion

As we have already seen, Jesus was *the* Messiah, but He avoided public use of the title because it was not unique—there were many others claiming to be messiahs. Jesus wanted to be seen for who He truly was —the divine Human. As the divine Human, He was greater than every other so-called messiah.

In the first section, we examined why Jesus avoided referring to Himself as *Messiah*, and now we need to see why Jesus also avoided using the title *Son of God*. Jesus' relationship to the title *Messiah* helps us understand His relationship to the title *Son of God*. The title *Messiah* was complicated because of the Jewish context, and *Son of God* was complicated because of the gentile context.

To modern, Western thinkers, *Son of God* is a very simple claim to deity, but in Jesus' time, it was not so simple. Son of God was applied to Jesus, but it was also frequently used to describe pagan kings and mythological gods. Jesus was familiar with the ancient, Roman idea of Caesars as "sons of god," and He was fully aware of the pagan mythology of the gentiles that included "gods" and "sons of the gods." Critics say the church made Jesus divine by adopting this cultural framework of "sons of god." However, Jesus' own words prove this is completely wrong.

Jesus *is* the unique, divine Son of God, and a result, He used the title occasionally to refer to Himself. Overall, however, He avoided identifying Himself as *Son of God* for the same reason He did not make *Messiah* His primary title: to avoid confusion. Because pagan kings claimed to be sons of god, Jesus did not base His identity on this same claim. He did not want to be viewed as yet another ruler claiming divine status.

When we consider Jesus in His Jewish context, His claim to deity was bold, public, and frequent. He was the Son of Man—a title His Jewish audience understood that meant He was divine. Jesus did not want to be confused with others who claimed to be Messiah, nor did He want to be confused with the Roman "sons of god." He was completely different. He was *the* Son of Man—the God of Israel who had descended from the heavens in human form.

Jesus was not like Caesar—a king born as a human and elevated to deity as a result of his political position. Nor was He like the mythological Greek gods who had sons and daughters as the result of sexual relationships among the gods. Jesus had to identify Himself as the One true, eternal, uncreated Son of God, setting Himself apart from the gentile concept of a son of god.

We cannot say Jesus did not claim to be divine according to our expectations when we live nearly two thousand years later in a very different cultural context.

Son of Man, Son of God

Jesus lived in a real historical context and must be understood in light of His context. If Jesus had adopted the title *Son of God* as His primary title, He would have appeared to be just another king claiming divine status like Caesar. His decision to prefer Son of Man over Son of God was not an attempt to obscure or hide His identity—it was intended to make His identity perfectly clear.

By identifying Himself as the Son of Man, Jesus identified Himself as the divine Son of God in an exclusive way, and He established Himself as a completely different kind of son of God. Critics who accuse the church of making Jesus out to be divine are ignoring the historical context Jesus lived in. Ironically, the same critics who claim Jesus did not call Himself the *Son of God* also often claim *son of god* is meaningless because it was common among ancient kings.

Jesus' decision to reveal His divinity using a relatively small book written by a unique prophet is something no one else would have done, and it demonstrates the divine origin of the vision. Jesus' revelation of Himself was a stunning revelation of a mystery. It was mysterious and yet simple. No false messiah would have taken that approach.

Jesus' preference for Son of Man over Son of God and over Messiah is a key indicator the Gospels are His actual words. If editors had changed the Gospels to "make" Jesus divine, they would have inserted phrases like *Son of God* into the Gospels and made *Messiah* much more prominent. They would not have depended on Daniel the way Jesus did.

Critical commentators have tried to deconstruct Jesus' identity by pointing out how much Jesus depended on *Son of Man* and how little He referenced *Son of God* and *Christ*. Ironically, this attempt to prove the church has fabricated an identity for Jesus has proved exactly the opposite—Jesus is who He said He was. He presented Himself as the divine Man in a way no one else would.

Daniel Settles the Issue of Jesus' Divinity

Jesus believed Daniel's book was so robust that it could serve as the key witness of His own identity.

Jesus' identification with Daniel 7 was certainly not His only claim to deity. Jesus allowed people to worship Him, demonstrated control over creation, plainly stated He descended from heaven, was referred to as God, was accused by His enemies of claiming to be God, and claimed a number of divine attributes.[3]

It is relatively easy to make the claim that Jesus presented Himself as divine without using Daniel, but Jesus' extensive use of Daniel leaves no doubt He was divine. Once you recognize Jesus' use of Daniel, His claim to deity is inescapable.

Some critics acknowledge Jesus' use of Daniel but question Daniel's authenticity. However, Jesus held a high view of Daniel. He affirmed Daniel as a historical figure and Daniel's book as a reliable, authentic prophecy. The only real way to question the divinity of Jesus in the Bible is to question the reliability of Scripture.

Anyone who believes Jesus did not claim divinity has not dealt robustly with Jesus' assessment of Daniel, use of Daniel, interpretation of Daniel, and identification with Daniel.

---

[3]Matthew 2:11; 8:27; 12:8; 28:9, 17–18; 26:65; Mark 1:27; 2:28; 14:63–64; Luke 6:5; 8:25; 24:52; John 1:1–4; 3:13, 31; 5:18, 23, 26; 5:22–27; 6:33, 38, 51, 62; 8:42, 58; 9:38; 10:30, 33; 13:3; 16:28–30; 17:3–5; 20:28.

THE GREAT CONTROVERSY

In the last few centuries, the interpretation of Daniel—and the identity of the Son of Man—has become a great controversy. Many have proposed alternate interpretations of the Son of Man that are completely different from the way Jesus interpreted the passage.

Many of these interpretations are a reaction to Jesus' interpretation of the passage. Because Jesus used Daniel so pervasively to support His claim to be divine, those who reject Jesus' divinity must also propose alternate interpretations of Daniel 7.

The controversy over Daniel tends to express itself in two challenges:

- The interpretation of Daniel
- The validity of Daniel

Jesus' use of Daniel in the Gospels answers both challenges.

Reinterpreting the Son of Man

There are usually two main alternative interpretations of Daniel. The first is to identify the Son of Man as Michael or some other powerful angel. This, of course, does not fit with the text because the Son of Man is served, which has the tone of religious service (i.e., worship), given dominion over the nations, and described in divine terms. No other angel is described this way in the Bible.[1]

No angel in Scripture would dare claim eternal dominion over the cosmos, be given an everlasting kingdom of immortal people to rule, be given the right to judge, sit on a throne with the Ancient of Days, or receive worship. For example, when the apostle John was tempted to

---

[1]The one exception would be the Angel of the Lord, but He is clearly divine. It is later made known the Angel of the Lord was Jesus.

give excessive honor to an angel, the angel rebuked him.[2] There is simply no biblical evidence for an angel's taking on divine status. Furthermore, Daniel made multiple references to angels, including Gabriel and Michael, and he did not make any connection between any of these heavenly beings and the Son of Man.[3]

The second common reinterpretation is the proposal that the Son of Man is a collective person, meaning He is not an individual but the representation of a corporate people who will be given an everlasting kingdom and exalted to immortality. The corporate people are generally identified as Israel—either historical Israel or some sort of "spiritual" Israel. However, the Ancient of Days and Son of Man are both presented as divine Persons in the vision, and they relate to each other. It simply does not make sense that One is a real Person and the other is an allegorical picture and not a Person.[4]

The earliest interpretations of Daniel 7 overwhelmingly interpreted the Son of Man as an individual, and this remained the consensus for nearly a thousand years. In fact, the collective interpretation of the Son of Man was rare until about a hundred years ago.[5] The collective interpretation typically comes from interpreters who deny Jesus is the divine Son of Man or critical scholars who deny the reliability of the Scripture.

This interpretation often focuses on the unusual language in Daniel 7, predicting the kingdom will be given to the Son of Man and to a people:

> "And to him was given dominion and glory and a kingdom, that all peoples, nations, and languages should serve him; his dominion is an everlasting dominion, which shall not pass away, and his kingdom one that shall not be destroyed.... until the Ancient of Days came, and judgment was given for the saints of the Most High, and the time came when the saints possessed the kingdom.... 'And the kingdom and the dominion and the greatness of the kingdoms under the whole heaven shall be given to the people of the saints of the Most High; his kingdom

---

[2]Revelation 19:10.

[3]Hamilton, *With the Clouds of Heaven: The Book of Daniel in Biblical Theology*, 145.

[4]Boyarin, "Intertextuality, and the History of Israel's Cult," 146.

[5]Collins and Collins, *Daniel: A Commentary on the Book of Daniel*, 306–9.

shall be an everlasting kingdom, and all dominions shall serve and obey him.'" (Daniel 7:14, 22, 27)

This language is certainly unusual, but the interpretation is clearly provided in the New Testament.[6] The Son of Man in Daniel 7:13 definitely is an individual, and this verse reveals a profound mystery the New Testament expounds on: The kingdom is given to the saints, but it remains "His kingdom" (the Son of Man's kingdom), and all dominions serve *Him.* While the Son of Man shares dominion with His people, the Son of Man and the saints remain two separate entities.

There is even a third hybrid reinterpretation of Daniel. It combines the angel theory and the collective people theory, and presents the Son of Man as Michael but as a representative of the collective nation of Israel.[7] Others try to resolve the apparent tension between the Son of Man and the saints by claiming it is a result of editing when the book of Daniel was compiled.[8]

There are only two reasons to embrace either of these reinterpretations of Daniel: The first is because you reject Jesus' interpretation of the Son of Man. The second is because you reject the book of Daniel as an authoritative book of Scripture containing true prophetic visions written by a real historical figure.

Both reasons can be addressed by a single question: Do we accept the authority of Jesus' words as recorded in the Gospels?

Jesus Was the Best Interpreter of Daniel

Some scholars also question the authenticity of Daniel. Many theories have been proposed, and most are some variation of the idea that Daniel was composed in the second century by an unknown author to encourage Israel during the revolt against Antiochus. This challenge to Daniel is so widespread that many interpreters no longer consider

---

[6]For example, Paul uses the same interpretation in 1 Corinthians 15 that I present here. For more on this, see *Son of Man: The Apostles' Gospel,* Volume 2.

[7]For example, John Collins proposes this theory. See "The Son of Man and the Saints of the Most High in the Book of Daniel," *Journal of Biblical Literature Vol. 93,* No. 1 (March 1974), 64.

[8]For example, Daniel Boyarin takes this approach to Daniel 7 in *The Jewish Gospels: The Story of the Jewish Christ.*

Daniel to be an authentic, prophetic text from the sixth century BC. *Jesus thought otherwise.*

Jesus was the best Bible interpreter in history, and He held Daniel in extremely high regard. Jesus referenced Daniel's prophecy more than any other prophecy, and He used Daniel's prophecy to present the most important message in the Gospels: His identity. Daniel was the only prophet Jesus mentioned by name in His longest teaching on the end times.[9] Jesus considered Daniel's prophecies to be predictions of future events, not descriptions of events that transpired in the second century BC, during the Maccabean revolt under the rule of Antiochus.[10]

If we accept Jesus as the authoritative interpreter of Daniel, the controversy around Daniel's book disappears. Jesus clearly thought Daniel was a real man, a real prophet, and the author of Scripture. Jesus interpreted Daniel 7 in a straightforward way and identified Daniel's biggest prophetic predictions as prophecies of the future.

Because Daniel has become controversial, some try to make the book of Daniel a secondary issue while others ignore it. Jesus' teaching in the Gospels is dependent on the book of Daniel, so we cannot just brush the issue aside. We must decide whether or not we consider Daniel's book Scripture because the integrity of the book of Daniel is not ultimately about Daniel—it is about the revelation of Jesus.

Much of the debate around the book of Daniel comes down to one question: Do we consider Jesus the authoritative interpreter of Daniel?

The Heart of the Issue

Jesus' use of Daniel forces two fundamental questions:

- Do we believe Jesus is who He claimed to be? He used Daniel to describe Himself.

---

[9]Matthew 24:15.

[10]While the rule of Antiochus has clear similarities to the prophecies in the book of Daniel, Antiochus must be considered a foreshadowing and not a fulfillment of Daniel based on Jesus' interpretation of Daniel. Jesus clearly stated Daniel's "abomination" was a future event. Therefore, the prophecies were not fulfilled by Antiochus (Mathew 24:14; Mark 13:14).

- Do we believe the Scripture is authentic and authoritative as it has been preserved? Jesus believed Daniel's book was authentic and authoritative.

These two questions are fundamental issues of Christianity, so in many ways, our interpretation of Daniel reveals the authenticity of our faith.

Daniel—perhaps more than any other book of Scripture—forces us to answer a decisive question: Do we really receive Scripture as the supernaturally preserved, divinely inspired Word of God that reveals Jesus in an authoritative way?

WHEN GOD BECOMES A MAN

Jesus not only used the title *Son of Man,* He also used Daniel 7 to undergird all the main themes of His teaching.[1] This may seem like an overstatement, but as we examine the main themes of Jesus' teaching, we will discover the unique and pervasive role Daniel played in Jesus' teaching. There are two reasons for this.

The first reason is because Jesus used the title *Son of Man* to present Himself as the divine Human to a predominantly Jewish audience. Jesus is the ultimate revelation of what God is like,[2] so His teaching describes what the divine Human is like and reveals what happens when God becomes a man. When we read the stories of what Jesus taught and did, we should hear Him saying, "This is what the divine Human is like."

The second reason is the Son of Man was revealed to Daniel in the context of a story and presented alongside the Ancient of Days, the beasts, and the saints. Therefore, when Jesus claimed to be the Son of Man, He brought all the aspects of Daniel's vision into His teaching. *We must remember ancient Jewish teachers would reference a phrase to expound on all the themes present in the referenced passage.* Therefore, Son of Man not only established Jesus' identity, it brought the entire Daniel 7 vision into Jesus' teaching.

In the next few chapters, we will examine these themes, see how they flowed from Jesus' identity as the divine Son of Man, and discover how Jesus used Daniel 7 to undergird these themes. Jesus used these themes to reveal Himself and to invite us to become part of His story,

---

[1]This does not mean Jesus used Daniel exclusively, but we will see He did use Daniel comprehensively.

[2]John 1:14; 10:30; Colossians 2:9; Hebrews 1:1–3.

and these themes comprise the message we now call the *gospel of the kingdom*.

As we move through the next few sections you are about to discover the gospel of the kingdom is not mysterious. It is much simpler and more straightforward than many people think. As we learn to read the Gospels with Daniel 7 in mind, Jesus' teaching will become much easier to grasp.

We have seen how Jesus used Daniel to reveal His identity. Now, we need to identify the key themes of Jesus' gospel and see how Jesus used Daniel to establish foundations of His gospel.

We cannot examine every theme in detail, but we can discover what God is like when He becomes a man and how Jesus used the Old Testament. In the process, we will learn to read the Gospels differently.

The Son of Man, His Father, and His People

THE SON OF MAN HAS A FATHER

Jesus' gospel began with His identity. We have already seen how He presented Himself as the Son of Man, but His identity is also deeply connected with His Father and His people. Both were prominent in Jesus' teaching, and He used Daniel 7 to undergird His revelation about His Father and His people.

Jesus radically reshaped our understanding of God by explaining He was the divine Son of a heavenly Father. Jesus made this claim in at least 134 verses.[1] The Trinitarian view of God and the concept of the Father and the Son have become so familiar to us that we can easily forget just how radical this revelation was.

The identity of Jesus as the Son is perhaps the core revelation that defines Christianity and sets it apart from other well-known monotheistic religions. It was so fundamental to Jesus' identity that we should be familiar with the way He used the Scripture to reveal who He was.

Old Testament Previews of the Son

There are a few Old Testament passages that point to Jesus' identity as the Son. God promised David a king would come from his line who would rule forever, and God would be a father to this son:

"I will be to him a father, and he shall be to me a son." (2 Samuel 7:14)

---

[1]Matthew 7:21; 10:32–33; 11:25–27; 12:50; 15:13; 16:17, 27; 18:10, 14, 19, 35; 20:23; 24:36; 25:34; 26:29, 39, 42, 53; 28:19; Mark 8:38; 13:32; 14:36; Luke 1:32; 2:49; 6:36; 9:26; 10:21–22; 22:29, 42; 23:34, 46; 24:49; John 1:14, 18; 2:16; 3:35; 4:21, 23; 5:17–23, 26, 36–37, 43, 45; 6:27, 31–32, 37, 40, 44–46, 65; 8:16, 18–19, 27–28, 38, 49, 54; 10:15, 17–18, 25, 29–30, 32, 36–38; 11:41; 12:26–28, 49–50; 13:1, 3; 14:2, 6–13, 16, 20–21, 23–24, 26, 28, 31; 15:1, 8–10, 15–16, 23–24, 26; 16:3, 10, 15, 17, 23, 25–28, 32; 17:1, 5, 11, 21, 24–25; 18:11; 20:17, 21.

David made a similar prophecy in Psalm 2, which became one of the most prominent prophecies of Jesus' identity:

> *I will tell of the decree: The LORD said to me, "You are my Son; today I have begotten you…. Serve the LORD with fear, and rejoice with trembling. Kiss the Son, lest he be angry, and you perish in the way, for his wrath is quickly kindled. Blessed are all who take refuge in him." (Psalm 2:7, 11–12)*

Isaiah prophesied a Son would be born who would be called *God with Us* and *Mighty God*:

> *Therefore the Lord himself will give you a sign. Behold, the virgin shall conceive and bear a son, and shall call his name Immanuel. (7:14)*

> *For to us a child is born, to us a son is given; and the government shall be upon his shoulder, and his name shall be called Wonderful Counselor, Mighty God, Everlasting Father, Prince of Peace. Of the increase of his government and of peace there will be no end, on the throne of David and over his kingdom, to establish it and to uphold it with justice and with righteousness from this time forth and forevermore. The zeal of the LORD of hosts will do this. (9:6–7)*

Matthew revealed Hosea's prophecy of Israel as God's son also had an application to Jesus as the Son.[2] The book of Proverbs also mentions a divine Son identified with the Creator, and Micah prophesied a Child would come whose origin was in eternity.[3] The New Testament revealed these were prophetic descriptions of Jesus, but many of them were not clear to the reader when they were first given.

Hosea's prophecy seemed to be entirely about Israel, and many questioned if 2 Samuel 7 or Psalm 2 meant God would have a divine Son or if they were descriptions of God's special care for a human king—a king like David—who would not be divine but would be exalted as God's representative on the earth. In other words, was God going to adopt a human and become like a father to him, or would there actually be a divine Son? Ancient kings often claimed divinity when they took the throne. Were these prophecies similar—or something entirely different? These passages all contained hints of Jesus' identity as the

---

[2]Hosea 11:1; Matthew 2:15.

[3]Proverbs 30:4; Micah 5:1–3.

Son, but the first coming was required to illuminate the full meaning of these passages.

It is very likely Jesus spoke to the disciples about these passages because He spoke about Himself in "all the Scriptures,"[4] and these passages were quoted in the New Testament. However, considering how much Jesus spoke about His identity as Son, it is intriguing Jesus did not quote any of these passages in the Gospels. Instead, Jesus justified His bold claim to be the heavenly Son of His Father in the heavens with the same passage He used to establish His identity.

A Heavenly Father and a Heavenly Son

Daniel's vision seems to describe a Father and Son type of relationship. The Ancient of Days appeared in the vision first. His name (Ancient of Days), His activity (taking His seat first), and His description (white clothing and hair like pure wool) present Him as a divine Father:

> *"As I looked, thrones were placed, and the Ancient of Days took his seat; his clothing was white as snow, and the hair of his head like pure wool." (Daniel 7:9)*

As the Ancient of Days sat, "thrones" were placed, indicating He would not sit alone—someone was going to be enthroned with Him. The Son of Man appeared as a second divine Person, and He approached the Ancient of Days the way a son would approach a father:

> *"I saw in the night visions, and behold, with the clouds of heaven there came one like a son of man, and he came to the Ancient of Days and was presented before him." (Daniel 7:13)*

The scene mimics a royal scene where a wise King is giving power to His Son to rule with Him. In Daniel's vision, Father and Son rule together, are enthroned together, and dwell in the heavens together. Psalm 2 and Psalm 110 contained similar predictions, but Daniel 7 was the most vivid image of the divine Son and His divine Father. As a result, Jesus primarily used Daniel to describe His relationship with the Father.

According to the Jewish scholar Daniel Boyarin, the concept of Father and Son came predominantly from Daniel 7:

---

[4]Luke 24:27.

In this prophetic narrative, we see two divine figures, one who is clearly marked as an ancient and one who has the appearance of a young human being. The younger one has his own throne (that's why there is more than one throne set up to start with), and he is invested by the older one with dominion, glory, and kingship over all the peoples of the world; not only that, but it will be an eternal kingship forever and ever. This is the vision that will become in the fullness of time the story of the Father and the Son.[5]

Moreover, Boyarin argues the Christian concept of the Son of Man comes from an ancient Jewish reading of Daniel 7:

The identification of the rider on the clouds with the one like a son of man in Daniel provides that name and image of the Son of Man in the Gospels as well. It follows that the ideas about God that we identify as Christian are not innovations but may be deeply connected with some of the most ancient of Israelite ideas about God. These ideas at the very least go back to an entirely plausible (and attested) reading of Daniel 7 and thus to the second century B.C. at the latest.[6]

Boyarin argues Daniel's vision prepared the Jewish people to receive Jesus as the divine Son:

The reasons that many Jews came to believe that Jesus was divine was because they were already expecting that the Messiah/Christ would be a god-man. This expectation was part and parcel of Jewish tradition. The Jews had learned this by careful reading of the Book of Daniel and understanding its visions and revelations as a prophecy of what would happen at the end of time. In that book, as we have just seen, the young divine figure is given sovereignty and made ruler of the world forever.[7]

Jesus' message of a divine Father and divine Son was not a new theological invention. It came directly from Daniel 7.

Boyarin's work is extremely valuable because it is an example of a larger trend in biblical scholarship to better understand the Jewish context of the Gospels. What we currently know as Judaism tends to be rigidly opposed to Jesus' divine identity, but modern Judaism does not

---

[5]Boyarin, *The Jewish Gospels*, Location 643.

[6]Boyarin, *The Jewish Gospels*, Location 734.

[7]Boyarin, *The Jewish Gospels*, Location 832.

accurately reflect Jewish ideas at the time of Jesus. In ancient Israel, many Jews interpreted Daniel's prophecy the way Jesus did.

This Is My Beloved Son

The Father spoke audibly over Jesus at three key times. Each time, there was a reference to Daniel 7. The Father first spoke audibly at Jesus' baptism. Daniel 7 was not quoted, but the heavens opened over Jesus as a statement Jesus was the One who comes with the clouds of heaven. Each account of Jesus' baptism seems to merge Psalm 2:7, Isaiah 42:1, and Daniel 7:13:[8]

> *And when Jesus was baptized, immediately he went up from the water, and behold, the heavens were opened to him, and he saw the Spirit of God descending like a dove and coming to rest on him; and behold, a voice from heaven said, "This is my beloved Son, with whom I am well pleased." (Matthew 3:16–17)*

The second time the Father spoke over Jesus was at the transfiguration, an event which has extensive connections to Daniel 7 as we will see in a future chapter. When Jesus was transfigured, He appeared as a divine Man, and the description of His appearance came from Daniel 7. He was accompanied by two other glorified humans who were a preview of the glorified saints described in Daniel. Finally, Jesus referred to Himself as the *Son of Man* at the end of the event.[9]

In the middle of the transfiguration, the Father spoke:[10]

> *He was still speaking when, behold, a bright cloud overshadowed them, and a voice from the cloud said, "This is my beloved Son, with whom I am well pleased; listen to him." (Matthew 17:5)*

The final time the Father spoke over Jesus occurred in the middle of a conversation in Jerusalem about Jesus' identity:

> *And Jesus answered them, "The hour has come for the Son of Man to be glorified.... Now is my soul troubled. And what shall I say? Father, save me from this hour'? But for this purpose I have come to this hour. Father, glorify your name." Then a voice came from heaven: "I have glorified it, and I will glorify it*

---

[8]See also Luke 3:21–22; Mark 1:9–11.

[9]Matthew 17:9; Mark 9:9.

[10]See also Mark 9:7–9; Luke 9:35.

again." The crowd that stood there and heard it said that it had thundered. Others said, "An angel has spoken to him." Jesus answered, "This voice has come for your sake, not mine.... And I, when I am lifted up from the earth, will draw all people to myself...." So the crowd answered him, "We have heard from the Law that the Christ remains forever. How can you say that the Son of Man must be lifted up? Who is this Son of Man?" (John 12:23, 27–30, 32, 34)

Jesus had identified Himself as the Son of Man who must be glorified, but the crowd was confused about His identity. In the middle of the discussion, the Father spoke audibly and declared His intention to glorify His Son. A few verses later, the crowd questioned Jesus again about His identity as the Son of Man, indicating Jesus was using Daniel 7 as the basis for His relationship to the Father.

The One Who Comes from Heaven

Jesus defended His authority, relationship to the Father, and shared glory with the Father on the basis He was the only man who had descended out of the heavens and would come with the clouds. In all four Gospels, Jesus consistently used His identity as Son of Man and the events of Daniel 7 to prove His unique relationship with the Father, thus demonstrating Daniel's vision was the main biblical basis for His claim.[11]

Matthew

Jesus predicted He would come in the glory of His Father as the Son of Man:

For the Son of Man is going to come with his angels in the glory of his Father, and then he will repay each person according to what he has done. Truly, I say to you, there are some standing here who will not taste death until they see the Son of Man coming in his kingdom. (Matthew 16:27–28)

Jesus would come as the Son of Man, but neither He nor the angels (a reference to Daniel 7:9–10) knew the timing of His coming. Only the Father of the Son of Man knows the time of His coming:

"Then will appear in heaven the sign of the Son of Man, and then all the tribes of the earth will mourn, and they will see the Son of Man coming on the clouds

---

[11]See also John 1:6.

of heaven with power and great glory.... But concerning that day and hour no one knows, not even the angels of heaven, nor the Son, but the Father only." (Matthew 24:30, 36)

When Jesus judges the nations as the Son of Man, He will welcome the righteous into the kingdom of the Father of the Son of Man:

"When the Son of Man comes in his glory, and all the angels with him, then he will sit on his glorious throne.... Then the King will say to those on his right, 'Come, you who are blessed by my Father, inherit the kingdom prepared for you from the foundation of the world.'" (Matthew 25:31, 34)

Mark

The Son of Man is going to come in the glory of His Father:

"For whoever is ashamed of me and of my words in this adulterous and sinful generation, of him will the Son of Man also be ashamed when he comes in the glory of his Father with the holy angels." (Mark 8:38)

Jesus is coming as the Son of Man, but the only One who knows the timing of that coming is the Father of the Son of Man:

"And then they will see the Son of Man coming in clouds with great power and glory.... But concerning that day or that hour, no one knows, not even the angels in heaven, nor the Son, but only the Father." (Mark 13:26, 32)

Luke

The Son of Man is coming in the glory of the Father:

"For whoever is ashamed of me and of my words, of him will the Son of Man be ashamed when he comes in his glory and the glory of the Father and of the holy angels." (Luke 9:26)

Jesus promised to give His disciples a kingdom just as the Father gave Him one:

And I assign to you, as my Father assigned to me, a kingdom. (Luke 22:29)

This was a summary of Daniel's prediction that the Ancient of Days would give the Son of Man a kingdom which He would share with the saints. Again, it reveals Jesus used Daniel 7 to refer to the Ancient of Days as Father.

John

When Nicodemus challenged Jesus' teaching, Jesus defended His authority on the basis that He had descended from heaven as the One Daniel had seen:

> No one has ascended into heaven except he who descended from heaven, the Son of Man. (John 3:13)

This statement helps us understand subsequent statements by Jesus in the book of John. In John 6, Jesus also establishes His identity and authority on the basis that He descended from heaven as the Son of Man:

> "Do not work for the food that perishes, but for the food that endures to eternal life, which the Son of Man will give to you. For on him God the Father has set his seal." ...Jesus answered them, "This is the work of God, that you believe in him whom he has sent...." "For the bread of God is he who comes down from heaven and gives life to the world...." "For I have come down from heaven, not to do my own will but the will of him who sent me.... For this is the will of my Father, that everyone who looks on the Son and believes in him should have eternal life, and I will raise him up on the last day...." "I am the living bread that came down from heaven. If anyone eats of this bread, he will live forever. And the bread that I will give for the life of the world is my flesh...." So Jesus said to them, "Truly, truly, I say to you, unless you eat the flesh of the Son of Man and drink his blood, you have no life in you. Whoever feeds on my flesh and drinks my blood has eternal life, and I will raise him up on the last day...." "Then what if you were to see the Son of Man ascending to where he was before?" (vv. 27, 29, 33, 38, 40, 51, 53–54, 62)

When we read this with John 3:13 in mind, we see Jesus repeatedly used Daniel 7 to establish the fact that God is His Father and He has unique authority because He descended from heaven. The promise He will raise up all those who believe in Him and give them eternal life is a reference to Daniel's prediction that the Son of Man will share the kingdom with an immortal, exalted people.

Jesus' defense of His identity as the divine Son in John is relatively straightforward. In John 3:13, Jesus used Daniel 7 to establish He had descended from heaven as the Son of Man. He then used that identity to establish God (the Ancient of Days) was His Father, thereby using Daniel 7 to make the argument He was the divine Son:

> So Jesus said to them, *"When you have lifted up the Son of Man, then you will know that I am he, and that I do nothing on my own authority, but speak just as the Father taught me...."* Jesus said to them, *"If God were your Father, you would love me, for I came from God and I am here. I came not of my own accord, but he sent me."* (John 8:28, 42)

Additionally, Jesus used Daniel 7 to establish He had come from God,[12] and His subsequent statements that He had come from heaven should also be read with Daniel in mind:

> Now before the Feast of the Passover, when Jesus knew that his hour had come to depart out of this world to the Father, having loved his own who were in the world, he loved them to the end.... Jesus, knowing that the Father had given all things into his hands, and that he had come from God and was going back to God. (John 13:1, 3)

> I came forth from the Father and have come into the world; I am leaving the world again and going to the Father. (John 16:28 NASB95)

> And now, Father, glorify me in your own presence with the glory that I had with you before the world existed. (John 17:5)

The Father in Heaven

The record we have of Jesus' teaching does not include many of the passages we would expect. Instead, Jesus relied almost exclusively on Daniel 7 to describe His relationship with the Father.

For example, Psalm 2 is probably the best known Old Testament passage describing Jesus as the divine Son alongside His Father. Jesus likely quoted it because the apostles frequently referenced it in the New Testament. However, Jesus never quoted Psalm 2 in the Gospels. More than likely, this is because, at the time some read Psalm 2 as a divine Father and Son, others read it as God exalting a human king to a place of authority. In light of that, Jesus chose another passage which made His identity crystal clear.

---

[12] John 3:13.

Daniel's prophecy was a clear revelation of a heavenly Father with a divine Son who dwelled in the heavens with Him, would be given His authority, and would descend from the heavens to the earth. Jesus identified Himself as the Son of Man because that made His identity clear and unlocked other key prophecies.

When passages like Psalm 2 and 2 Samuel 7 were read through the lens of Daniel 7, they became references to a human Ruler who is also a divine Son. Jesus' emphasis on *Son of Man* was not intended to discard these passages but meant to enable them to be interpreted correctly.

The lack of controversy over Jesus' statements about a heavenly Father indicates people understood the concept of God's existing as a Father and Son. Based on Jesus' teaching and the historical evidence, Daniel 7 was a primary source of that understanding. The controversy in the Gospels was not whether or not the heavenly Father existed, but whether or not Jesus was the Son of Man and, therefore, His divine Son.[13] If Jesus was the Son of Man, the claim to have a heavenly Father made perfect sense.

---

[13]Matthew 13:55–56; Mark 6:3; Luke 4:22; John 6:42; 7:27; 8:41.

THE SON OF MAN HAS A PEOPLE

Daniel 7 revealed the everlasting kingdom will be given to the Son of Man *and* the saints:

> *"And to him was given dominion and glory and a kingdom, that all peoples, nations, and languages should serve him; his dominion is an everlasting dominion, which shall not pass away, and his kingdom one that shall not be destroyed.... until the Ancient of Days came, and judgment was given for the saints of the Most High, and the time came when the saints possessed the kingdom." (Daniel 7:14, 22)*

The word *everlasting* in Daniel is the same word as *eternal* in the New Testament, so references to the *eternal kingdom* in the New Testament are references to the *everlasting kingdom* in Daniel. Verse 27 gives perhaps the best summary of the mystery:

> *"And the kingdom and the dominion and the greatness of the kingdoms under the whole heaven shall be given to the people of the saints of the Most High; his kingdom shall be an everlasting kingdom, and all dominions shall serve and obey him."*

Dominion over all the "kingdoms under the whole heaven" will be given to the saints, but the kingdom is "his kingdom," and all powers "serve and obey him." This description of the kingdom was not a redefinition of the Son of Man as a collective entity. It was a profound prediction that the Son of Man will have a people who will become like Him.

Daniel's description of the kingdom is a prediction of the mystery we now call the church.

Jesus will be given a kingdom and dominion over all the earth, but He will rule with a people who share His inheritance. This people will be distinct from Him yet will be exalted with Him. They will be immortal like Him and placed over all dominions alongside Him. It was a profound prophecy of an exalted people from every nation[1] who will be like the Son of Man and rule with Him forever.

The Promise of Thrones

Jesus gave His disciples a profound promise that they would rule alongside him:[2]

> Then Peter said in reply, "See, we have left everything and followed you. What then will we have?" Jesus said to them, "Truly, I say to you, in the new world, when the Son of Man will sit on his glorious throne, you who have followed me will also sit on twelve thrones, judging the twelve tribes of Israel." (Matthew 19:27–28)

Jesus promised the disciples that they would sit on thrones with Him *when the Son of Man sits on His throne,* indicating this promise came from Daniel 7:

> "As I looked, thrones were placed, and the Ancient of Days took his seat ... and behold, with the clouds of heaven there came one like a son of man.... And to him was given dominion and glory and a kingdom.... 'And the kingdom and the dominion and the greatness of the kingdoms under the whole heaven shall be given to the people of the saints of the Most High; his kingdom shall be an everlasting kingdom, and all dominions shall serve and obey him.'" (vv. 9, 14, 27)

When the Ancient of Days took His seat in Daniel 7, *thrones* were placed. As the vision unfolded, it was obvious there were at least two thrones—one for the Ancient of Days and one for the Son of Man. Perhaps Daniel only saw two thrones, but as we discussed much earlier in this book, he did not say *two* thrones but *thrones*, which seems to indicate there were multiple thrones, not only two. Daniel 7:27 appears to answer the question of how many thrones were placed. Because the saints will be given dominion alongside the Son of Man, it is likely they will sit on thrones with the Son of Man.

---

[1] Daniel 7:14.

[2] See also Luke 22:28–30.

The disciples were so captivated by this promise that James, John, and their mother asked Jesus on two different occasions to sit at the throne on His right and left hand:

> *"See, we are going up to Jerusalem, and the Son of Man will be delivered.... And after three days he will rise." And James and John, the sons of Zebedee, came up to him and said to him, "Teacher, we want you to do for us whatever we ask of you." And he said to them, "What do you want me to do for you?" And they said to him, "Grant us to sit, one at your right hand and one at your left, in your glory." (Mark 10:33–37)*

> *"See, we are going up to Jerusalem. And the Son of Man will be delivered ... and he will be raised on the third day." Then the mother of the sons of Zebedee came up to him with her sons.... She said to him, "Say that these two sons of mine are to sit, one at your right hand and one at your left, in your kingdom." Jesus answered, "You do not know what you are asking ... to sit at my right hand and at my left is not mine to grant, but it is for those for whom it has been prepared by my Father." "...and whoever would be first among you must be your slave, even as the Son of Man came not to be served but to serve, and to give his life as a ransom for many." (Matthew 20:18–23, 27–28)*

On both occasions, the request to sit on a throne was a response to Jesus' prediction that He would be exalted as the Son of Man, indicating the hope of ruling alongside Jesus came from Daniel. In fact, Daniel 7 is the only Old Testament passage that clearly predicts the saints will sit on thrones alongside the divine Son.

Jesus' promise that the disciples had been given authority over other dominions and their names had been written in heaven was likely a reference to the exaltation of the saints described in Daniel 7:27:

> *"Behold, I have given you authority to tread on serpents and scorpions, and over all the power of the enemy, and nothing shall hurt you. Nevertheless, do not rejoice in this, that the spirits are subject to you, but rejoice that your names are written in heaven." (Luke 10:19–20)*

Your Father in Heaven

We have already seen Jesus' references to the *heavenly Father* were references to Daniel.[3] Not only did Jesus claim God was *His* Father in the heavens, He also proclaimed the Father was *our* Father in the heavens:

> *In the same way, let your light shine before others, so that they may see your good works and give glory to your Father who is in heaven. (Matthew 5:16)*

> *Pray then like this: "Our Father in heaven, hallowed be your name." (Matthew 6:9)*

> *Then the righteous will shine like the sun in the kingdom of their Father. He who has ears, let him hear. (Matthew 13:43)*

> *Then the King will say to those on his right, "Come, you who are blessed by my Father, inherit the kingdom prepared for you from the foundation of the world." (Matthew 25:34)*

> *But love your enemies, and do good, and lend, expecting nothing in return, and your reward will be great, and you will be sons of the Most High, for he is kind to the ungrateful and the evil. (Luke 6:35)*

> *And he said to them, "When you pray, say: 'Father, hallowed be your name. Your kingdom come.'" (Luke 11:2)*

> *Fear not, little flock, for it is your Father's good pleasure to give you the kingdom. (Luke 12:32)*

Jesus referred to the Father as *our* Father in at least 29 verses.[4] In another 22 verses, Jesus referred to the Father as *the* Father in a way that invited the disciples into relationship with the Father.[5] The Father is not only Jesus' Father, He is also the Father of the saints, and He has

---

[3]Matthew 5:16, 45, 48; 6:1, 9, 14, 26, 32; 7:11, 21; 10:32–33; 11:25; 12:50; 15:13; 16:17; 18:10, 14, 19, 35; 23:9; 24:36; Mark 11:25; 13:32; Luke 6:36; 10:21; 11:13; 15:18; John 6:32; 12:28; 17:1.

[4]Matthew 5:16, 45, 48; 6:1, 4, 6, 8–9, 14–15, 18, 26, 32; 7:11; 10:20, 29; 13:43; 23:9; Mark 11:25; Luke 11:2, 13; 12:30, 32; John 14:2, 6–7, 23; 17:11, 21.

[5]Matthew 11:27; Luke 10:22; John 4:21, 23; 5:21; 6:37, 44; 10:29, 38; 14:6, 9, 16, 26; John 15:9, 16; 16:3, 15, 23, 25–27; 20:21.

made a way for the saints to enter into His family because He is gladly going to give them the kingdom.

The Ancient of Days is not just the Father of the Son of Man, He is also the Father of the saints who will be exalted.

Jesus' statements about the Father were not generic statements about God as the Father (Creator) of all humanity. They were specific promises for the saints who will be exalted. There are a number of things the Ancient of Days will do for the Son of Man *and* the saints that can be derived from Daniel 7:

- He gives them a kingdom.
- He raises them from the dead.
- He gives them eternal life.
- He gives them authority in the heavens.
- He gives them dominion over His creation.
- He judges on their behalf.
- He allows them to suffer under the beast.

When we come to the Son of Man, we gain a Father in the heavens. Because the saints will receive dominion with the Son of Man, they must become a "heavenly" people like the Son of Man. They will be immortal and capable of ruling over all other kingdoms and authorities. Because the exalted saints are like the Son of Man, the Ancient of Days becomes their Father as well.

The Father, the Saints, and the Kingdom
When Jesus revealed God was His Father *and* the Father of the saints, He interpreted the mystery of Daniel 7:27:

> *"And the kingdom and the dominion and the greatness of the kingdoms under the whole heaven shall be given to the people of the saints of the Most High; his kingdom shall be an everlasting kingdom, and all dominions shall serve and obey him.'"*

This mystery is so profound Jesus invited the saints into direct relationship with Him and the Father:

> *That they may all be one, just as you, Father, are in me, and I in you, that they also may be in us, so that the world may believe that you have sent me…. Father,*

I desire that they also, whom you have given me, may be with me where I am, to see my glory that you have given me because you loved me before the foundation of the world. (John 17:21, 24)

The Son of Man will be given dominion as an exalted Man, but there will also be an exalted people. God will be their Father because they will be exalted, immortal, and share in His dominion. Daniel 7 is the only passage which combines the divine Father in the heavens, the divine Son, and an exalted people who must also become sons of the Father in a way that the rest of humanity is not.

Because of Daniel 7, Jesus associated God's identity as Father with the saints' receiving the kingdom:

"Pray then like this: 'Our Father in heaven, hallowed be your name. Your kingdom come, your will be done, on earth as it is in heaven.'" (Matthew 6:9–10)

"Not everyone who says to me, 'Lord, Lord,' will enter the kingdom of heaven, but the one who does the will of my Father who is in heaven." (Matthew 7:21)

"The Son of Man will send his angels, and they will gather out of his kingdom all causes of sin and all law-breakers…. Then the righteous will shine like the sun in the kingdom of their Father. He who has ears, let him hear." (Matthew 13:41, 43)

"When the Son of Man comes in his glory, and all the angels with him, then he will sit on his glorious throne…. Then the King will say to those on his right, 'Come, you who are blessed by my Father, inherit the kingdom prepared for you from the foundation of the world.'" (Matthew 25:31, 34)

"You know that after two days the Passover is coming, and the Son of Man will be delivered up to be crucified…." "I tell you I will not drink again of this fruit of the vine until that day when I drink it new with you in my Father's kingdom." (Matthew 26:2, 29)

And he said to them, "When you pray, say: 'Father, hallowed be your name. Your kingdom come.'" (Luke 11:2)

"And I tell you, everyone who acknowledges me before men, the Son of Man also will acknowledge before the angels of God…." "Fear not, little flock, for it is your Father's good pleasure to give you the kingdom." (Luke 12:8, 32)

"And I assign to you, as my Father assigned to me, a kingdom." (Luke 22:29)

Jesus' statements about the Father, the saints, the heavens, and the kingdom were not new theological inventions. They were simple expositions of Daniel 7. To make the connection more clear, Jesus also referred to Himself as the *Son of Man* in many of these passages. Because Jesus was the Son of Man, He would bring about everything Daniel predicted.

This profound promise is one of the reasons Jesus was accompanied by Elijah and Moses in His transfiguration. As we will see in a future chapter, the transfiguration was a demonstration that Jesus was the Son of Man whom Daniel saw. Accordingly, when He was transformed, Jesus was accompanied by two saints who represented the exalted people Daniel predicted.

Because of what Jesus accomplished on the cross, Jesus' Father is now our Father:

"Go to my brothers and say to them, 'I am ascending to my Father and your Father, to my God and your God.'" (John 20:17)

While this does not make us divine, it does mean we will be given a body like Jesus' and exalted alongside Him. *Daniel had seen a glimpse of the eternal mystery and majesty of the church.*

It Is to Your Advantage That I Leave

One of the strangest things Jesus ever said to the disciples was it would be to their *advantage* for Him to leave:

But I tell you the truth, it is to your advantage that I go away; for if I do not go away.... (John 16:7 NASB95)

The statement is especially odd because the next chapter in John contains Jesus' majestic prayer for His people. That prayer focused on the exaltation of the saints and Jesus' desire for them to be with Him:

That they may all be one, just as you, Father, are in me, and I in you, that they also may be in us, so that the world may believe that you have sent me. The glory that you have given me I have given to them, that they may be one even as we are one, I in them and you in me, that they may become perfectly one, so that the world may know that you sent me and loved them even as you loved me. Father, I

*desire that they also, whom you have given me, may be with me where I am, to see
my glory that you have given me. (John 17:21–24)*

Jesus prayed for the saints to be given unity with Him and the Father, as well as His own glory. Jesus wanted the world to know the truth of who He is and the love the Father has for the saints—the same love the Father has for Jesus. *In other words, Jesus asked the Father to share His glory with the church so the church would become a tangible demonstration of the glory of the Son of Man.* When the world encounters the church, they should encounter a glory which proves the reality of the Son of Man.

Jesus' deep desire to have His people exalted to be with Him where He is demonstrates separation from Jesus is not the ultimate goal, so something else must be going on. John 17 is a prayer for the fulfillment of Daniel 7 (the exaltation of the saints), and if we re-examine John 16 in light of Daniel 7, we more clearly understand Jesus' words:

But I tell you the truth, it is to your advantage that I go away; for if I do not go away, the Helper will not come to you; but if I go, I will send Him to you. And He, when He comes, will convict the world concerning sin and righteousness and judgment; concerning sin, because they do not believe in Me; and concerning righteousness, because I go to the Father and you no longer see Me; and concerning judgment, because the ruler of this world has been judged. (John 16:7–11 NASB95)

The first benefit of Jesus' absence is the gift of the Holy Spirit, who enables the believer to become part of the exalted people. However, the Holy Spirit also "convicts the world of sin, righteousness, and judgment." Righteousness in a biblical sense means more than moral perfection. It means being faithful to do what has been promised.

First, the Holy Spirit convicts of sin because people do not believe in Jesus. In other words, the fundamental sin is not believing in the Son of Man—the One whom God has chosen. Secondly, the Spirit convicts the world of righteousness because Jesus has gone to the Father. This statement is the key to understanding the passage: *God is faithful (righteous) because Jesus ascended into the heavens.*

According to Daniel, the fulfillment of God's promises all depends on the Son of Man's coming with the clouds of heaven. That event results in the judgment of wickedness, the establishment of the kingdom, and the rewarding of the saints. But prior to the ascension of

Jesus, there wasn't a man in the heavens who could come to fulfill God's promises. Jesus has not fulfilled all God's promises yet, but His ascension proved His faithfulness. There is now a Man in the heavens who is capable of coming with the clouds and fulfilling all God's promises.

Finally, the Spirit convicts the world of judgment because the ruler of this world has been judged. That judgment has been rendered but not yet enforced. Now that Jesus has ascended to the Father, He can come with the clouds to execute the Father's judgment on the beasts. The ascension served the "beasts" notice—the Judge is now in place waiting to be sent.

Jesus' ascension to the Father is to our advantage because it set the stage for the fulfillment of all the promises.

The Son of Man's Kingdom

THE SON OF MAN HAS A KINGDOM

The next most important theme in Jesus' teaching was the kingdom. The kingdom is the context for the fulfillment of God's promises related to the redemption of the earth. As a result, the subject of the kingdom was a prominent theme in Jesus' teaching. Jesus referred to the kingdom over 120 times in the New Testament, and He spent His final forty days teaching on the kingdom.[1]

The theme of the kingdom is so foundational in Jesus' teaching that He described the gospel as the *gospel of the kingdom* and sent the disciples out to preach the kingdom:

> *And this gospel of the kingdom will be proclaimed throughout the whole world as a testimony to all nations, and then the end will come. (Matthew 24:14)*

> *And he called the twelve together and gave them power and authority over all demons and to cure diseases, and he sent them out to proclaim the kingdom of God and to heal. (Luke 9:1–2)*

When Jesus spoke about His kingdom, He described it a specific way: He called it the *kingdom of God*. Jesus used this title over eighty times in the Gospels,[2] and yet the phrase does not appear anywhere in the Old Testament. The kingdom is clearly the fulfillment of the predictions of the kingdom made by "nearly every Old Testament

---

[1]Acts 1:3.

[2]Matthew 3:2; 4:17; 5:3, 10, 19–20; 6:33; 7:21; 8:11; 10:7; 11:11–12; 12:28; 13:11, 24, 31, 33, 44–45, 47, 52; 16:19; 18:1, 3–4, 23; 19:12, 14, 23–24; 20:1; 21:31, 43; 22:2; 23:13; 25:1; Mark 1:15; 4:11, 26, 30; 9:1, 47; 10:14–15, 23–25; 12:34; 14:25; 15:43; Luke 4:43; 6:20; 7:28; 8:1, 10; 9:2, 11, 27, 60, 62; 10:9, 11; 11:20; 13:18, 20, 28–29; 14:15; 16:16; 17:20–21; 18:16–17, 24–25, 29; 19:11; 21:31; 22:16, 18; 23:51; John 3:3, 5. Note Matthew frequently used *kingdom of heaven* in place of *kingdom of God*.

prophet,"[3] but because prophets did not use the phrase *kingdom of God*, it raises a question: *Why did Jesus use this phrase, and how did He develop it from the Old Testament?*

The Kingdom of Heaven

The answer begins in the book of Matthew. In Matthew's Gospel, John the Baptist and Jesus began preaching by announcing the kingdom of heaven:

> *Repent, for the kingdom of heaven is at hand. (Matthew 3:2)*

> *From that time Jesus began to preach, saying, "Repent, for the kingdom of heaven is at hand." (Matthew 4:17)*

Matthew's Gospel is unique because Matthew typically referred to the kingdom as the *kingdom of heaven* rather than the *kingdom of God*. Because Matthew was written principally for a Jewish audience, some people assume Matthew used the word *heaven* instead of *God* because it was a Jewish preference. But this is not the case. The custom of using *heaven* as a euphemism for *God* seems to be a later tradition. Furthermore, Matthew preferred the phrase *kingdom of heaven*, but he did not have a problem using the phrase *kingdom of God*. For example, he used the phrase *kingdom of God* five times. He even used it in one of Jesus' premier sermons, the Sermon on the Mount.[4]

According to scholars, there is no known historical reason for Matthew's decision to use *kingdom of heaven*. Some have proposed it could have been a stylistic preference Matthew chose,[5] and others conclude it was an expression used by Matthew's community.[6] Like the

---

[3]J. Dwight Pentecost. *Things to Come* (Grand Rapids: Zondervan, 1964), 442.

[4]Matthew 6:33; 12:28; 19:24; 21:31, 43.

[5]R. T. France, *The Gospel of Matthew*, The New International Commentary on the New Testament (Grand Rapids, MI: Wm. B. Eerdmans Publication Co., 2007), 101.

[6]Ulrich Luz, *Matthew 1–7: A Commentary on Matthew 1–7*, Hermeneia—a Critical and Historical Commentary on the Bible, ed. Helmut Koester, Rev. ed., (Minneapolis, MN: Fortress Press, 2007), 135.

phrase *kingdom of God, kingdom of heaven* does not exist in the Old Testament.[7]

We need to understand why Matthew chose this unusual phrase. His preference for kingdom of heaven was much more than a stylistic preference—it was part of his message.

The Son of Man and His Kingdom

Jesus used the title *Son of Man* to redefine the expectation of who the Messiah was. He was the Messiah, but He was a very different Messiah than everyone was expecting. He was not simply a better version of David who would ascend to the throne. He was a divine King who would *descend* from the heavens to take the throne of Israel.

The expectation of the Messiah was connected to a kingdom, so if the understanding of Messiah was redefined, the kingdom had to be redefined as well. Jesus used the title *Son of Man* to redefine the identity of the Messiah, and He used the phrase *kingdom of God* (and *kingdom of heaven*) to redefine how the kingdom was to be understood.

These two subjects only come together in one passage:

Daniel 7:13–14 are the only Old Testament verses where we hear both about Son of man and eternal kingdom of God, and these two phrases are the most frequent phrases on Jesus' lips throughout His ministry.[8]

As we have already seen, the kingdom is one of the key themes of Daniel 7. It is the great reward given to the Son of Man and also the inheritance of the saints. There are seven verses describing the Son of Man and the saints in Daniel 7, and five of them reference the kingdom:

"And to him was given dominion and glory and a kingdom, that all peoples, nations, and languages should serve him; his dominion is an everlasting dominion, which shall not pass away, and his kingdom one that shall not be destroyed." (v. 14)

"But the saints of the Most High shall receive the kingdom and possess the kingdom forever, forever and ever.'" (v. 18)

---

[7]Psalm 103:19 is the closest to this expression, "The LORD has established his throne in the heavens, and his kingdom rules over all."

[8]Witherington, *"Did Jesus Believe He Was the Son of Man?"*

"And judgment was given for the saints of the Most High, and the time came when the saints possessed the kingdom." (v. 22)

"'And the kingdom and the dominion and the greatness of the kingdoms under the whole heaven shall be given to the people of the saints of the Most High; his kingdom shall be an everlasting kingdom.'" (v. 27)

"Here is the end of the matter. As for me, Daniel, my thoughts greatly alarmed me, and my color changed, but I kept the matter in my heart." (v. 28)

Because Matthew wrote for Jewish readers who knew the Old Testament well, he used the phrase kingdom of heaven as an allusion to Daniel 7 to help his readers understand exactly how Jesus redefined the kingdom.

Daniel 7 provided Jesus the best summary of His identity and His kingdom. Daniel saw the Son of Man come "with the clouds of heaven" to receive His kingdom (Daniel 7:13–14); therefore, Matthew referred to His kingdom as the *kingdom of heaven*. Furthermore, while *kingdom of heaven* is the traditional English translation, it is not completely accurate. The literal translation is *the kingdom of the heavens* because "heaven" is plural in the book of Matthew, not singular. (This was an odd translation decision in the book of Matthew, because every instance of "heaven" in the book of Matthew is plural, not singular as it is usually rendered in English.)

"Heaven" is also plural in Daniel 7:13,[9] so if we read the two passages with a literal translation, the connection is clear: Daniel predicted "with the clouds of the heavens there came one like a son of man…. And to him was given a kingdom," and Jesus identified Himself as the Son of Man and proclaimed "the kingdom of the heavens."

A Heavenly Man and a Heavenly Kingdom

Jesus radically redefined the expectation of the Messiah *and* His kingdom. Israel assumed the Messiah would be a human exalted by God to rule His people. Jesus revealed the Messiah was not a human who would *ascend* to a place of privilege, but rather a divine Person who would *descend* to the earth to rule.

If the Messiah—the Son of Man—would descend, then His kingdom must descend as well. *The heavenly Man must come with a heavenly*

---

[9]The Greek in the Septuagint is singular, but the Aramaic is plural.

kingdom. Daniel's revelation of a heavenly Man and a heavenly kingdom revealed *how* God would fulfill the many prophecies of the kingdom.

Jesus' redefinition of Messiah helps us understand how He redefined the kingdom. He redefined the Messiah as the divine Son of Man who will descend to rule, revealing the liberation of Israel will come by a Deliverer who was more than a political leader. The same redefinition applies to the kingdom. The authority of the kingdom will come from heaven with the Son of Man. Israel's promises will be fulfilled in a kingdom as the prophets have predicted, but it will come through a kingdom which *descends* and is ultimately ruled by resurrected humans who are like the Son of Man.

Jesus' message was not a dismissal of Israel's promises, but a fulfillment of Israel's promises in a way Israel never anticipated. Israel had always been unique because they were the only nation with the divine presence in their midst. The nation was formed in the desert camped around the visible presence of God on Mount Sinai. The nation then moved into the land, and the manifest presence of God was in the temple. That presence left when Jerusalem was destroyed, but the prophets promised the presence would return.

Jesus revealed the divine presence would return through a divine Man who would rule as God.

Jesus' audience expected Him to speak about a restored kingdom of Israel—and He did.[10] However, Jesus' declaration He was the Son of Man, and His invitation to participate in the kingdom of heaven He had been given by His Father radically defined people's expectation of the kingdom. This redefinition obviously came directly from Daniel 7.

Jesus used Daniel as an interpretive key to unlock all that the prophets had said about the Messiah and the kingdom.

The promised Messiah was not only human, He was divine. God would rule Israel and dwell in their midst just as He had always promised, but He would rule *as* a human, not merely *through* a human. Because this Man is God, He can rule forever and rule with perfection in a way David and Moses could not.

This heavenly kingdom was not a replacement of Israel, but the ultimate fulfillment of Israel's promise. The Son of Man would become an Israelite in order to become Messiah. The kingdom of heaven

---

[10]Acts 1:6.

would descend but become a kingdom on earth through God's restoration of Israel. Jerusalem's promises would ultimately be fulfilled by a city descending from heaven, but that city would have twenty-four Jewish names on its gates.[11]

Jesus' redefinition of Israel's expectations should be seen as a radical enlargement of Israel's hope, not a nullification of Israel's story. Jesus will fulfill Israel's hope in a way that goes far beyond anything Israel would have imagined, but it will be true to the core promises made to Israel—promises that have not yet been fulfilled.[12]

Those who take a supersessionist or "fulfillment" view of Israel's promises[13] correctly recognize Jesus radically *redefined* the expectation of the kingdom. However, Jesus did not *eliminate* Israel's role in the story. On the contrary, He continued to predict He would fulfill Israel's promises in a specific way at His second coming.[14]

Jesus *expanded* Israel's promises. He did not *replace* Israel's promises. Jesus profoundly shifted expectations regarding the kingdom, but His teaching was given in a specific context. When Jesus' audience heard Him speak about the kingdom of heaven and the kingdom of God, they immediately understood this was the ultimate restoration of Israel. This is demonstrated by the disciples' response to Jesus' teaching about the kingdom in Acts 1:

Lord, will you at this time restore the kingdom to Israel? (v. 6)

Jesus never corrected their expectation. After nearly two thousand years of theology formed mostly by gentile theologians who believed God had finished His plan with Israel, we tend to hear the word *kingdom* very differently from the way Jesus' audience heard it. As a result, we tend to leave it almost entirely out of its historical, cultural, and—most importantly—biblical context. Jesus' audience understood this kingdom would bring the fulfillment of what the prophets had predicted.

---

[11]Revelation 21:12–14.

[12]I deal with this subject extensively in the books *OneKing* and *It Must Be Finished.*

[13]The idea that Israel's unique part in the story of God ends with Jesus' first coming is sometimes referred to by its opponents as *replacement theology.*

[14]Matthew 23:39; 24:30; Acts 1:6–8.

Kingdom of Heaven and Kingdom of God

Matthew's use of *kingdom of heaven* helped his Jewish audience make an immediate connection to Daniel 7, but the connection exists in the other Gospels where *kingdom of God* is used. Like *kingdom of heaven*, *kingdom of God* does not appear in the Old Testament. However, when Jesus' audience heard the Son of Man declare the kingdom of God, they would have made the connection to Daniel 7.

Most of the predictions of the kingdom in the Old Testament revolve around the liberation of Jerusalem. The kingdom was expected to be the Jerusalem-centered rule of Messiah over the nations. Jesus did not remove this expectation (in fact, He encouraged it), but He used Daniel to give a much bigger description of the kingdom. The kingdom that will be established in Jerusalem means much more than the political restoration of Israel. *God Himself will descend from heaven to rule in Jerusalem.*

The presentation of the kingdom in Daniel is unique in the Old Testament. In Daniel's vision, the kingdom was handed to the Son of Man by the Ancient of Days (the Father) when the Son of Man came with the clouds. The kingdom was a gift given *to* God (the Son of Man) *from* God (the Ancient of Days), and Daniel saw it given to Him in the heavens. Thus, it could be referred to as the *kingdom of heaven(s)* or *the kingdom of God.*

Though Jesus will rule Jerusalem, His kingdom and His authority do not derive from His throne in Jerusalem. He will take the throne of Jerusalem on the basis of His heavenly authority.

Many passages describe God's subduing the nations on Messiah's behalf,[15] but Daniel reveals how this will happen. Some assume Jesus will have authority over the nations because He will sit in the seat of David in Jerusalem.[16] Others assume Jerusalem and the kingdom of Israel no longer matter because Jesus' kingdom is the kingdom of God. Both of these conclusions, however, are in error. *Jesus will rule from Jerusalem on the earth, but He will rule on the basis of His heavenly authority.*

---

[15] 2 Samuel 7:13–16; Psalm 2:6–8; 110; Isaiah 49:6.

[16] 2 Samuel 7:13; Jeremiah 33:17.

When Jesus referred to the *kingdom of God*, He did not mean there would not be an earthly expression of the kingdom. The phrase primarily indicated the source of Jesus' authority. George Ladd explains:

> *The primary meaning of the New Testament word for kingdom, basileia, is "reign" rather than "realm" or "people." A great deal of attention in recent years has been devoted by critical scholars to this subject, and there is a practically unanimous agreement that "regal power, authority" is more basic to basileia than "realm" or "people". In the general linguistic usage, it is to be noted that the word basileia, which we usually translate by realm, kingdom, designates first of all the existence, the character, the position of the king. Since it concerns a king, we would best speak of his majesty, his authority.*[17]

When Jesus described the kingdom of God, it was not necessarily a metaphysical statement (i.e., the kingdom would not be on the earth); it was a statement of authority. It was a statement that He was not just another messiah (like Israel's false messiahs) nor another son of god (like Rome's Caesars). He was divine and uncreated, and His right to rule comes from what He has been given in the heavens by His Father.

Jesus' conversation with Pilate is an example of this:

> *Jesus answered, "My kingdom is not of this world. If my kingdom were of this world, my servants would have been fighting, that I might not be delivered over to the Jews. But my kingdom is not from the world." (John 18:36)*

This was not a metaphysical statement that the kingdom only exists in an alternate realm. It was a statement of divine authority. Jesus did not need to fight Rome because He had a higher authority. His refusal to fight Rome was not a statement of His weakness but of His strength. He did not need to fight a war to gain authority He already had.

What's more, Pilate could only crucify Jesus because the kingdom of heaven had allowed it:

> *Jesus answered him, "You would have no authority over me at all unless it had been given you from above." (John 19:11)*

---

[17]George E. Ladd, *Crucial Questions about the Kingdom of God* (Grand Rapids: MI, Eerdmans, 1952), 78.

The issue in Jesus' conversation with Pilate was authority. The authority of heaven was governing the earthly realm even in Jesus' crucifixion. That same heavenly authority has been given to Jesus to judge the earth and establish a kingdom that is "not of this world" though it will be on the earth. In context, *world* did not mean *not of this earth*; it meant not according to the authority of this age.

Jesus' acts of power were a demonstration that the kingdom of God had come upon the people which meant He had the authority of the kingdom:

> *"But if it is by the Spirit of God that I cast out demons, then the kingdom of God has come upon you." (Matthew 12:28)*

When Jesus told the Pharisees that the kingdom could not be observed, He was not redefining the kingdom as an invisible force. He was confronting them with their inability to recognize the kingdom of God—meaning the authority of the kingdom—was in their midst. He had come, but they had not seen or recognized Him. The power of the kingdom was not centered in a political structure but in a Person:

> *Being asked by the Pharisees when the kingdom of God would come, he answered them, "The kingdom of God is not coming in ways that can be observed, nor will they say, 'Look, here it is!' or 'There!' for behold, the kingdom of God is in the midst of you." (Luke 17:20–21)*

Jesus' claim of the authority from the heavens redefined the kingdom, but it did not reinterpret the promise that the kingdom will be established on the earth according to what the prophets predicted. Jesus claimed He had the full authority ("kingdom") of heaven and a day would come when He would establish a kingdom on the earth, rule from Jerusalem, and restore Israel in an ultimate way.

God Will Be King

The concept of God as King and the prediction God would rule as King appear throughout the Old Testament.[18] These predictions, though, raised a significant question: How would God rule as King

---

[18]Psalm 10:16; 29:10; 45; 47:2, 7; 74:12; 93; 96; 97–99; 103; Isaiah 2:2–4; 49:7; Jeremiah 10:10; Ezekiel 20:33; Daniel 2:44; Micah 4:1–3; Zechariah 8:3, 20–23; 14:9, 17.

over His people? Ancient Israel was a theocracy, but God had exercised His rule through human agents who were given an exalted status before God and became a representative of God to Israel and Israel's enemies.

This pattern began with Moses. When God commissioned Moses, He made Moses the representative of God:

And the LORD said to Moses, "See, I have made you like God to Pharaoh." (Exodus 7:1)

As a result, when Israel complained about Moses' leadership, Israel spoke against God:

And the people spoke against God and against Moses, "Why have you brought us up out of Egypt to die in the wilderness? For there is no food and no water, and we loathe this worthless food." (Numbers 21:5)

The prophets predicted a day would come when God would rule in the midst of Israel, but they also described a future human king—a Messiah. This human was described as an apparently flawless ruler who seemed to rule forever. This created a tremendous tension in the prophecies and a profound sense of mystery about the coming Messiah. He seemed to have divine attributes but was human. As a result, most Israelites assumed he would be a much greater ruler along the lines of a Moses or David.

The kingdom is much more than a return to the golden age of David and Solomon. It will fulfill Israel's promises but be much bigger than anyone anticipated. The Son of Man is a greater David and a greater Moses who will rule as a man *and* is the God who was on Mount Sinai. In Him, God can rule His people directly as a human without any other human intermediary.

The kingdom of the Son of Man creates a context for God Himself to directly rule over His people—the ultimate theocracy and the physical kingdom of God.

Heavenly and Earthly

Theologians have endlessly debated whether the kingdom of God is "heavenly" or "earthly," but Jesus never created this question. When He referred to the kingdom of God, He indicated the *source* and *scope* of His authority. Jesus was unique because He did not receive His authority from the realm of men. He was not just another human messiah. He had divine authority. Because He rules as God, His kingdom can go far beyond anything anyone has anticipated and be referred to as the kingdom of God.

The Son of Man will establish a kingdom on the earth, but that kingdom will rule more than just men. It will rule over *all dominions*.[19] The prophets predicted the Messiah's kingdom would have dominion over Israel and the nations, but Daniel significantly enlarged Messiah's dominion. Because Messiah is the Son of Man, He is divine and has all authority in heaven *and* the earth. Therefore, His kingdom has dominion over *all* powers and dominions—not just human ones.

Jesus—a resurrected Man—and the saints—also resurrected humans—will be put in authority over the earth and all other spiritual powers and dominions as well.

According to Daniel 7, the beasts will rule and the saints will suffer until the Son of Man comes with the clouds, and this is precisely what Jesus taught about the timing of the kingdom. Peter summarized Jesus' message in Acts 3:

> *Repent therefore, and turn back, that your sins may be blotted out, that times of refreshing may come from the presence of the Lord, and that he may send the Christ appointed for you, Jesus, whom heaven must receive until the time for restoring all the things about which God spoke by the mouth of his holy prophets long ago. (vv. 19–21)*

Jesus ascended into heaven as a resurrected man to prepare for the day He will come with the clouds with the authority of God to establish the kingdom according to all the prophets had spoken.

Traditionally, Christian theologians either emphasize an "earthly" kingdom or a "heavenly" kingdom, but Daniel does not present this tension. The kingdom will still come to earth when the Son of Man comes with the clouds and judges the beasts of this age. His kingdom will come with heavenly authority and an exalted humanity. It will be both earthly and heavenly. We have created an unnecessary division by emphasizing certain aspects of the kingdom while overlooking other aspects.

When we recognize Jesus' use of Daniel, it makes the kingdom much easier to understand because Daniel unlocked the mystery of the

---

[19]Daniel 7:27.

kingdom predicted by the prophets. The other prophets emphasized salvation on the earth. Resurrection was implied in their prophecies but not usually explicitly stated. Daniel unlocked the mystery that the kingdom descends from heaven and the people who receive the kingdom are resurrected to immortality to receive their inheritance.

Just as the Son of Man is both heavenly and earthly (divine and human), the kingdom will be both heavenly and earthly.

The proper perspective of the kingdom of God is not that it is an earthly or a heavenly kingdom but rather the union of heaven and earth in the context of a kingdom ruled by the Son of Man and His people.

THE KINGDOM ACCORDING TO DANIEL

Once we recognize the heavenly Father, the saints, and the kingdom were all Daniel 7 concepts, we can see that Jesus described the promise of the kingdom using language from Daniel:[1]

> *"Until the Ancient of Days came, and judgment was given for the saints of the Most High, and the time came when the saints possessed the kingdom…. 'And the kingdom and the dominion and the greatness of the kingdoms under the whole heaven shall be given to the people of the saints of the Most High; his kingdom shall be an everlasting kingdom, and all dominions shall serve and obey him.'" (Daniel 7:22, 27)*

> *"Not everyone who says to me, 'Lord, Lord,' will enter the kingdom of heaven, but the one who does the will of my Father who is in heaven." (Matthew 7:21)*

> *"Then the righteous will shine like the sun in the kingdom of their Father. He who has ears, let him hear." (Matthew 13:43)*

> *"I tell you I will not drink again of this fruit of the vine until that day when I drink it new with you in my Father's kingdom." (Matthew 26:29)*

> *And he said to them, "When you pray, say: 'Father, hallowed be your name. Your kingdom come.'" (Luke 11:2)*

> *"Fear not, little flock, for it is your Father's good pleasure to give you the kingdom." (Luke 12:32)*

> *"And I assign to you, as my Father assigned to me, a kingdom." (Luke 22:29)*

Jesus also used Daniel to define the timing of the kingdom. Because Jesus has been exalted, we are real citizens of the kingdom now

---

[1] See also Matthew 25:34.

and can enjoy substantial blessings that flow from being part of His kingdom. As we wait for Jesus to return, the church is called to be a present demonstration of the culture, values, and power of the kingdom throughout the nations of the earth.[2] With that in mind, the kingdom will be established on earth when the Son of Man comes in power with the clouds of heaven, and not before:[3]

> *"Just as the weeds are gathered and burned with fire, so will it be at the end of the age. The Son of Man will send his angels, and they will gather out of his kingdom all causes of sin and all law-breakers, and throw them into the fiery furnace. In that place there will be weeping and gnashing of teeth. Then the righteous will shine like the sun in the kingdom of their Father. He who has ears, let him hear." (Matthew 13:40–43)*

> *"For the Son of Man is going to come with his angels in the glory of his Father, and then he will repay each person according to what he has done. Truly, I say to you, there are some standing here who will not taste death until they see the Son of Man coming in his kingdom." (Matthew 16:27–28)*

> *Jesus said to them, "Truly, I say to you, in the new world, when the Son of Man will sit on his glorious throne, you who have followed me will also sit on twelve thrones, judging the twelve tribes of Israel. And everyone who has left houses or brothers or sisters or father or mother or children or lands, for my name's sake, will receive a hundredfold and will inherit eternal life. But many who are first will be last, and the last first." (Matthew 19:28–30)*

> *"Immediately after the tribulation of those days the sun will be darkened, and the moon will not give its light, and the stars will fall from heaven, and the powers of the heavens will be shaken. Then will appear in heaven the sign of the Son of Man, and then all the tribes of the earth will mourn, and they will see the Son of Man coming on the clouds of heaven with power and great glory. And he will send out his angels with a loud trumpet call, and they will gather his elect from the four winds, from one end of heaven to the other." (Matthew 24:29–31)[4]*

---

[2] See *Son of Man: The Apostles' Gospel*, Volume 2 for much more on the present demonstration of the kingdom.

[3] See also Luke 21:36.

[4] Daniel saw Jesus come in the "night visions" (Daniel 7:13), and it will be darkened as night when Jesus comes.

"When the Son of Man comes in his glory, and all the angels with him, then he will sit on his glorious throne. Before him will be gathered all the nations, and he will separate people one from another as a shepherd separates the sheep from the goats." (Matthew 25:31–32)

Jesus said to him, "You have said so. But I tell you, from now on you will see the Son of Man seated at the right hand of Power and coming on the clouds of heaven." (Matthew 26:64)

"For whoever is ashamed of me and of my words in this adulterous and sinful generation, of him will the Son of Man also be ashamed when he comes in the glory of his Father with the holy angels." (Mark 8:38)

"But in those days, after that tribulation, the sun will be darkened, and the moon will not give its light, and the stars will be falling from heaven, and the powers in the heavens will be shaken. And then they will see the Son of Man coming in clouds with great power and glory. And then he will send out the angels and gather his elect from the four winds, from the ends of the earth to the ends of heaven." (Mark 13:24–27)

And Jesus said, "I am, and you will see the Son of Man seated at the right hand of Power, and coming with the clouds of heaven." (Mark 14:62)

"For whoever is ashamed of me and of my words, of him will the Son of Man be ashamed when he comes in his glory and the glory of the Father and of the holy angels." (Luke 9:26)

"For as the lightning flashes and lights up the sky from one side to the other, so will the Son of Man be in his day." (Luke 17:24)

"Just as it was in the days of Noah, so will it be in the days of the Son of Man." (Luke 17:26)

"Likewise, just as it was in the days of Lot—they were eating and drinking, buying and selling, planting and building, but on the day when Lot went out from Sodom, fire and sulfur rained from heaven and destroyed them all—so will it be on the day when the Son of Man is revealed." (Luke 17:28–30)

"And then they will see the Son of Man coming in a cloud with power and great glory." (Luke 21:27)

Jesus' teaching on the kingdom in the Sermon on the Mount should also be read with Daniel 7 in mind:[5]

> *"Blessed are those who are persecuted for righteousness' sake, for theirs is the kingdom of heaven.... Rejoice and be glad, for your reward is great in heaven, for so they persecuted the prophets who were before you.... In the same way, let your light shine before others, so that they may see your good works and give glory to your Father who is in heaven.... For I tell you, unless your righteousness exceeds that of the scribes and Pharisees, you will never enter the kingdom of heaven.... so that you may be sons of your Father who is in heaven. For he makes his sun rise on the evil and on the good, and sends rain on the just and on the unjust.... Beware of practicing your righteousness before other people in order to be seen by them, for then you will have no reward from your Father who is in heaven." (Matthew 5:10, 12, 16, 20, 45; 6:1)*

The promise of heavenly rewards was a reference to the reward of ruling alongside the Son of Man when He comes in His kingdom. Because the saints will be exalted and co-rule with the Son of Man, Jesus referred to the saints who will rule with Him as family members:

> *For whoever does the will of my Father in heaven is my brother and sister and mother. (Matthew 12:50)*

> *All of this was a straightforward exposition of Daniel 7:27.*

The People of the Kingdom

Daniel predicted the Son of Man would be served by a people who come from "all peoples, nations, and languages." This people from all the nations are described as "saints" in Daniel 7:22 and 27. This was an unusual prediction because the prophets usually predicted the kingdom with Israel-centric language and then expanded the kingdom to include dominion over the nations.

It is not revolutionary now to think of the people of God as a people from every nation, but Daniel, like other righteous Israelites, was longing for the redemption of His people Israel.[6] This prediction of a kingdom consisting of people from all nations would have been

---

[5]See also Matthew 5:45, 48; 6:10, 14, 20; 7:21; 8:11; 10:32–33; 12:50; 13:11; 16:19; 18:1, 3–4; 19:14, 21; 23:9, 13; Mark 10:21; Luke 6:23; 10:20; 12:33.

[6]Daniel 9:1–3, 19.

surprising even though it was a fulfillment of the promise originally given to Abraham.[7]

Daniel understood this prediction did not mean God was finished with Israel. Nearly fourteen years later, Daniel was in fasting and mourning over Israel's condition when Gabriel gave him a profound prophecy about God's commitment to Israel and Jerusalem.[8] However, it did mean, when the Son of Man came, He would receive a kingdom consisting of people from all nations.

Daniel was given a profound hint of what would unfold as the gospel extended to the gentiles.

A Testimony to All Nations

Jesus used Daniel's language in Matthew 24 to make one of His best known predictions:

> *"And to him was given dominion and glory and a kingdom, that all peoples, nations, and languages should serve him." (Daniel 7:14)*

> *"And this gospel of the kingdom will be proclaimed throughout the whole world as a testimony to all nations, and then the end will come." (Matthew 24:14)*

If you compare the Greek translation[9] of Daniel 7:14 to Matthew 24:14, Daniel's phrase *all the peoples* and Matthew's phrase *all the nations* are the same. The reason is simple—Daniel 7 is a summary of the gospel of the kingdom.

Matthew 24:14 is part of Jesus' answer to an important question from His disciples:

> *As he sat on the Mount of Olives, the disciples came to him privately, saying, "Tell us, when will these things be, and what will be the sign of your coming and of the end of the age?" (Matthew 24:3)*

Using Daniel language, their question was, "When will the Son of Man come to rule, and when will the dominion of the beasts end?" The answer in Matthew 24:14 was surprising: He will come when the gospel of the kingdom is proclaimed to all nations. Because Daniel said

---

[7]Genesis 12:3.

[8]Daniel 9.

[9]Septuagint.

"all nations" must be included in the people given to the Son of Man, Jesus used the phrase to commission His disciples to take the gospel of the kingdom "to all nations."

In order for the kingdom to consist of people from all nations when the Son of Man comes with the clouds, a witness of the good news (gospel) of this kingdom must be given to all nations.

The Old Testament repeatedly predicted the kingdom would include the nations.[10] Yet, most of the prophecies of the nations' worshipping the God of Israel could conceivably be fulfilled *after* Messiah saved Israel and began His rule from Jerusalem.

They were genuinely confused that anything else would be necessary for the Son of Man to rule, especially after He entered Jerusalem the way Zechariah predicted the Messiah would.[11] The disciples' question demonstrates they expected Jesus to rule the nations after He saved Israel, so they did not see any need for the nations to hear this gospel of the kingdom before Messiah established His throne in Jerusalem.

Jesus used Daniel to explain the mystery of His plan for the gentiles. There would be an exalted people from all nations who serve the Son of Man when He comes with the clouds. This required they would hear the news about Him and submit to Him *before* He came to rule. Consequently, before "the end will come," the gospel of the kingdom must be carried "to all the nations." *Then* the Son of Man will come with the clouds to rule, and exalt a people from all nations and languages to rule with Him.[12]

Daniel 7 defined the kingdom in a way that gave unique insight into the timing of the kingdom—an insight not stated this clearly in any other Old Testament passage.

---

[10]Genesis 12:3; 28:14; Deuteronomy 32:21; Psalm 22:27; Isaiah 24:14–16; 42:10–12; 49:6; 56:6–7; 60:1–3; 65:1; Jeremiah 16:19–21; Amos 9:11–12; Zechariah 2:11; 14:16; Malachi 1:11.

[11]Zechariah 9:9; Matthew 21:1–11.

[12]The disciples asked a similar question in Acts 1, and Jesus gave the same answer in Acts 1:6–8.

Daniel's Great Commission

The last command Jesus gave in the gospel of Matthew is known as the *Great Commission*. It is one of Jesus' best known instructions and often described as a main assignment of the church in this age. As in Matthew 24:14, the influence of Daniel can be seen in the key phrases of the commission:

> *And Jesus came and said to them, "All authority in heaven and on earth has been given to me. Go therefore and make disciples of all nations, baptizing them in the name of the Father and of the Son and of the Holy Spirit, teaching them to observe all that I have commanded you. And behold, I am with you always, to the end of the age." (Matthew 28:18–20)*

"All authority in heaven and on earth has been given to me" is clearly connected to Daniel 7:14 and 27:

> *"And to him was given dominion and glory and a kingdom, that all peoples … should serve him; his dominion is an everlasting dominion, which shall not pass away, and his kingdom one that shall not be destroyed…. 'his kingdom shall be an everlasting kingdom, and all dominions shall serve and obey him.'" (Daniel 7:14, 27)*

Jesus is more than an exalted Messiah—He is a divine Man who has full authority in heaven *and* on the earth. He not only has a kingdom, He has everlasting dominion over all dominions. Every other dominion must serve and obey Him.

"Go therefore and make disciples of all nations" points to the Son of Man's kingdom, which consists of people from all nations. In the Greek, Jesus' command to make disciples of "all the nations" is the same as the phrase in Daniel 7:14 (and Matthew 24:14).

Jesus instructed the disciples to baptize, "in the name of the Father and of the Son and of the Holy Spirit." While Daniel did not name the Holy Spirit, Daniel 7 is one of the most prominent predictions of the divine Father and Son.

The church must operate in this age under the dominion of the beasts because the great beast, Satan, prowls around like a roaring lion seeking to destroy.[13] Jesus knew the church would need the promise of

---

[13] 1 Peter 5:8.

His presence and His strength until He ends the age (the rule of the beasts), so He promised, "I am with you always, to the end of the age."

The connection between Daniel 7, Matthew 24, and Matthew 28 are another reason we can say Daniel 7 is the gospel of the kingdom.

Eternal Life

Jesus repeatedly offered the promise of eternal life to those who followed Him.[14] This is frequently assumed to be a new promise (eternal life in a heavenly kingdom) and a reinterpretation of the Old Testament, but this promise was firmly grounded in the Old Testament. The Old Testament presented the rule (kingdom) of God as an everlasting rule,[15] and it described or alluded to the immortality of the saints in many passages.[16]

Daniel added a key insight to these predictions: He predicted an exalted people would rule the eternal (everlasting) kingdom.[17] No other Old Testament passage directly made the connection that the eternal kingdom would be ruled by an immortal people.[18]

Jesus frequently made an explicit connection between eternal life, rewards, the eternal kingdom, and His coming as the Son of Man to demonstrate that He used Daniel's prophecy as a basis for the promise of eternal life:

And behold, a man came up to him, saying, "Teacher, what good deed must I do to have eternal life?"... Jesus said to them, "Truly, I say to you, in the new world, when the Son of Man will sit on his glorious throne, you who have

---

[14]Matthew 18:8; 19:16, 29; 25:41, 46; Mark 3:29; 10:17, 30; 16:20; Luke 10:25; 16:9; 18:18, 30; John 3:15–16, 36; 4:14, 36; 5:24, 39; 6:27, 40, 47, 54, 68; 10:28; 12:25, 50; 17:2–3.

[15]Exodus 15:18; 2 Samuel 7:16; Psalm 10:16; 89:35–37; 145:13; 146:10; Isaiah 9:7; Jeremiah 33:15–21.

[16]1 Samuel 2:6; Job 19:25–27; Psalm 16:10; 21:4–7; 49:14–15; 73:24–26; Isaiah 26:19; Daniel 12:1–3.

[17]The words Jesus used for *eternal* and *kingdom* (αἰώνιος and βασιλεία) only appear together in the Old Testament in two verses: Daniel 7:14 and 27. This is a minor point because those words appear individually throughout the Old Testament, but it is interesting.

[18]Some passages describe the Messiah (Son of David) using language that hints at immortality, but not an immortal people.

followed me will also sit on twelve thrones, judging the twelve tribes of Israel. And everyone who has left houses or brothers or sisters or father or mother or children or lands, for my name's sake, will receive a hundredfold and will inherit eternal life." (Matthew 19:16, 28–29)

"When the Son of Man comes in his glory, and all the angels with him, then he will sit on his glorious throne.... And these will go away into eternal punishment, but the righteous into eternal life." (Matthew 25:31, 46)

And he said to them, "Truly, I say to you, there is no one who has left house or wife or brothers or parents or children, for the sake of the kingdom of God, who will not receive many times more in this time, and in the age to come eternal life." And taking the twelve, he said to them, "See, we are going up to Jerusalem, and everything that is written about the Son of Man by the prophets will be accomplished." (Luke 18:29–31)

"No one has ascended into heaven except he who descended from heaven, the Son of Man. And as Moses lifted up the serpent in the wilderness, so must the Son of Man be lifted up, that whoever believes in him may have eternal life. For God so loved the world, that he gave his only Son, that whoever believes in him should not perish but have eternal life." (John 3:13–16)

"For as the Father raises the dead and gives them life, so also the Son gives life to whom he will.... Truly, truly, I say to you, whoever hears my word and believes him who sent me has eternal life. He does not come into judgment, but has passed from death to life. Truly, truly, I say to you, an hour is coming, and is now here, when the dead will hear the voice of the Son of God, and those who hear will live. For as the Father has life in himself, so he has granted the Son also to have life in himself. And he has given him authority to execute judgment, because he is the Son of Man." (John 5:21, 24–27)

"Do not work for the food that perishes, but for the food that endures to eternal life, which the Son of Man will give to you. For on him God the Father has set his seal." "... And this is the will of him who sent me, that I should lose nothing of all that he has given me, but raise it up on the last day. For this is the will of my Father, that everyone who looks on the Son and believes in him should have eternal life, and I will raise him up on the last day." "...Truly, truly, I say to you, whoever believes has eternal life." (John 6:27, 39–40, 47)

And Jesus answered them, "The hour has come for the Son of Man to be glorified. Truly, truly, I say to you, unless a grain of wheat falls into the earth and dies, it remains alone; but if it dies, it bears much fruit. Whoever loves his life loses it, and whoever hates his life in this world will keep it for eternal life. If anyone serves me, he must follow me; and where I am, there will my servant be also. If anyone serves me, the Father will honor him." (John 12:23–26)

When Jesus had spoken these words, he lifted up his eyes to heaven, and said, "Father, the hour has come; glorify your Son that the Son may glorify you, since you have given him authority over all flesh, to give eternal life to all whom you have given him." (John 17:1–2)

Just as Daniel prophesied, an immortal people will inherit an eternal kingdom and eternal life. They will be raised from the dead and exalted alongside the Son of Man.

Daniel's Lake of Fire

Jesus promised eternal life to those who followed Him, but also warned about a fiery judgment for the wicked (commonly referred to as *hell*). In fact, He warned of this more than anyone else.[19] The promise of a day of severe judgment was all throughout the Old Testament, but the explicit warning of fiery judgment for the wicked was relatively rare.[20] When we carefully examine Jesus' teaching, we find He used Daniel 7 as a basis of His warnings about fiery judgment. Just as the saints will share in the reward of the Son of Man, those who follow the beast will share in His fiery judgment.

In Daniel 7, the beast—the final, ultimate adversary of God—was cast into a burning fire just as the Son of Man appeared to receive the reward of His kingdom:[21]

"A stream of fire issued and came out from before him; a thousand thousands served him, and ten thousand times ten thousand stood before him; the court sat in judgment, and the books were opened. I looked then because of the sound of the great words that the horn was speaking. And as I looked, the beast was killed, and its body destroyed and given over to be burned with fire.... I saw in

---

[19]Matthew 5:22, 29–30; 10:28; 16:18; 18:9; 23:15, 33; Mark 9:43, 45, 47; Luke 12:5.

[20]Deuteronomy 32:22; Isaiah 34:10; 66:24.

[21]The book of Revelation calls this the *lake of fire* in Revelation 20:10.

the night visions, and behold, with the clouds of heaven there came one like a son of man, and he came to the Ancient of Days and was presented before him. And to him was given dominion and glory and a kingdom, that all peoples, nations, and languages should serve him; his dominion is an everlasting dominion, which shall not pass away, and his kingdom one that shall not be destroyed." (vv. 10– 11, 13–14)

This narrative was part of the basis of Jesus' warnings about hell. Let's consider Matthew 10:[22]

"And do not fear those who kill the body but cannot kill the soul. Rather fear him who can destroy both soul and body in hell. Are not two sparrows sold for a penny? And not one of them will fall to the ground apart from your Father. But even the hairs of your head are all numbered. Fear not, therefore; you are of more value than many sparrows. So everyone who acknowledges me before men, I also will acknowledge before my Father who is in heaven, but whoever denies me before men, I also will deny before my Father who is in heaven." (vv. 28–33)

This passage draws extensively on Daniel 7. Jesus' warning in verse 28 was taken from Daniel's prediction that God will cast the beast into the burning fire when the beast is killed. The warning is clear and terrifying: *If we follow the beast, we will share in his judgment.* We should fear the One who can also cast us into the burning fire.

The same Judge also presides in both passages. In Daniel, the Ancient of Days (the Father) passed judgment on the beast. In Matthew, the Father (Ancient of Days) is seated as Judge. Jesus promised the disciples that He will speak up before the Father on behalf of those who are His to save them from the Father's judgment. But He will deny those who deny Him, implying they will face the judgment of the Father in the burning fire. This judgment scene with a divine Father and Son executing judgment came directly out of Daniel.

Those who belong to the Son of Man receive eternal life and a kingdom, but those who follow the beast enter the lake of fire with Him:[23]

---

[22]See also Luke 12:4–9.

[23]Jesus even referred to His enemies as *children of hell* (Matthew 23:15).

And the beast was captured and ... thrown alive into the lake of fire that burns with sulfur. (Revelation 19:20)

And if anyone's name was not found written in the book of life, he was thrown into the lake of fire. (Revelation 20:15)

The people who belong to the beast will share His fate just as the people who belong to the Son of Man will share His future. As a result, Jesus often contrasted the threat of hell with entering into the kingdom:[24]

And if your hand causes you to sin, cut it off. It is better for you to enter life crippled than with two hands to go to hell, to the unquenchable fire. And if your foot causes you to sin, cut it off. It is better for you to enter life lame than with two feet to be thrown into hell. And if your eye causes you to sin, tear it out. It is better for you to enter the kingdom of God with one eye than with two eyes to be thrown into hell, "where their worm does not die and the fire is not quenched." (Mark 9:43–48)

Deliverance—The Authority of the Kingdom

The magnitude of Jesus' miracles were unique, but the majority of His miracles had been done before. There was one thing, though, Jesus did that had never been done before: *He cast out evil spirits.*

Evil spirits were present in the Old Testament, but they were not driven out and only appeared sporadically. However, when the Son of Man appeared, evil spirits reacted to His presence and manifested in unusual ways. When they appeared, Jesus cast them out to demonstrate His dominion over evil spiritual powers.[25]

Jesus' deliverance ministry was an evidence of His identity and His authority over the beasts. It was also a preview of what is coming. The spirits recognized this:

---

[24]See also Matthew 5:29–30.

[25]Matthew 4:23–24; 8:16, 28–34; 9:32–34; 10:1, 8; 12:22–32; 15:22–28; 17:14–21; 25:41; Mark 1:23–28, 32–34, 39; 3:22–30; 5:1–19; 6:7, 13; 7:25–30; 9:14–30, 38–42; 13:14–15; 16:8–10, 17; Luke 4:33–37, 41; 8:1–3, 26–39; 9:1, 38–43, 49–50; 10:17–20; 11:14–26; 13:10–13, 32; 16:18.

Two demon-possessed men met him…. And behold, they cried out, "What have you to do with us, O Son of God? Have you come here to torment us before the time?" (Matthew 8:28–29)

This was a demonstration of the authority of the kingdom because the kingdom is associated with the end of the rule of the beasts:

"But if it is by the finger of God that I cast out demons, then the kingdom of God has come upon you." (Luke 11:20)

Jesus and His followers had the power to deliver as an evidence of our future exaltation over the beasts. Like Jesus, we will rule over them. While we wait for the deliverance of the earth from the reign of the beasts, the power of the kingdom is available now to deliver individuals from the beasts. The gospel of the kingdom is associated with healing and deliverance because it gives a preview of a kingdom free of sickness, death, and the oppression of the beasts:[26]

And he went throughout all Galilee, teaching in their synagogues and proclaiming the gospel of the kingdom and healing every disease and every affliction among the people. (Matthew 4:23)

And he called to him his twelve disciples and gave them authority over unclean spirits, to cast them out, and to heal every disease and every affliction…. These twelve Jesus sent out, instructing them, "… proclaim as you go, saying, 'The kingdom of heaven is at hand.' Heal the sick, raise the dead, cleanse lepers, cast out demons." (Matthew 10:1, 5, 7–8)

The Kingdom According to Daniel

Jesus used Daniel to teach a number of characteristics of the kingdom:

- The kingdom comes from heaven. It is the kingdom of God. It comes to the earth and will be established on the earth when the Son of Man comes, but its authority comes from the heavens.

- The kingdom comes from the Father in heaven, and it is His gift to the Son of Man.

- The kingdom is eternal (everlasting).

---

[26]See also Matthew 9:35; Mark 3:14–15; Luke 10:1–17.

- The people of the Son of Man will be rewarded and receive an inheritance in the kingdom.

- The kingdom will be established on the earth when the Son of Man comes with clouds in power.

- When the kingdom comes, the beasts of this age will be destroyed.

- The saints will receive their inheritance in the kingdom when the Son of Man comes.

- The people who inherit the kingdom will also receive eternal life.

- The enemies of the kingdom will face judgment by fire.

- The people who inherit the kingdom come from every people group.

- The kingdom will have dominion over the earth and over every other dominion.

Daniel provided Jesus with a unique, concise summary of the key aspects of the kingdom, so Jesus used it as the basis of His teaching. Other passages expounded further on aspects of the kingdom, but no other prophecy contained this many details of the kingdom in a single vision. As a result, when Jesus described the *kingdom of heaven* or *kingdom of God*, it was a reference to Daniel's prophecy, and we can confidently say Daniel 7 was Jesus' primary source for the gospel of the kingdom.

For nearly two thousand years, Christian theologians have been debating the nature of the kingdom and what Jesus meant when He spoke about the kingdom of God. *Jesus' audience never asked Him that question.* They understood He was speaking from Daniel's prophecy, and that prophecy enabled them to understand the nature of the kingdom Jesus proclaimed.

Many struggle with *tension* between the "heavenly" and "earthly" elements of the kingdom. Jesus' teaching did not describe a *tension* between heaven and earth. Instead, His teaching depicted a *convergence*. As Daniel predicted, God was going to bring heaven and earth together through the Son of Man and His kingdom. The kingdom is the intersection of heaven and earth, and if we overlook the heavenly or earthly aspects of the kingdom, we miss important aspects of the kingdom.

There are a number of other passages that describe Jesus as God's King. Psalm 2 and Psalm 110 are two of the most significant ones, but Jesus never quoted Psalm 2, and He only referenced Psalm 110 seven times. In four of those references, He combined Psalm 110 with Daniel 7.[27] Jesus used Daniel more often than these Psalms for one simple reason: It gave more insight into the nature of the kingdom.

---

[27]Matthew 22:44; 26:64; Mark 12:36; 14:62; Luke 20:42–43; 22:69; John 12:34.

WHEN WILL THE SON OF MAN RULE?

Matthew 24–25 contains Jesus' longest teaching on His return.[1] It is commonly known as the *Olivet Discourse* because it was given on the Mount of Olives. This passage also contains Jesus' prediction that the gospel of the kingdom must be preached to all nations:

And this gospel of the kingdom will be proclaimed.... (Matthew 24:14)

Understanding the context of the passage will make it even clearer that this is a reference to the message of Daniel 7.

The teaching was given to answer the disciples' confusion about the timing of Israel's deliverance and the messianic kingdom. Jesus had entered Jerusalem on a donkey, the way Zechariah predicted the Messiah would, accompanied by shouts of "Hosanna to the Son of David."[2] As a result, the disciples fully expected Jesus to destroy Rome and begin His rule from Jerusalem.

Yet, after He entered the city, Jesus gave a long sequence of rebukes, making it clear He was not going to establish the kingdom at that time. Then, He left Jerusalem and walked up the Mount of Olives. He left Jerusalem like a betrayed King, leaving the way David did when Absalom betrayed him.[3] (David returned to the city as the rightful king, from which we can infer Jesus must as well.)

The Disciples' Question

Because they were confused by Jesus' refusal to rule, the disciples asked Jesus to explain what was happening:

---

[1]Mark 13 and Luke 21:10–36 contain shorter versions of the sermon.

[2]Zechariah 9:9; Matthew 21:4–9.

[3]2 Samuel 15:30.

As he sat on the Mount of Olives, the disciples came to him privately, saying, "Tell us, when will these things be, and what will be the sign of your coming and of the end of the age?" (Matthew 24:3)

The disciples were not asking Jesus when He would return because they did not expect Him to leave and come again. They were genuinely confused. Their question was about timing, and they focused on two key signs: (1) the sign of His coming and (2) the sign of the end of the age. Both were Daniel 7 questions.

By this time, the disciples understood Jesus was the Son of Man who had descended from heaven,[4] but He was not ruling the way that Daniel predicted. And so they asked, "What will be the sign of your coming?" When the Son of Man comes, He will end the rule of the beasts who represent evil, gentile empires. (For example, the disciples viewed Rome as a beast empire.) This "age" referred to the time the beasts rule, so of course they wanted to know what sign would bring about the "end of the age."

From the disciples' perspective, the Son of Man had come, but He was not doing what Daniel predicted He would do when He came. If Jesus' coming from heaven was not the sign He was going to rule and end the age (rule of the beasts), then what sign would be necessary?

They were asking about the fulfillment of Daniel 7. (This is especially clear considering Jesus referenced Daniel 7 more than any other Old Testament passage.)

Jesus' Answer from Daniel

Jesus' answer to the disciples' question is His longest teaching on His return. Most of the teaching came from quotations and allusions to existing Old Testament prophecies. Jesus' answer drew from a number of the prophets, but He used Daniel extensively and mentioned him by name—something He did not do with any other prophet.

Daniel provided the basic framework for the answer because the question was based on Daniel, and Jesus answered their question with two key signs from Daniel. Before we consider Jesus' entire answer, we need to see how He used Daniel to answer the two specific details that the disciples asked about.

---

[4]John 3:13; 6:33, 38, 51, 62; 13:3; 16:28–30; 17:5.

The Son of Man Will Come with the Clouds

The first sign the disciples asked about was the sign of Jesus' coming, and He used Daniel 7 to answer their question:

> *For as the lightning comes from the east and shines as far as the west, so will be the coming of the Son of Man.... Immediately after the tribulation of those days the sun will be darkened, and the moon will not give its light, and the stars will fall from heaven, and the powers of the heavens will be shaken.... Then will appear in heaven the sign of the Son of Man, and then all the tribes of the earth will mourn, and they will see the Son of Man coming on the clouds of heaven with power and great glory. (Matthew 24:27, 29–30)[5]*

Jesus repeated Daniel's glorious prediction: *The Son of Man will come on the clouds with power and great glory* to bring the end of the age (end of the rule of the beasts), judge the beasts, establish a kingdom, and reward the saints. This was the heart of Jesus' answer to the disciples' question because it revealed the key sign that the age is over: The Son of Man must *physically*[6] come with the clouds of heaven as Daniel predicted. Until He comes with the clouds in power and great glory, the end has not come. Jesus did not come that way the first time, so it was not time for the age to end.

Jesus' answer combined a direct quote of Daniel 7:13–14 with a quotation of Zechariah 12:10–12.[7] Zechariah 12 predicts a day when Israel sees God as the One whom Israel pierced and responds with weeping, mourning, and repentance:

> *"And I will pour out on the house of David and the inhabitants of Jerusalem a spirit of grace and pleas for mercy, so that, when they look on me, on him whom they have pierced, they shall mourn for him, as one mourns for an only child, and weep bitterly over him, as one weeps over a firstborn. On that day the mourning in Jerusalem will be as great.... The land shall mourn, each family by itself: the family of the house of David by itself, and their wives by themselves; the family of the house of Nathan by itself, and their wives by themselves." (vv. 10–12)*

---

[5]See also Luke 17:24, 30; 21:27.

[6]Acts 1:11.

[7]The mourning of the tribes of the earth is a reference to Zechariah 12:10–12, a prophecy of Israel's repentance and restoration at Jesus' return.

This was the only time Jesus quoted Zechariah 12, and His interpretation of Zechariah was profound. When Jesus comes with the clouds, Israel will see *Him* as the One Israel had pierced and be restored to Him through mourning and repentance. Zechariah predicted YHWH would be pierced, but Jesus revealed He was the One about whom Zechariah spoke—*Israel will weep over the Son of Man when Israel is restored to Him as Israel's God.*

Jesus had already revealed He would judge as YHWH, and He would also suffer as YHWH.[8] By combining both prophecies, Jesus revealed He will return as YHWH the Judge *and* as YHWH who was pierced. It was also a reminder that Jesus is fully committed to Israel's salvation. This combination of Daniel and Zechariah helps us better grasp the gospel of the kingdom. His crucifixion and His return as God are central. We are called to proclaim both aspects of His identity to all nations (Matthew 24:14).

Paul used this same combination to summarize His message:

> *For I decided to know nothing among you except Jesus Christ and him crucified.*
> *(1 Corinthians 2:2)*

Paul *decided* to limit himself to this message. If Paul intentionally decided to limit himself to searching out Christ and Him crucified, it means these two things are capable of carrying the entire weight of the gospel.

Every time Jesus predicted His return, He referred to this same sign from Daniel 7:13.[9] Until that sign happens, He has not come as King. He combined Daniel with Zechariah 12 to make a solemn promise that His coming would result in the salvation of Israel. This addressed the disciples' concern about Israel's future.

This sign is so certain that it keeps us from deception. We should not pay attention to anyone who claims to be Messiah—only the One who descends from heaven:

> *"Then if anyone says to you, 'Look, here is the Christ!' or 'There he is!' do not*
> *believe it. For false christs and false prophets will arise and perform great signs*

---

[8]See also Isaiah 63:9.

[9]Matthew 13:41–49; 16:27–28; 19:28; 23:39; 24:30, 36–44; 25:31; 26:64; Mark 8:38; 13:26–32; 14:62–64; Luke 9:26; 12:40; 17:24–30; 18:8; 21:27; 22:69; John 14:1–3.

and wonders, so as to lead astray, if possible, even the elect. See, I have told you beforehand. So, if they say to you, 'Look, he is in the wilderness,' do not go out. If they say, 'Look, he is in the inner rooms,' do not believe it. For as the lightning comes from the east and shines as far as the west, so will be the coming of the Son of Man." (Matthew 24:23–27)

You Will Not See Me Again

Jesus' combination of Daniel 7 with Zechariah 12 also helps us interpret His final statement from the previous chapter:

For I tell you, you will not see me again, until you say, "Blessed is he who comes in the name of the Lord." (Matthew 23:39)

This statement came at the end of a series of harsh rebukes that Jesus gave the Pharisees. The prediction that the leaders of Jerusalem would not "see" Jesus was in light of Matthew 21,[10] which tells the story of Jesus' entering Jerusalem riding a donkey as Zechariah said the Messiah would. He entered as Messiah, but was not received as King by the leaders of the city.

This rejection led Jesus to predict they would not see Him enter the city again as King again until He is received in Jerusalem as "he who comes in the name of the Lord." This was a direct quotation of Psalm 118:26, and Jesus' combination of Daniel 7 and Zechariah 12 explained how Psalm 118:26 will be fulfilled.

When Will the Son of Man Come?

Though it may seem as if the beast kingdoms will go on forever, the Father has fixed a day when the Son of Man will return to claim His inheritance:

"But concerning that day and hour no one knows, not even the angels of heaven, nor the Son, but the Father only." (Matthew 24:36)

This prediction also came from Daniel because the Son of Man will not come with the clouds until the Ancient of Days sits in judgment.[11] He must decide to sit in judgment, and then the Son of Man will come. Therefore, no one knows the time except the Father.

---

[10]Matthew 21:4–10.

[11]Daniel 7:25–26.

The End of the Age

The second sign that Jesus was asked about was the end of the age. Jesus assured the disciples that He would end the age when He comes with the clouds by reminding them He was the Judge of Daniel 7:

> *When the Son of Man comes in his glory, and all the angels with him, then he will sit on his glorious throne. Before him will be gathered all the nations....* *(Matthew 25:31–32)*

When He came with the clouds, Jesus would also come as the Son of Man to judge the nations and end the age. This is not the first time Jesus predicted He would judge,[12] but this time Jesus went even further. He intentionally blurred the lines between the Ancient of Days and the Son of Man.

In Daniel 7, the Ancient of Days is the One seated in judgment, surrounded by the angels:

> *"As I looked, thrones were placed, and the Ancient of Days took his seat; his clothing was white as snow, and the hair of his head like pure wool; his throne was fiery flames; its wheels were burning fire. A stream of fire issued and came out from before him; a thousand thousands served him, and ten thousand times ten thousand stood before him; the court sat in judgment, and the books were opened." (Daniel 7:9–10)*

In Matthew 25, Jesus predicted the Son of Man is the One who will be seated, surrounded by *His* angels. Jesus presented Himself as equal to the Ancient of Days. The Ancient of Days' throne is His throne and the Ancient of Days' angels are His angels. Furthermore, this entire judgment scene is a reference to Joel 3. In Joel 3, YHWH is the Judge, but in Matthew 25 the Son of Man is the Judge.

A few verses later, Jesus reminded the disciples He is the Judge *and* the King:

> *Then the King will say to those on his right, "Come, you who are blessed by my Father, inherit the kingdom prepared for you from the foundation of the world." (Matthew 25:34)*

---

[12]John 5:27.

When the Son of Man executes the Ancient of Days' judgment, He will rule as King, presiding over a kingdom given from the Father. This is the final section of the message, and it affirms everything Daniel predicted according to the sequence of events Daniel saw.

Jesus finished the message with a statement that He is King because He is the Son of Man coming with the clouds to execute judgment. Therefore, the gospel of the kingdom must be the announcement that the Son of Man is coming with the clouds as judge to become King and establish the kingdom that comes from His Father—in other words, Daniel 7.

To summarize, the sign of the end of the age was directly out of Daniel: The Son of Man will come with the clouds, sit in judgment with His angels, and become King.

Also, the signs were all designed to answer the question, "What will be the sign of [His] coming?" Every time Jesus used the word *coming* He added, "coming of the Son of Man":[13]

> *For as the lightning comes from the east and shines as far as the west, so will be the coming of the Son of Man... For as were the days of Noah, so will be the coming of the Son of Man.... and they were unaware until the flood came and swept them all away, so will be the coming of the Son of Man. (Matthew 24:27, 37, 39)*

Links to Daniel

Jesus used Daniel for more than these two signs. His sermon contained a number of references to Daniel. Jesus predicted kingdoms will rise against each other:

> *For nation will rise against nation, and kingdom against kingdom. (Matthew 24:7)*

This was a reference to Daniel's vision of the wind's stirring up the sea and the beasts coming out of a stormy sea.[14] Stormy seas were frequently used to symbolize the chaos of the nations.

---

[13]There are two Greek words in the passage typically translated as *coming*, so *coming* appears more often in English translations. The disciples' question used the word παρουσία, and Jesus only used that word three times in the sermon.

[14]See Daniel 7:2. See also Daniel 8 and 11.

Jesus also repeated Daniel's warning that the saints will be under the dominion of the beast, and the beast will prevail over the saints, trying to wear them out through his persecution.[15]

All these are but the beginning of the birth pains. Then they will deliver you up to tribulation and put you to death, and you will be hated by all nations for my name's sake. (Matthew 24:8–9)

Jesus warned His coming will be preceded by great trouble:

For then there will be great tribulation, such as has not been from the beginning of the world until now, no, and never will be. (Matthew 24:21)

The phrase *great tribulation* was quoted from Daniel 12:1, and Jesus' description of this trouble in Matthew 24:15–30 was an exposition of Daniel 7:

"After this I saw in the night visions, and behold, a fourth beast, terrifying and dreadful and exceedingly strong. It had great iron teeth; it devoured and broke in pieces and stamped what was left with its feet. It was different from all the beasts that were before it, and it had ten horns.... As I looked, this horn made war with the saints and prevailed over them.... 'He shall speak words against the Most High, and shall wear out the saints of the Most High..., and shall think to change the times and the law; and they shall be given into his hand for a time, times, and half a time.'" (Daniel 7:7, 21, 25)

The final "beast" will be much more terrifying and dreadful than any other beast in history, but Jesus reminded the disciples that the beast will only rule for a brief period of time, and he cannot change that time:

And if those days had not been cut short, no human being would be saved. But for the sake of the elect those days will be cut short. (Matthew 24:22)

Mark and Luke add other allusions to Daniel. For example, Luke contains a powerful promise:

"Settle it therefore in your minds not to meditate beforehand how to answer, for I will give you a mouth and wisdom, which none of your adversaries will be able to withstand or contradict." (21:14–15)

---

[15]Daniel 7:21, 25.

This promise is in context to the final beast:[16]

"And behold, in this horn were eyes like the eyes of a man, and a mouth speaking great things…. I looked then because of the sound of the great words that the horn was speaking…. Then I desired to know the truth about the fourth beast, which was different from all the rest, exceedingly terrifying… 'He shall speak words against the Most High.'" (Daniel 7:8, 11, 19, 25)

One of the main characteristics of the dreadful end-time beast is his boastful words. The beast will be "given" his mouth and his bold words, but Jesus will give His people words no adversary—not even the beast—will be able to withstand or contradict. Jesus went so far as to instruct us not to prepare to answer the beast. This is a powerful prediction that the Lord will answer the challenge of the end-time beast through the saints.

Jesus will come with the clouds *after* this time of trouble, and He only gave one sign that absolutely confirms the time of trouble has begun: an event referred to as the "abomination of desolation":

"So when you see the abomination of desolation spoken of by the prophet Daniel…." (Matthew 24:15)

This sign is so serious Jesus predicted it is *the* event that will set into motion the end of the age. Not only is the abomination one of Daniel's best known prophecies, Daniel is the only prophet who spoke about the abomination.[17]

These links to Daniel emphasize the significance of Daniel's prophecy. *The key signs Jesus identified in His most important teaching on His return are only found in Daniel:*

- The Abomination of Desolation—The only absolute sign the end-times have begun.

- The Son of Man Will Come with the Clouds—The only undeniable sign of Jesus' coming.

- The Son of Man Will Judge with His Angels—The final sign the age has ended.

---

[16]See also Revelation 13:5.

[17]Daniel 9:27; 11:31; 12:11.

Let the Reader Understand

With all this in mind, let's examine what Jesus said about the gospel of the kingdom:

> *And this gospel of the kingdom will be proclaimed throughout the whole world as a testimony to all nations, and then the end will come. So when you see the abomination of desolation spoken of by the prophet Daniel, standing in the holy place (let the reader understand)…. (Matthew 24:14–15)*

Jesus predicted *this* gospel of the kingdom must be proclaimed, indicating He had a specific message in mind. This message is "good news" about His kingdom. We have already seen Daniel 7 is the passage Jesus used to proclaim His kingdom. If Jesus used Daniel 7 to proclaim the kingdom, it is reasonable to assume He intended us to do the same.

This message must be *proclaimed*. The world *proclaimed* referred to the task of an ancient herald. When an ancient king wanted to visit a city, he would send his herald with a message. The herald would go to the city ahead of the king and proclaim the message to give the city instructions on how to prepare for the arrival of the king. This is the task of the church. We have been sent ahead of Jesus to proclaim the message He is coming, and this is the way the apostles preached the gospel.[18]

Every time Jesus proclaimed His coming, He used Daniel 7. Ancient heralds had to carry the message they were given by their king, and the same is true for us. Jesus used Daniel 7 as an example for us. We are to proclaim His coming, using His message, and Jesus' own words tell us that message begins with Daniel 7.

Jesus wants this message of the kingdom proclaimed as a *witness* to the nations. The word *witness* was a legal word which referred to a witness in a court of law. The gospel of the kingdom is more than an invitation to individual salvation although it includes that. The gospel of the kingdom is a witness—a statement, a warning—to the nations of the earth that the Son of Man is coming and the age will end.

---

[18]Acts 1:11; 10:42; 17:30–31; 28:20; Romans 2:5, 16; 8:18–25; 1 Corinthians 15:19; Galatians 5:5; 1 Thessalonians 2:19; 3:13; 2 Thessalonians 1:5–10; Titus 2:13; 1 Timothy 6:14–16; 2 Timothy 1:12; Hebrews 10:37; 1 Peter 1:13; 2 Peter 3:4–14; 1 John 3:2–3.

This is especially apparent when we read verses 14 and 15 together. Verse 15 begins with a word "so" also translated as "therefore," indicating verse 15 is connected to verse 14:

"And this gospel of the kingdom will be proclaimed throughout the whole world as a testimony to all nations, and then the end will come. So when you see the abomination of desolation spoken of by the prophet Daniel, standing in the holy place (let the reader understand)...." (Matthew 24:14–15)

The gospel of the kingdom is a witness ("warning") that must be given to all nations because the abomination Daniel spoke about is coming. Because these two verses were meant to be read together, the emphasis on Daniel in verse 15 helps us interpret verse 14. The witness of the gospel of the kingdom prepares the nations for the dreadful events that begin with the abomination.

The prophecy of the abomination is only found in Daniel, but Jesus still felt it necessary to emphasize Daniel by name. What's more, Jesus referenced a number of Old Testament passages in this message, but Daniel is the *only* prophet he mentioned by name. He specifically instructed us to read and *understand* Daniel.

Jesus' words indicate there is something so foundational about Daniel's revelation that He felt it necessary to mention Daniel by name and instruct us to spend the effort necessary to understand Daniel's prophecy. Jesus could have mentioned Moses, David, Isaiah, Jeremiah, Ezekiel, or a number of other prophets, but He specifically named Daniel as the one we must understand to grasp His second coming.

Jesus' warning also indicates it is possible to read Daniel but not understand. "Understanding" is one of the main themes of Daniel,[19] but Jesus warned it is possible to read Daniel but not understand it. For example, this happens when we read Daniel mainly as a prophecy of the antichrist or when we do not live in light of his message. It is not enough to read Daniel. We must *understand* him.[20]

---

[19]Daniel 1:4; 2:21; 8:15–17; 9:22–23; 10:1, 11–12, 14, 20; 11:33; 12:8, 10.

[20]Some have speculated the phrase *let the reader understand* may have been inserted by Matthew and not spoken by Jesus. Even if this is the case, it does not diminish the instruction in any way because it reveals Daniel's prophecy was central enough to Jesus' teaching that Matthew felt compelled to instruct his readers to grasp the prophecy. Furthermore, the admonition is part of Scripture.

These references to Daniel further reinforce Daniel 7 is the the gospel of the kingdom to which Jesus referred. We need to read and understand Daniel to grasp the abomination *and* to know the message Jesus wants proclaimed to prepare the world for the abomination.

Daniel's predictions of the abomination are found in prophetic encounters that came after the dream of Daniel 7, and these encounters are expositions of Daniel 7. For example, the abomination is an event performed by the terrible beast described in Daniel 7. Jesus followed this same sequence. Matthew 24:14 is a reference to Daniel 7, and Matthew 24:15 is a reference to an exposition of Daniel 7.

Daniel's book not only gives us the key events related to Jesus' return, it also gives us the message that prepares the nations for those events.

The message of Daniel 7—especially the central message of the Son of Man and His kingdom—has power to prepare people for the most difficult hour of human history. It must be proclaimed to warn the nations and prepare the saints to endure and overcome this dreadful beast.

Discovering the Gospel of the Kingdom

If we put everything together, there is no question Daniel 7 is the main message Jesus had in mind in Matthew 24:15:

- The disciples asked Jesus a question about the timing of Daniel 7 in order to understand why He refused to rule at that time. They specifically asked about two signs in Daniel's prophecy.

- Jesus answered their question by quoting two key signs from Daniel. He affirmed and expounded on Daniel's prediction.

- The disciples asked about Jesus' coming, and every time Jesus described His coming He called Himself the *Son of Man*.

- Jesus instructed us to proclaim "the gospel of the kingdom." Daniel 7 is the passage that Jesus used to proclaim the key aspects of His kingdom.

- The gospel of the kingdom is designed to prepare the nations for Jesus' return. Daniel 7 is the only prophecy Jesus used to describe His return every time He predicted it.

- Daniel is the only prophet Jesus named in His longest message on His return.

- Jesus referenced more specific predictions from Daniel than any other prophet.

- Jesus only gave one decisive sign that the end-time trouble has begun—the abomination—which was only predicted by Daniel.

- In His conclusion, Jesus predicted He would return as Son of Man to judge the nations and rule as King over a kingdom given from the Father.

- Jesus told the disciples to watch for three unique, decisive signs that occur only once: the abomination, the Son of Man coming with the clouds, and the Son of Man judging the nations as YHWH. All three of these signs are only found in Daniel.

Matthew 24–25 is key because it is Jesus' longest teaching on what it will take for Him to rule, *and* it is the place He predicts the gospel of the kingdom must be proclaimed. Daniel 7 provides the basic structure for the entire teaching and provides far more key points in the message than any other prophet.

This is another example of how Jesus used Daniel. Daniel wasn't more important than the other prophets, but he was given the most concise, complete summary of Jesus' gospel. That gospel includes the first *and* second coming. Daniel was not given all the details. Jesus expected His audience to fill in details from the other prophets, but He taught us to use Daniel as a framework to interpret the prophets.

Jesus' return is the most dramatic event in history, and the time of His glory is finally unveiled in the sight of the nations. He has waited a long time for this day. It is *His* day and incredibly precious to the Father. The fact that Jesus mainly chose Daniel to describe this day is a profound statement about the significance of Daniel's small book.

The Son of Man's Judgment

THE SON OF MAN IS A JUDGE

Many people recognize Jesus as a King, but the subject of Jesus as a Judge tends to be overlooked and ignored. However, it was a very prominent part of Jesus' gospel, and He used Daniel's prophecy to present Himself as the divine Judge. Our gospel is incomplete without the message of Jesus the Judge.

Jesus spoke about judgment and His identity as Judge in over twenty passages,[1] and He repeatedly presented Himself as the divine Judge:[2]

> *For the Son of Man is going to come with his angels in the glory of his Father, and then he will repay each person according to what he has done. (Matthew 16:27)*

> *When the Son of Man comes in his glory, and all the angels with him, then he will sit on his glorious throne. Before him will be gathered all the nations, and he will separate people one from another as a shepherd separates the sheep from the goats. (Matthew 25:31–32)*

> *But stay awake at all times, praying that you may have strength to escape all these things that are going to take place, and to stand before the Son of Man. (Luke 21:36)*

> *For not even the Father judges anyone, but He has given all judgment to the Son ... and He gave Him authority to execute judgment, because He is the Son of Man. (John 5:22, 27 NASB95)*

---

[1]Matthew 10:15, 32; 11:22, 24; 12:27, 36, 41, 42; 13:41; 16:27; 19:28; 25:31–32; Mark 8:38; Luke 9:26; 10:14; 11:31–32; 12:8–9; 18:8; 21:36; John 3:18–19; 5:22, 24, 27, 29–30; 8:16; 9:39; 12:31, 48; 16:8, 11.

[2]See also Matthew 9:6; Mark 8:38; Luke 9:26; 12:8–9.

Because Daniel 7 introduced the Son of Man in a judgment scene, every time Jesus predicted He would come with the clouds, it was also a statement He was the divine Judge.[3] Jesus referred to salvation or being saved in about sixteen verses and interestingly never directly used the title *Savior*. [4] The reason for this is simple: Jesus' mission to save men and His commitment to bring judgment are not in conflict.

We tend to think of Jesus as a Savior, and His judgments are part of His salvation because He brings salvation through judgment.

Without judgment, there is no salvation because the perpetrators of evil continue to bring destruction on God's good creation. Therefore, Jesus is committed to judging every individual and every structure that promotes sin and destroys His creation:

> *"The Son of Man will send his angels, and they will gather out of his kingdom all causes of sin and all law-breakers." (Matthew 13:41)*

> *"Now is the judgment of this world; now will the ruler of this world be cast out." (John 12:31)*

Until Jesus judges in an ultimate, final way, He has not brought full salvation, freedom, and restoration to the earth.

Judging the Beasts

Before Jesus began His public ministry, He first went out into the wilderness to face Satan and demonstrate authority over the beasts. Mark records Jesus was with the "wild beasts" and the "angels" because Jesus is the One with authority over the beasts and served by the heavenly hosts who accompany the Ancient of Days.[5]

The beasts had to be judged by a man because God gave dominion over the earth to man, but no man was qualified to judge the beasts. For thousands of years, the beasts had exploited the fact that man has authority on the earth but not the ability to judge and remove the beasts.

---

[3]Matthew 24:30; 26:64; Mark 13:26; 14:62; Luke 21:27.

[4]Matthew 10:22; 16:25; 18:11; 24:13; Mark 8:35; 13:13; 16:16; Luke 7:50; 8:12; 9:24, 56; 19:10; John 3:17; 5:34; 10:9; 12:47.

[5]Mark 1:13.

Throughout history, God has used men to execute His judgments on other nations, but no man has been able to execute His judgments on the spiritual powers ("beasts") behind the nations, so these judgments have never brought resolution. Because all men are born under the spiritual dominion of the beasts, men cannot break the beasts' power. As a result, the cycle of evil and oppression has continued through history.

The only way to stop the rule of the beasts is to judge them by a man with divine authority. Because Jesus is divine, He has full authority over the beasts. Because He is fully human, He has the dominion over the earth necessary to remove the beasts. In Jesus, God can judge in righteousness while leaving man's delegated authority intact. Jesus will judge the world as God and as a man.

Jesus now sits in the heavens as God and as Man—the ultimate Judge. This is the key difference between Jesus and every other "anointed one" (messiah). He is *the* Messiah because He is the Man who can do more than defeat "beast" empires; He can also judge the beasts behind the empires.

The Glory of the Son of Man in Judgment

The prophets repeatedly predicted the day of YHWH's judgment, but they struggled to adequately describe what they saw and what they felt:

> *The LORD reigns, let the earth rejoice; let the many coastlands be glad! Clouds and thick darkness are all around him; righteousness and justice are the foundation of his throne. Fire goes before him and burns up his adversaries all around. His lightnings light up the world; the earth sees and trembles. The mountains melt like wax before the LORD, before the Lord of all the earth. (Psalm 97:1–5)*

> *Behold, the day of the LORD comes, cruel, with wrath and fierce anger, to make the land a desolation and to destroy its sinners from it. For the stars of the heavens and their constellations will not give their light; the sun will be dark at its rising, and the moon will not shed its light. I will punish the world for its evil, and the wicked for their iniquity; I will put an end to the pomp of the arrogant, and lay low the pompous pride of the ruthless. I will make people more rare than fine gold, and mankind than the gold of Ophir. Therefore I will make the heavens tremble, and the earth will be shaken out of its place, at the wrath of the LORD of hosts in the day of his fierce anger. (Isaiah 13:9–13)*

And the LORD will cause his majestic voice to be heard and the descending blow of his arm to be seen, in furious anger and a flame of devouring fire, with a cloudburst and storm and hailstones. (Isaiah 30:30)

Draw near, O nations, to hear; and listen, O peoples! Let the earth and all it contains hear, and the world and all that springs from it. For the LORD's indignation is against all the nations, and His wrath against all their armies; He has utterly destroyed them, He has given them over to slaughter. So their slain will be thrown out, and their corpses will give off their stench, and the mountains will be drenched with their blood. And all the host of heaven will wear away, and the sky will be rolled up like a scroll; all their hosts will also wither away as a leaf withers from the vine, or as one withers from the fig tree. (Isaiah 34:1–4 NASB95)

"But the LORD is the true God; he is the living God and the everlasting King. At his wrath the earth quakes, and the nations cannot endure his indignation." (Jeremiah 10:10)

The LORD utters his voice before his army, for his camp is exceedingly great; he who executes his word is powerful. For the day of the LORD is great and very awesome; who can endure it? (Joel 2:11)

Multitudes, multitudes, in the valley of decision! For the day of the LORD is near in the valley of decision. The sun and the moon are darkened, and the stars withdraw their shining. The LORD roars from Zion, and utters his voice from Jerusalem, and the heavens and the earth quake. (Joel 3:14–16)

The LORD is a jealous and avenging God; the LORD is avenging and wrathful; the LORD takes vengeance on his adversaries and keeps wrath for his enemies. The LORD is slow to anger and great in power, and the LORD will by no means clear the guilty. His way is in whirlwind and storm, and the clouds are the dust of his feet…. The mountains quake before him; the hills melt; the earth heaves before him, the world and all who dwell in it. Who can stand before his indignation? Who can endure the heat of his anger? His wrath is poured out like fire, and the rocks are broken into pieces by him. (Nahum 1:3, 5–6)

When the prophets spoke of God's terrifying judgment, they made the most extreme comparisons possible. They struggled to find language capable of describing the glory and terror of God as Judge. However, even the prophets could not fully anticipate what Jesus revealed: *Jesus revealed He was the One the prophets predicted would come in judgment.*

The prophets' most dramatic oracles were not just descriptions of God; they were descriptions of a *divine Man* who will liberate the cosmos and punish the wicked.

When we neglect the message of Jesus as the divine Judge and do not long for Jesus to come with His judgments, it demonstrates we disagree with God. It shows we disregard what Jesus did, because His suffering set the stage for His judgments. We cannot receive His mercy but disregard His judgments. It's a rejection of who He truly is, and it's a partial gospel.

The terrifying majesty of Jesus' judgments are part of His glory, and we dare not take that glory away from Him.

This age is under the dominion of the beasts until it is liberated by Jesus' judgments.[6] These beasts profane God's name and fuel the rebellion against Him. It is to our shame when we do not share God's zeal for His own judgments. When we do not desire those judgments, it indicates we are comfortable with the rule of the beasts and do not share God's longing to see His creation liberated from darkness.

The Revelation of the Son of Man in Judgment

Daniel saw YHWH seated in judgment as the Ancient of Days with a river of fire flowing from Him. The Son of Man suddenly appeared in this judgment scene to execute the terrifying judgment of YHWH and receive His inheritance. The passage Jesus chose as the key revelation of His identity reveals Him in a judgment scene, indicating how central judgment is to His identity.

God's judgments do at least five profound things in this scene.

His judgments bring everlasting salvation. When He judges, it brings salvation, and creation will flourish. (We will examine this more in the next chapter.)

His judgments reveal the glory of the Son of Man. We cannot separate Jesus' glory from His judgments. There are profound aspects of Jesus' glory that will only be revealed when He comes in the clouds, executes His judgments, and delivers a people in His mercy. John also summarized the dramatic events surrounding Jesus' appearance as the "revela-

---

[6]2 Corinthians 4:4; Ephesians 2:2; 6:12; 1 John 5:19; 1 Peter 5:8.

tion (unveiling) of Jesus."[7] Many have carefully studied the glory of Jesus in securing mercy in His first coming, but far fewer have studied the glory of Jesus in His second coming. He is glorified in His judgments *and* in His mercy.

His judgments will dethrone the beasts. Jesus' judgments dethroned the spiritual powers who oppress and destroy God's good creation. Jesus' work on the cross *purchased* the liberation of the cosmos, but that liberation must be *enforced* in judgment. Until Jesus judges, the full work of the cross has not been accomplished.

His judgments will establish the kingdom. The kingdom of God which supplants every other kingdom is established through judgment. It cannot come any other way because God must first remove the kingdoms that are in opposition to it. Because it removes and replaces every other kingdom, the kingdom itself is a judgment.[8]

His judgments will enthrone a people. When Jesus comes in judgment, He will demonstrate the mystery of His mercy by exalting a people (the saints) who will receive glorified bodies and dominion with Him. His judgments begin a new age free of evil.

In this scene, Jesus is involved in judgment and salvation. Wrath and mercy. *Both are the gospel.* Jesus' judgments are an aspect of His mercy because they liberate creation and exalt a new kind of humanity. This exposes the fact that the modern tension between judgment and mercy is not biblical.

The Son of Man Will Judge

The idea Jesus is the Judge seems strange to some people because of a few statements Jesus made:[9]

> *For God did not send his Son into the world to condemn the world, but in order that the world might be saved through him. (John 3:17)*

> *If anyone hears my words and does not keep them, I do not judge him; for I did not come to judge the world but to save the world. The one who rejects me and does not receive my words has a judge; the word that I have spoken will judge him on the last day. (John 12:47–48)*

---

[7]Revelation 1:1.

[8]2 Timothy 4:1.

[9]See also John 5:45; 8:15.

If these verses are read out of context, they seem to indicate Jesus does not judge. However, we must interpret these statements in light of everything Jesus taught. There are a number of reasons these statements do not contradict Jesus' identity as Judge.

First, Jesus repeatedly predicted He would judge and identified Himself as Judge while He only made a handful of statements about not judging. There is no indication in the Gospels these statements are contradictory or caused confusion, so the authors of the Gospels did not interpret them as statements that Jesus would never judge.

Second, Jesus told the disciples to testify He was the appointed Judge,[10] and the apostles preached Jesus as Judge.[11] Jesus would not have given this command if He was not going to judge.[12]

Last, one of the most unusual aspects of God's redemptive plan is the plan to send Jesus twice. Jesus did not need to come twice to justify His judgment because, before He came, we deserved God's wrath and stood condemned as our actions and words demonstrate.[13] The first coming was not necessary to establish the need for judgment; it was necessary to secure mercy and save us from God's just judgment.

Jesus did not come to judge the first time, but His first coming does not replace the second coming, and He repeatedly predicted He would judge when He comes with the clouds.

---

[10]Acts 10:42.

[11]Acts 17:31; Romans 2:5, 16; 1 Corinthians 4:5; 2 Thessalonians 1:5–9; 2 Timothy 4:1.

[12] We will examine this more in the second volume, *Son of Man: The Apostles' Gospel* dealing with the apostles' use of Daniel.

[13]Matthew 12:36–37.

SALVATION THROUGH JUDGMENT

Daniel saw the Son of Man bring salvation through judgment while also delivering a remnant in mercy, but it was not clear how God would accomplish this. Jesus opened up the mystery of God's plan to bring salvation through judgment.

At the center of God's plan of redemption is His commitment to bring salvation *through* judgment. We cannot understand the nature of God or the nature of our salvation until we grasp it comes through judgment.

Judgment includes two distinct actions:

- Those who do evil must be punished.

- Those who do evil must be removed so they do not continue to perpetuate evil.

Because judgment is necessary for salvation, God repeatedly promised He would punish those who do evil:[1]

> *"The LORD is slow to anger and abounding in steadfast love, forgiving iniquity and transgression, but he will by no means clear the guilty."* *(Numbers 14:18)*

> *"I will not keep silent, but I will repay; I will indeed repay into their lap both your iniquities and your fathers' iniquities together, says the LORD; because they made offerings on the mountains and insulted me on the hills, I will measure into their lap payment for their former deeds."* *(Isaiah 65:6–7)*

Because God is good, He must *punish* the evil that has been done, and He must *remove* everyone who does evil so creation can flourish. We all know instinctively this is what must be done.

---

[1]See also Exodus 34:7; Jeremiah 32:18.

The concept that judgment brings salvation is not difficult for people to grasp, and the vast majority of humans agree with it to some extent. For example, when someone is guilty of a crime, they must be punished for that crime *and* removed from society so people can live in peace and safety without fear. When a criminal is *judged*, society enjoys *salvation*.

The challenge is we do not agree with God's definition of evil, and we refuse to acknowledge the ways we embrace and promote evil.

The Judge Is a Savior

God's judgment includes punishment for evil *and* bringing an end to the life of the evildoer so they do not continue to corrupt His creation. Human judges do this every day. They punish dedicated criminals and then "end the life" of criminals to prevent them from carrying out future crimes. For some crimes, this is done dramatically, and the criminal is put to death. For other crimes, a criminal is sent to prison for life. Either way, the "life" of a criminal must end so they no longer threaten society.

We all know a judge who does not respond to evil by punishing the criminal and removing him from society is a bad judge. The same is true of God. As Judge, God must respond to evil by punishing it. The Bible reveals the "criminals" in this age are the evil spiritual powers and fallen man. We are born in sin (crime). We love it, and we perpetuate it as long as we live. Because we are familiar with our sin, we do not recognize the extent of the damage we do to creation, but for the sake of creation, God must punish and remove the "criminals" in His creation.

God's great challenge is how to be true to His promise to repay the guilty, bring an end to their lives, *and* rescue a people for Himself.

God's desire for relationship with man drives His redemptive plan. He has to punish man and end man's life, but He also wants to live with man forever. Because man embraced sin and it became part of every human being,[2] this seemed impossible. However, God revealed His glory by resolving this impasse in a stunning way. Through Jesus, God can be faithful to His judgments *and* show profound mercy.

We tend to think of Jesus as Savior in the sense that He offers mercy for our sin. We also tend to associate judgment only with con-

---

[2]Romans 3:23, 9; 5:12.

demnation. However, God is a Savior in judgment. His judgments save creation because they end the freedom of sinners who corrupt the cosmos.

This is central to the gospel but not well understood by most believers, so we need to briefly see how the cross accomplishes what Daniel saw.

The Mystery and Majesty of Mercy

When Daniel saw the Ancient of Days seated and the Son of Man's coming in judgment, he saw a profound mystery. He saw the beasts punished, and every "beast" kingdom destroyed. The judgment in the vision was absolute. However, he also saw a people given to the Son of Man. This people came from all nations, meaning they were taken out of the beast kingdoms that were judged and destroyed. Yet, this people received mercy, everlasting life, and exaltation instead of punishment.

The obvious question is how did these people survive? Why were they not punished with their kingdoms and their lives ended? How did they obtain mercy and exaltation? It was not clear how God could be faithful to His commitment to save creation through His judgments yet show mercy to a people who had been part of the beast empires.

Some people ask why God cannot just make a decision to forgive, but the reason is simple. There must be an appropriate response to evil *and* an appropriate action that brings a final end to evil so creation is not endlessly destroyed.

Because many people think salvation and judgment are opposites, it is important we understand how Jesus' death on the cross provides salvation *through* judgment. We tend to think the cross provides salvation *from* judgment for the redeemed, but that is not the complete message because judgment *produces* salvation.

When God judges, individuals suffer the punishment of their sin, but His creation flourishes. The cross secured mercy, but judgment must still be executed. Everyone—the redeemed and the condemned—experience God's salvation through judgment.

In Jesus, God accomplishes both judgment actions—this is the mystery and majesty of God's mercy.

The First Act of Judgment—Punishment

God must be faithful to judge sin through punishment. Because sin has corrupted His creation, there must be an appropriate payment.

All sin must be punished, and God has chosen to render all judgment for sin through Jesus. Through God's majestic plan, Jesus is both the *recipient* and *instrument* of God's judgment.

First, Jesus became the recipient of God's judgment. God still punishes the sin of the redeemed, but the punishment was given to Jesus. In the crucifixion, Jesus endured our judgment because the Lord put our sin (iniquity) on Him:

> *All we like sheep have gone astray; we have turned—every one—to his own way; and the LORD has laid on him the iniquity of us all. (Isaiah 53:6)*

While many are offended at God's judgments, His judgments are so perfect He submitted to His own judgments. Jesus' crucifixion answers every accusation against God's judgments. God chose to endure our judgment when we were His enemies.[3] While we do not face the full penalty of our sin, punishment was still executed. Because Jesus took the required punishment for our sin, we are saved *through* judgment, not simply saved *from* judgment. He suffered what we deserved.

Because sin brought death, the only appropriate punishment is death. Death ends human life, so the punishment of death meant no human being could survive God's punishment.[4] However, Jesus was completely different from every other man. He was a *divine* Human. Because He was human, He could suffer God's punishment and die as a man. Because He was divine, the death of His human body would not end His life. He is the One who sustains all life in the cosmos[5]; therefore, His life cannot end. His life is eternal and indestructible.

Jesus' sinlessness was required, but His divinity was key to His ability to experience our punishment. He alone could endure God's judgments and survive. Jesus emphasized this before the cross because, every time Jesus predicted His suffering and His death, He predicted

---

[3]Romans 5:6–10.

[4]Romans 5:12; 6:23; 1 Corinthians 15:56; James 1:15.

[5]Ephesians 1:23; Colossians 1:16–17; Hebrews 1:3;

He must suffer as the Son of Man.[6] He did not predict He would suffer as Messiah nor as the Suffering Servant. Both were true, but He had to die *as God* to secure redemption.

Jesus used Daniel's language to predict the divine Human must suffer and must die because only the death of a divine Human was capable of enduring God's punishment for sin and surviving.

God faithfully punished our sins when Jesus became the *recipient* of our judgment. In Him, we are saved *through* judgment. If God punishes us, we will not survive, but because Jesus was the Son of Man—the divine Human—He could endure God's punishment and survive. The punishment for sin is death, so Jesus' human body died; however, His life could not be destroyed. The resurrection was inevitable.

Because Jesus became the *recipient* of God's judgment in His first coming, He is qualified to be the human *instrument* of God's judgment in His second coming.[7] When He returns, He will execute God's fierce judgment. As we have seen, Jesus repeatedly and boldly identified Himself as the One who would execute YHWH's judgment.

The Father has given *all* judgment into the hands of the Son, and *all* will experience God's salvation through judgment. No one's sin escapes. All will be judged. Jesus became the recipient of judgment so punishment could be executed for those who receive God's mercy, and He will become the instrument of judgment so punishment can be executed on those who reject His mercy.

Jesus' death and suffering was the shocking way in which God can show mercy and still be faithful to bring salvation through judgment.

God Must End the Life of the Sinner

God accomplished our punishment in Jesus, but He must also be faithful to end the life of every sinner. This is the second element of His judgment, and it is also accomplished through Jesus.

Creation will not be saved until God ends the life of every creature who tolerates, embraces, or promotes sin. This includes the evil spiritual powers and all humanity. It is obvious God must end the life of the

---

[6]Matthew 16:21; 17:12, 20:18–19; 26:2; Mark 8:31; 9:12; Luke 9:22; 17:25; 22:15, 22; 24:7.

[7]Philippians 2:8–11.

wicked for creation to flourish, but because all have sinned,[8] He must end the sinful life of *all* humans—both those who are condemned and those who receive mercy in Jesus.

God does this in a stunning way through Jesus. In Jesus, God can be faithful to judge and end our sinful lives in a way that brings redemption so we can survive His judgments and receive mercy when He comes. Jesus accomplishes this in the life of a saint in two stages.

The first stage is the re-creation of a person through what the Bible calls the "new birth." Jesus explained this process in John 3:

> *Unless one is born again he cannot see the kingdom of God.... unless one is born of water and the Spirit, he cannot enter the kingdom of God. That which is born of the flesh is flesh, and that which is born of the Spirit is spirit. Do not marvel that I said to you, "You must be born again." (vv. 3, 5–7)*

We cannot enter the kingdom of God unless we are born of the Spirit. The reason is simple. The kingdom is the everlasting kingdom that comes when God brings an end to the reign of sin by judging every sinful kingdom and every sinful creature. Only creatures free of sin can live in the everlasting kingdom. Because we are born in sin, we must be born "again," free of sin.

Jesus accomplishes this by giving us the gift of His own Spirit. When we are born of the Spirit, Jesus puts His own life in us. His life is free of sin, and when it enters a human, it re-creates that human. A redeemed human is a human sustained by a divine, eternal, sin-free life. We are a new type of humanity with a new life that comes from God—our new life is free of sin and everlasting.

While this new life makes us a new species of human, God does not eliminate our humanity. Instead, He transforms it. God has committed to end the life of every sinful creature, so only creatures free of the impulse of sin will be able to live in the new creation. Consequently, the Holy Spirit transforms our desires over time so we *love* what God loves and *hate* sin. This transformation is usually referred to as "sanctification," and it is required to live in the new creation because God's salvation includes the end of sin. No one who loves sin will be able to live in the new creation (everlasting kingdom) because they would destroy it by reintroducing sin.

---

[8]Romans 3:23.

The Holy Spirit is very patient, but if our desire for sin does not change over time, either we have not been born again by the Spirit, or we are resisting His work and in serious danger. This is likely part of the reason Jesus said anyone who blasphemes the Holy Spirit cannot be forgiven.[9] If we resist Him in an ultimate and final way, He cannot remove the desire for sin and re-create us so we can live eternally. (Jesus warned of an ultimate, extreme rejection of the Spirit, not a temporary resistance to the Spirit as He reshapes us in the process of the maturity process. The Holy Spirit is *very* patient with our process of maturity.)

Most people think changes in behavior are the main goal of spiritual growth, but the primary goal of spiritual growth is a change in *desire*. Changes in behavior should be the fruit of new appetites not simply new rules. God is not looking for a people who are "perfect" in every way. He is looking for a people who love what He loves and hate what He hates. Jesus' biggest problem was people who had good behavior but no appetite for God. His biggest mission field was people who had bad behavior but were willing to receive new appetites.

If anyone is in Jesus, they are a new creation:

Therefore, if anyone is in Christ, he is a new creation. The old has passed away; behold, the new has come. (2 Corinthians 5:17)

New species is usually a better phrase than *new creation*, because it is a better description of what Paul was trying to say. When Jesus saves us and gives us the Holy Spirit, the Spirit re-creates us and we are "born again." In the process, we become like Jesus in a profound way. Jesus was born in a fallen body,[10] but He was free of sin because He was divine. While we are not made divine, when we are born again, God comes to dwell in our fallen bodies. His life becomes our life in a mysterious way that does not make us divine, but gives us a new sinless, source of life through the indwelling Spirit. The Spirit then labors with us over time to transform our desires so we no longer love sin and, instead, love what He loves.

The work of the Holy Spirit in the new birth and in sanctification is the first stage of ending our sinful lives. Our "life of sin" must end

---

[9]Mark 3:29; Luke 12:10.

[10]Romans 8:3.

because we cannot live in the eternal kingdom if we still love sin. This stage is critical, and it prepares us for the second stage.

The second stage is the physical death of our bodies. When the Holy Spirit enters us and re-creates us, He forms a new life and gives us new desires, but there remains a profound problem: Sin is deeply embedded in our fallen bodies. The Holy Spirit brings about profound transformation, but the weakness of our sinful bodies keeps us from living entirely free of any vulnerability to sin.

Because God must end the life of anything that tolerates, embraces, or promotes sin, every human must die—even the redeemed. God's judgment in the death of our bodies reveals the true majesty of redemption.

Jesus does something astonishing for the saints. When God judges our bodies through death, He gives us a new body like His. This new body is free from sin and can live without sin. This new body is the majestic, outward demonstration of the Holy Spirit's inward work of sanctification. Because of His work, we will be able to live without sin in this new body. This body will not die because death comes from sin.

This reveals how salvation comes through judgment for the saints. We already saw how Jesus endured our judgment. The death of our bodies is the judgment we must endure, but through Jesus, God turns this judgment into salvation.

Jesus ends our sinful lives by recreating us through the indwelling Holy Spirit who becomes the source of our lives. He is everlasting and sinless. He then begins the process of transformation so we love what God loves and hate what He hates. This prepares us to receive new bodies when He judges our old bodies through death. These new bodies are free from sin. They are fully capable of living according to our new desires and the new life in us by the Holy Spirit.

God does not want the new creation corrupted, so those who reject the Holy Spirit's work of sanctification in this age should not expect to inherit eternal bodies. God is not going to give glorious, sinless bodies to people who want to continue in sin. That would completely defeat the purpose of the gift of a new body.

This is God's pattern—death and resurrection. The judgment of death brings about life for those who are in Jesus.

For the saints, death is a judgment, but it is not the end of our lives. It is the beginning. The judgment of death does not destroy us; it transforms us so we can live free of sin in our glorious new bodies.

Jesus was sinless, but His life provides the pattern:

- Jesus was born as God, dwelling in a fallen, human body. When we receive the Holy Spirit, we are reborn, and God comes to live in our fallen, human bodies.

- When Jesus was judged for sin (our sin, not His), it resulted in His death. God is going to judge every man's sin through death.

- Jesus' death prepared Him to receive a new, glorified body similar and yet different from the body He received at birth. After we die, we will receive a new body like Jesus' new body.

Because salvation must come through judgment, we do not receive our new body until Jesus comes with the clouds in judgment. The author of Hebrews summarized this:

> *And just as it is appointed for man to die once, and after that comes judgment, so Christ, having been offered once to bear the sins of many, will appear a second time, not to deal with sin but to save those who are eagerly waiting for him. (9:27–28)*

Every man must die and then pass through the judgment—redeemed or not.[11] Jesus will come a second time, not to deal with sin, but to judge it. Those who are eagerly waiting for Him will be saved by that judgment.

The judgment of death produces salvation for the saints (a new body), but it is terrifying for those not in Jesus. God cannot allow them to live in His creation because they would destroy it. As a result, they are finally condemned after their bodies die. The Bible calls this the *second death.*[12] Their death and judgment result in salvation for creation.

Judgment Brings Salvation

There is much more to judgment and salvation, but for our purposes, we need to grasp how Jesus expanded on what Daniel saw. Daniel saw

---

[11]The only exception is those who are alive at the Lord's return. They are changed suddenly, but their old bodies do not survive (1 Thessalonians 4:17).

[12]Revelation 20:14.

the Son of Man appear in a judgment scene. He condemned the beasts, judged the kingdoms, and redeemed the saints.

Jesus' terrifying judgment will result in a "new heaven and a new earth":

> *But the day of the Lord will come like a thief, and then the heavens will pass away with a roar, and the heavenly bodies will be burned up and dissolved, and the earth and the works that are done on it will be exposed.... the heavens will be set on fire and dissolved, and the heavenly bodies will melt as they burn! But according to his promise we are waiting for new heavens and a new earth in which righteousness dwells. (2 Peter 3:10, 12–13)*

> *Then I saw a great white throne and him who was seated on it. From his presence earth and sky fled away, and no place was found for them. And I saw the dead, great and small, standing before the throne, and books were opened. And the dead were judged by what was written in the books. (Revelation 20:11–12)*

> *Then I saw a new heaven and a new earth, for the first heaven and the first earth had passed away, and the sea was no more. (Revelation 21:1)*

God's pattern is to bring salvation through death and resurrection. It was the pattern for Jesus, it is the pattern for Israel, it is the pattern for the saints, and it is even the pattern for the cosmos. This is simply another way of saying salvation comes through judgment. God's judgments bring about death, but they ultimately produce new life and redemption for creation. (This of course does not minimize the fact that individuals who are not redeemed experience the glory of God's wrath but not the glory of His mercy.)

Until God comes in judgment to punish sin and bring an end to the lives of sinful creatures, creation remains in bondage.[13] Judgment results in condemnation for the wicked but salvation for the cosmos. Judgment is God's means of salvation for humanity because it removes the humans who embrace sin and corrupt other humans.

The most stunning part of God's plan to bring salvation through judgment is what He does with the saints. God's judgment does not condemn the saints; it transforms them. Those in Jesus are redeemed by judgment, not destroyed by it. God's salvation through judgment has

---

[13]Romans 8:19–22; Revelation 11:18.

different expressions, but when He judges, it causes creation to flourish. Jesus is a picture of that. He endured God's judgment on the cross, and it led to His resurrection in a glorified body.

Jesus' suffering *as God* provides mercy, and His judgment *as God* will bring God's salvation. Therefore, the *Son of Man* had to suffer, and the Son of Man has to judge. God will be glorified in His mercy *and* in His wrath. He should be honored and celebrated for *both*.

The Son of Man's Suffering

THE SON OF MAN MUST SUFFER

The cross has become a symbol of Christianity, and Jesus' suffering is well-known as a central theme of the gospel. However, it is often overlooked that Jesus primarily used Daniel to set the stage for His suffering. Surprisingly, He rarely used many of the most commonly known passages about His suffering. *Instead, it was very important to Jesus that we would know He suffered as the Son of Man.*

There are many prophetic passages that predict and describe Jesus' suffering.[1] The details in these passages reveal the crucifixion of Jesus was always central to the redemptive plan, but these passages alone are not enough to form a *paradigm* of suffering. Yet, Jesus invited people to follow Him and embrace the same paradigm of suffering He had embraced.

Daniel 7 was the predominant passage used to establish a paradigm of suffering not only for the Son of Man, but also for those who follow Him. Other passages pointed to the need for an atonement but did not present the paradigm of suffering Jesus repeatedly described.

As a result, every time Jesus spoke of His suffering, He connected it to His identity as the Son of Man.

Jesus spoke about His crucifixion 3 times, and each time referred to Himself as the Son of Man.[2] Jesus spoke in general about His suffering 9 times. In 7 of those verses, He either directly stated the Son of Man must suffer or connected His suffering to His identity as the Son of Man.[3]

---

[1]For example, Psalm 22; 41:9; 118:22; Isaiah 50:6; 52:14–53:12; Daniel 9:26; Zechariah 13:7.

[2]Matthew 20:18–19; 26:2; Luke 24:7.

[3]Matthew 16:21; 17:12; Mark 8:31; 9:12; Luke 9:22; 17:25; 22:15, 22.

Suffering as Daniel Predicted

After the resurrection, Jesus opened up everything the Old Testament said about Him:

> *And beginning with Moses and all the Prophets, he interpreted to them in all the Scriptures the things concerning himself. (Luke 24:27)*

Daniel 7 was not the only passage that predicted Jesus' suffering. Many other passages provided more significant and detailed information about Jesus' suffering. Yet, Jesus used Daniel's prophecy more than any other prediction to force His audience to wrestle with His suffering *as God*. This is especially remarkable when you compare His use of Daniel to other passages.

For example, Isaiah 53 contains one of the most prominent Old Testament prophecies of Jesus' suffering:

> *Surely he has borne our griefs and carried our sorrows; yet we esteemed him stricken, smitten by God, and afflicted. But he was pierced for our transgressions; he was crushed for our iniquities; upon him was the chastisement that brought us peace, and with his wounds we are healed. All we like sheep have gone astray; we have turned—every one—to his own way; and the LORD has laid on him the iniquity of us all. (vv. 4–6)*

Given how detailed and astounding this prophecy is, we would expect Jesus to refer to it a number of times. Yet, Jesus only directly referenced Isaiah 53 *one time,* and that was to predict His death:[4]

> *"For I tell you that this Scripture must be fulfilled in me: 'And he was numbered with the transgressors.' For what is written about me has its fulfillment." (Luke 22:37)*

Another prominent Old Testament prophecy is Psalm 22, which described the agony of Jesus' crucifixion in great detail.

> *My God, my God, why have you forsaken me? Why are you so far from saving me, from the words of my groaning? (v. 1)*

---

[4]Mark 10:45 can be considered an allusion to Isaiah 53:10, but it is not a direct quote.

Psalm 22 is quoted 8 times in the Gospels but only during Jesus' actual crucifixion.[5] Jesus fulfilled the details of Psalm 22 and quoted the Psalm on the cross, but He did not use Psalm 22 to predict or explain His suffering.

Jesus' suffering was "according to the Scriptures,"[6] and His use of Scripture in reference to His suffering is fascinating. A number of scriptures gave tremendous revelation about the nature and purpose of Jesus' suffering, but Jesus chose to use Daniel 7 far more than any other passage to predict His suffering.

Jesus could have easily explained the mystery of His suffering by combining Daniel 7 and Isaiah 53 to describe Himself as the Son of Man *and* the Suffering Servant, but He did not. Passages like Isaiah 53 and Psalm 22 seem to be more obvious predictions of His death, but Jesus chose to present Himself as the *Son of Man* who must suffer. He wanted us to connect His suffering with His identity as the Son of Man.

Understanding Jesus' use of Daniel to describe His own death is key to grasping how Jesus presented the gospel.

Exaltation through Suffering

As the Son of Man, Jesus was fully man *and* fully divine, but this raised questions. Two of these questions help us grasp Jesus' exaltation through suffering.

First, how did the divine Son of Man become a human? When Daniel saw the Son of Man, He was in the heavens coming with the clouds—an event Jesus always associated with His second coming. Daniel either did not see or did not record what we call the first coming. (We cannot be completely sure because Daniel did not write down every detail of the vision.[7])

Because the Son of Man is a human, it implies He must have been born on the earth as a man before He comes with the clouds. The reason is simple: Real humans are not created in the heavens; they are

---

[5]Matthew 27:35, 39, 43, 46; Mark 15:24, 34; Luke 23:34–35; John 19:23–24.

[6]Matthew 26:56; Mark 14:49; Luke 22:37; 24:26–27, 46; John 13:18; John 19:24, 28, 36–37; 1 Corinthians 15:3–4.

[7]Daniel 7:1.

born on the earth because our flesh is connected to the earth.[8] Even the first man Adam was formed on the earth in God's image[9] and not made in the heavens.

Second, how was a human capable of riding the clouds as God? The man whom Daniel saw was immortal and riding the heavens as God. Men are born mortal and fallen; therefore, the Son of Man would have to pass through a tremendous transformation from an "earthly" man to a "heavenly" one. Somehow, the divine Son of Man had to become a real human who was exalted, immortal, and could ride the heavens as God.

Jesus answered these questions with a shocking revelation: *The Son of Man would suffer and be killed.* This revelation was so shocking one of Jesus' closest disciples rebuked Him for predicting it.[10] Jesus' own disciples could not fathom the idea that Jesus would pass through death and suffering. However, suffering was necessary for the Son of Man to enter the heavens as an exalted, immortal human who was both fully human and fully God.

The Son of Man would be exalted through suffering—suffering was predicted by Daniel.

The Firstborn among Many Brethren

In Daniel 7, the saints overcome the beast and gain their inheritance through suffering. Their suffering sets the stage for the judgment of the final beast, the destruction of his kingdom, the establishment of the everlasting kingdom, and the exaltation of the saints to inherit the kingdom. The saints are also deeply identified with the Son of Man— they inherit His reward and rule with Him as immortals. The inverse is also true: The Son of Man is also deeply identified with the saints.

When Jesus revealed His suffering, He revealed the depth of His identification with His people—He will gain His inheritance the same way His people will.

Paul referred to this mystery by calling Jesus the "firstborn among many brothers":[11]

---

[8]Genesis 2:7.

[9]Genesis 1:26–27.

[10]Matthew 16:22; Mark 8:31–32.

[11]See also Colossians 1:8; Revelation 1:5.

For those whom he foreknew he also predestined to be conformed to the image of his Son, in order that he might be the firstborn among many brothers. (Romans 8:29)

This was a stunning revelation. While the Son of Man is divine, He is more than divine. *He is also the first of the saints.* John and Peter predicted the same thing. Jesus is the firstborn of a glorified humanity, and we will follow and become like Him:[12]

Beloved, we are God's children now, and what we will be has not yet appeared; but we know that when he appears we shall be like him, because we shall see him as he is. (1 John 3:2)

His divine power has granted to us all things that pertain to life and godliness, through the knowledge of him who called us to his own glory and excellence, by which he has granted to us his precious and very great promises, so that through them you may become partakers of the divine nature, having escaped from the corruption that is in the world because of sinful desire. (2 Peter 1:3–4)

Because the Son of Man is a real man and the *firstborn* of the saints, He had to take the same path to exaltation the saints will take. As the first of the saints, He had to take that path before the rest of the saints. He had to be given over into the hands of the beast who would prevail over Him for a short time.

As Daniel predicted, Jesus' suffering would bring an end to the rule of the beast, destroy his kingdom, and establish the everlasting kingdom.

That victory will be enforced after the saints pass through their suffering, but it was secured by the suffering of the firstborn of the saints. The saints will be overcome for three and a half units of time,[13] and Jesus' suffering would last just over three units of time. Like the saints, He had to be "overcome" by the beast in death and then raised up to rule forever.

This revealed the perplexing mystery of how a man appeared in the heavens as God. Because the Son of Man had to become a man,

---

[12]See also Romans 8:18, 29; 1 Corinthians 2:9; 15:49; 2 Corinthians 3:18; Philippians 3:21.

[13]Daniel 7:25.

He had to first descend to earth[14] to obtain a human body and become fully human. He then had to ascend into the heavens to His place of authority as an immortal man through death and resurrection.

The Pattern

Daniel 7 predicted a pattern of death, resurrection, exaltation, and reward. God is going to give the saints over to the beast who will make war over them, prevail over them, and wear them out. Surprisingly, God will give them into his hand and allow the beast to triumph over the saints for a limited period of time. This was all allegorical language for death and persecution.

Even the persecution of the beast will not destroy the saints. He will "prevail" over the saints for a short time, but then they will rule in an everlasting kingdom which requires resurrection to immortality. They will be given authority over all other dominions, indicating they are raised to an exalted status over other spiritual powers in their immortality.

Because the kingdom comes from the heavens and has power over all dominions, they will receive new bodies capable of existing in the heavens and exercising dominion over all powers. These saints are more than people who will live forever. They are immortals who will have authority over the cosmos, including the spiritual powers that humans are now subject to.

The kingdom will be given to the saints as a reward after they suffer, implying the suffering of the saints prepares them to inherit the everlasting kingdom and rule with the Son of Man.

Jesus revealed a profound mystery in Daniel 7:27. The Son of Man is so intricately identified with His people that He is the first of the saints, and therefore, Daniel's prophecy about the saints was also a prediction about the Son of Man. Daniel could have never imagined the divine Human he saw would also be handed to the beasts and overcome for a brief time before receiving His reward, and yet the prophecy applied both to the Son of Man and His people.

Jesus, as the first of the saints, would ascend again to the place He had before the incarnation[15] through a process of death and resurrec-

---

[14]John 3:13; 6:33, 38, 51, 62; 8:42; 13:3; 16:28–30; 17:5.

[15]See also John 1:1–4; 3:31; 13:3; 16:5, 10; 20:17.

tion by which the Son of Man would seem to be overcome by the beasts but then suddenly given all dominion over them. Daniel saw the saints would share the reward of the Son of Man, but he also saw the Son of Man would share in the saints path of exaltation.

We will share in His exaltation, and He shares in our suffering.

Jesus revealed the cross (inheritance through suffering) was at the center of Daniel's gospel. Daniel's gospel was a cruciform gospel. The beasts would seem to prevail over the Son of Man, but they would be unable to destroy His life because He is divine. Their victory would become their defeat. In the same way, the beast will attempt to prevail over the saints and set into motion his own judgment and their everlasting inheritance.

Death is the main threat the beasts wield. The Son of Man shattered their power because the divine life in Him could not be overcome. Though He died, He was raised up in a new kind of body, and He will share His power over death with everyone who follows Him. They will be raised to immortality just as He was.

When Jesus personally identified with the suffering of the saints, He established the New Testament's paradigm of suffering.

THE CROSS AS THE MEANS OF JESUS' EXALTATION

Perhaps the greatest mystery hidden in Daniel 7 was the mystery of Jesus' exaltation through suffering. Jesus repeatedly predicted He would ascend back into the heavens to a place He had been before.[1] In eternity past, Jesus was exalted as God and rode the heavens, but not as a man.

A mortal man cannot ascend into the heavens, so Jesus would have to pass through death and resurrection to become an immortal, divine Man who can ride the heavens as God *and* Man. Then He would have to be raised back into the heavens as a man so He could descend with the clouds as a divine Man to execute judgment and inherit the kingdom.

Because the disciples expected Jesus to function as a political Messiah, they did not fully grasp this until after Jesus' ascension. Once they understood it, Jesus' teaching took on a whole new depth of meaning.

John's Description of Jesus' Exaltation

The Gospel of John connects Jesus' suffering on the cross to His exaltation in a unique way. John recorded at least three occasions where Jesus explained He would be "lifted up"[2] in death because His death would set the stage for His exaltation. Death was required for resurrection, resurrection was required for ascension, and ascension was required to become the Man who rode the heavens and would come with the clouds in judgment.

John Collins summarizes the connection:

---

[1] See also John 1:1–4; 3:31; 13:3; 16:5, 10.

[2] John 3:14; 8:28; 12:32, 34.

Three sayings in John refer to the "lifting up" of the Son of Man (3:14; 8:28; 12:34; cf. 12:32). This "lifting up" is typically Johannine paradoxical language. The Greek verb in question, ὑψόω, can have the sense "lift up" or "exalt." In these sayings, both meanings are intended. Jesus will be lifted up on the cross and this will be his exaltation.[3]

Jesus described this processing of descending and then ascending when Nicodemus came to Him. Jesus defended His divine authority by referencing His divine identity as the Son of Man who had descended:

Truly, truly, I say to you, we speak of what we know, and bear witness to what we have seen, but you do not receive our testimony. If I have told you earthly things and you do not believe, how can you believe if I tell you heavenly things? No one has ascended into heaven except he who descended from heaven, the Son of Man. (vv. 11–13)

Jesus had authority because He had *descended* from heaven and was the Son of Man. Nicodemus understood what this reference to Daniel 7 implied. Jesus was much more than a teacher or even an anointed prophet sent by YHWH. The conversation with Nicodemus revealed the Son of Man was the divine Person whom John called the *Word*[4] who "became flesh and dwelt among us."

Again, Collins explains:

The most distinctive use of the phrase "the Son of Man" in the Gospel of John is in reference to the preexistence of Jesus. This usage appears twice in the Gospel, in Jesus' dialogue with Nicodemus (3:13) and in the discourse on the bread of life (6:62).[5]

The Son of Man had descended from heaven, but He would also be "lifted up" as a man:

"And as Moses lifted up the serpent in the wilderness, so must the Son of Man be lifted up, that whoever believes in him may have eternal life. For God so loved the world, that he gave his only Son, that whoever believes in him should not perish but have eternal life." (John 3:14–16)

---

[3]Collins and Collins, *Daniel: A Commentary on the Book of Daniel*, 101.

[4]John 1:14.

[5]Collins and Collins, *Daniel: A Commentary on the Book of Daniel*, 100.

Again, this was a double reference to Jesus' being "lifted up" when He was fastened to the cross and the subsequent exaltation that would come through His resurrection and the ascension. He had to be raised up—die as an atonement and ascend into the heavens—so all who believe in Him can inherit eternal life (the everlasting kingdom of Daniel 7). If Jesus did not die, there would be no atonement, and the saints could not be exalted, and if He did not die and ascend, He could not come with the clouds to bring judgment and the kingdom.

Jesus' death was so central to His exaltation that He predicted His death would prove He was who He said He was:

> *So Jesus said to them, "When you have lifted up the Son of Man, then you will know that I am he, and that I do nothing on my own authority, but speak just as the Father taught me." (John 8:28)*

Once again, Jesus combined the imagery of the cross with His return to the heavens as an exalted man (v. 28). He would be "lifted" up when He died on the cross. He would be "lifted up" *toward* the "heavens" in death, and that "lifting up" would set into motion His resurrection and ascension ("lifting up") *into* the heavens. When the people saw a resurrected man ascend, they would be fully convinced Jesus was the Son of Man and fully convinced He was "from above" and "not of this world." As we will see, this is precisely what happened in Acts 1.

Just before His execution, Jesus explained again His death would be the means of His exaltation:

> *And Jesus answered them, "The hour has come for the Son of Man to be glorified. Truly, truly, I say to you, unless a grain of wheat falls into the earth and dies, it remains alone; but if it dies, it bears much fruit.... Now is my soul troubled. And what shall I say? 'Father, save me from this hour'? But for this purpose I have come to this hour. Father, glorify your name." Then a voice came from heaven: "I have glorified it, and I will glorify it again." ...Jesus answered, "This voice has come for your sake, not mine.... And I, when I am lifted up from the earth, will draw all people to myself." (John 12:23–24, 27-28, 30, 32)*

Here, too, Jesus used Daniel 7 to set the context. The hour had come for the Son of Man to be glorified through His death (vv. 23–24). He had always existed in glory in the heavens but without an exalted people. His death would bear tremendous fruit because it would enable

Him to raise a people up who could inherit the kingdom and rule with Him (v. 26). The suffering associated with the cross was overwhelming, but it was the reason Jesus had come into the world (v. 27).

Jesus had come so He could be exalted as a man and exalt a people with Him. The cross was a path of suffering, but it was not only about suffering. It was about the future glory.[6] The Father had already glorified Jesus, and He would glorify Him again by raising Him up into the heavens (v. 28). Jesus would be lifted up from the earth (in death and in ascension), and the process would draw "all" men to Him (v. 32). This "all" obviously does not mean every human being—the Bible is clear every human being will not be saved. It was an allusion to Daniel 7:14 because His death would do more than save Israel; it would save a remnant from "all" peoples :

> *"All peoples, nations, and languages should serve him."*

Jesus' teaching confused the crowd because they still mostly saw Him as a possible Messiah. They understood the Messiah would come and rule forever, so why was Jesus calling Himself the *Son of Man* and predicting His death?

> *So the crowd answered him, "We have heard from the Law that the Christ remains forever. How can you say that the Son of Man must be lifted up? Who is this Son of Man?" So Jesus said to them, "The light is among you for a little while longer. Walk while you have the light, lest darkness overtake you. The one who walks in the darkness does not know where he is going." (John 12:34–35)*

Their question is another indicator Jesus spoke of His suffering according to His identity as the Son of Man, not His messianic identity. As Leon Morris comments, Jesus called them to come to the light—to come into the knowledge of the Son of Man:

> *His reply points them to the urgent necessity to act on the light they have. It is reasonable to infer that to do this is to enter into a knowledge of the Son of*

---

[6]Hebrews 12:2.

Man. Let them give up their preconceived notions of messiahship and act on the revelation Jesus is giving them, and their question will be answered.[7]

Jesus' identification as "the light" was a reference back to John 8, the previous passage we examined where Jesus said He was "the light of the world" (v. 12). Jesus' claim to be the light was a claim to divine status, and He backed it up with the revelation that He was "from above" and "not of this world." Furthermore, this divine status would be proven when He was exalted through the cross and lifted up as the Son of Man. Jesus' claim to be "the light" in John 12 is the same claim. As the Son of Man, He was God in the midst of the darkness.

In John 12:36, Jesus combined His claim to be the light with a powerful allusion to Daniel 7:

While you have the light, believe in the light, that you may become sons of light.

If people would believe in His light (He is the Son of Man), they could become "sons of the light." This was an invitation to become part of the exalted people (saints) who would be like "the light" in the age to come.

The Suffering Messiah

In the last two chapters, we have seen Jesus overwhelmingly used Daniel as the biblical basis for His suffering. He referenced Daniel in all three predictions of the *crucifixion* and in every prediction about His suffering.

There are only two times Jesus spoke about His suffering as the Messiah instead of referencing Daniel. They both occur in Luke 24 after Jesus' resurrection. Before His suffering, Jesus used Daniel to address the expectations of His disciples. In this chapter, Jesus referred to His suffering as Messiah to address the disciples' disillusionment.

The chapter begins with the story of the women who discovered Jesus' empty tomb. They encountered two angels who reminded them that the Son of Man would be executed and then rise in three days:

---

[7]Leon Morris, *The Gospel according to John*, The New International Commentary on the New Testament (Grand Rapids, MI: Wm. B. Eerdmans Publishing Co., 1995), 533.

Remember how he told you, while he was still in Galilee, that the Son of Man must be delivered into the hands of sinful men and be crucified and on the third day rise. (Luke 24:6–7)

The women carried this message to Jesus' disciples, and later that day, two of the disciples encountered Jesus on the road to Emmaus. They described their confusion over His crucifixion and their shock at the news they had heard from the women:

Moreover, some women of our company amazed us ... they came back saying that they had even seen a vision of angels, who said that he was alive. (Luke 24:22–23)

Jesus' response was unusual because it was the first time He referred to Himself as Christ (Messiah) in context to His suffering:

And he said to them, "O foolish ones, and slow of heart to believe all that the prophets have spoken! Was it not necessary that the Christ should suffer these things and enter into his glory?" (Luke 24:25–26)

The disciples were discouraged by Jesus' suffering and death because He seemed to fail to deliver Israel.[8] Jesus' unusual statement that the "Christ should suffer" was designed to shift their thinking. Jesus still would deliver Israel, but the process would be very different from what they expected. Though He had suffered, died, and was about to ascend, He was still the true Messiah of Israel.

A few verses later, Jesus appeared to His disciples and had a similar conversation. Like the disciples on the road to Emmaus, they were also discouraged and doubted Jesus' messianic identity:

And he said to them, "Why are you troubled, and why do doubts arise in your hearts?" (Luke 24:38)

Once again, Jesus opened the Scriptures and described His suffering:

Then he opened their minds to understand the Scriptures, and said to them, "Thus it is written, that the Christ should suffer and on the third day rise from the dead." (Luke 24:45–46)

---

[8]Luke 24:21.

Jesus explained their understanding of the Messiah by opening up the Scriptures to show His death was not a cause for doubt or despair. He had suffered just as the Scriptures had predicted. The context of Luke 24 explains why Jesus connected His suffering to His identity as Messiah in this chapter. Before the resurrection, Jesus' supporters were convinced He was the Christ but did not grasp His identity as the suffering Son of Man. As a result, Jesus emphasized His divine identity and His coming suffering.

After Jesus' death, He faced the opposite problem. His followers now questioned whether He was the Messiah, so He had to address their discouragement and their expectation. He was the Messiah, but He would deliver Israel in a way they did not expect. His suffering was not an unexpected development. It was a necessary part of the plan for Him to become Israel's Messiah.

The Wisdom of God

The wisdom of Jesus' suffering was not the wisdom of this age. It was a hidden wisdom God had decreed from the beginning.

> *Yet among the mature we do impart wisdom, although it is not a wisdom of this age or of the rulers of this age, who are doomed to pass away. But we impart a secret and hidden wisdom of God, which God decreed before the ages for our glory. None of the rulers of this age understood this, for if they had, they would not have crucified the Lord of glory. (1 Corinthians 2:6–8)*

According to this wisdom, Jesus was crucified by the "rulers of this age." These "rulers" correspond to the beasts of Daniel 7 who rule this age. Modern commentators view the "rulers" more often as human rulers rather than the spiritual powers. In the same way, the beasts in Daniel's vision were interpreted as kings though it was clear there were spiritual powers behind the beasts.

Jesus, like the saints, suffered at the hands of the rulers of this age. He was given over to the beasts for a specific amount of time as the saints will be. The rulers of this age seemed to prevail over Him just as Daniel said will happen to the saints. However, in the hidden wisdom of God, Jesus' suffering and death at the hands of the beasts set the stage for His resurrection and subsequent exaltation.

This is the wisdom of God for His Son and His saints.

JESUS' PARADIGM OF SUFFERING

Old Testament saints and prophets suffered, but they did not articulate a paradigm of suffering the way Jesus did. As we saw in a previous section, suffering was usually connected to sin and judgment.

Daniel predicted the saints would suffer at the hands of the beast under God's sovereign direction. Daniel's prophecy has a specific application for a final, future beast, but it has implications for life under all the beasts. If the saints will suffer under the final beast, they should expect to suffer under the other beasts, and God is sovereign over that suffering as well.

Daniel's message was simple but radical: Suffering is not always the result of sin or judgment. God sovereignly allows His people to suffer under the beasts in preparation to inherit the kingdom.[1] This applies to the Son of Man *and* His people, and this suffering will not end until the Son of Man comes with the clouds, judges the beasts, and breaks their power.

The idea of God's handing over a people to suffer—a people who were meant to inherit the kingdom—was so radical that the disciples could not make sense of it. After they saw Him ascend, however, they completely embraced His paradigm of suffering.

Daniel was the main scriptural basis for Jesus' paradigm of suffering, and it became a foundation for the radical approach to suffering in the New Testament.[2]

---

[1]Daniel 7:18, 22, 27.

[2]We can say it was the *primary* basis because of the way Jesus used Daniel in the Gospels. It was not the only passage, however. For example, Isaiah 53 predicted Jesus' exaltation through suffering. This is dealt with more in depth in *Son of Man: The Apostles' Gospel*, Volume 2.

The Gospel Is a Cruciform Gospel

The wisdom and glory of God was revealed in the suffering and death of Jesus. The cross is a revelation of *who* God is and *the way He will glorify Himself.* Both are revealed in the Person of Jesus.[3]

Paul described his gospel as "Christ and Him crucified."[4] The gospel must include the message of Jesus' divinity *and* the message of His suffering. If either are missing, the gospel is incomplete.

If we speak about Jesus' suffering without His divine identity, our gospel is false. If Jesus was not God, His suffering was not capable of securing His own exaltation or the exaltation of a people. If Jesus is not divine, He is either a failed revolutionary or some sort of religious martyr. This reduces His life to either an inspiring example or a waste. The neglect of Jesus' divine identity produces a humanistic gospel by presenting Jesus as some sort of suffering saint rather than the divine Redeemer securing atonement through His suffering.

If we speak about the divine identity of Jesus without His suffering, our gospel is also unbiblical. There is something foundational about the nature of God revealed only in the cross. As Jürgen Moltmann famously wrote, He is the crucified God.[5] The idea of ruling in the everlasting kingdom is appealing, but any gospel that promises exaltation apart from Jesus' suffering, death, and resurrection is unbiblical and humanistic. It denies our deep need of atonement, ignores a fundamental revelation of God's identity, and excludes us from the necessary means of salvation. It is so serious, when Peter rebuked Jesus for His embrace of suffering, Jesus rebuked him as *satan.*[6]

Jesus' divine identity and His suffering are fundamental to the gospel. Jesus used Daniel 7 to explain His suffering because it revealed His divine identity, connected His identity to His suffering, and revealed the process of exaltation through suffering.

---

[3]Philippians 2:5–11; Colossians 2:15; Hebrews 12:2.

[4]1 Corinthians 2:2.

[5]Jürgen Moltmann, *The Crucified God: The Cross of Christ as the Foundation and Criticism of Christian Theology* (Minneapolis: Fortress Press, 1993).

[6]Matthew 16:23.

A People like Their God

God sovereignly determines the individual's experience of suffering, but the church is called to embrace Jesus' paradigm of exaltation through suffering and resurrection through death. The embrace of suffering is not for the sake of suffering, but for the sake of the inheritance. Jesus pleaded with His disciples to embrace His paradigm of suffering in order to receive great reward:[7]

> *Then Jesus told his disciples, "If anyone would come after me, let him deny himself and take up his cross and follow me. For whoever would save his life will lose it, but whoever loses his life for my sake will find it. For what will it profit a man if he gains the whole world and forfeits his soul? Or what shall a man give in return for his soul? For the Son of Man is going to come with his angels in the glory of his Father, and then he will repay each person according to what he has done." (Matthew 16:24–27)*

Jesus used a scene from Daniel 7 to motivate His disciples in verse 27. We are called to embrace His path of suffering so we can be exalted when He comes in His Father's glory as the exalted Son of Man and Judge. Jesus did not receive His glory until He passed through death and resurrection. Likewise, the people of God will not get their inheritance until they pass through a similar apocalyptic trial compared to death and resurrection.[8]

The gospel of the kingdom is cross-centered. We will overcome and receive our inheritance the way Jesus did. In this age, we need patient endurance to live under the beasts as preparation for an inheritance in the eternal kingdom that will be given when the Son of Man comes in glory.

Those who follow the path of the Son of Man will be exalted by the Son of Man when He comes.

The Father Is Looking for a People

This entire age is designed to produce a people who can be God's eternal companion. Once that people has matured, the age will end:

---

[7]See also John 6:40.

[8]Daniel 12:1; Matthew 24:21.

"Let us rejoice and exult and give him the glory, for the marriage of the Lamb has come, and his Bride has made herself ready." (Revelation 19:7)

The Father's mission to form a people for Jesus can be compared to a rich father's search for a bride for his son. How does a father find a suitable bride for a son who is worth a billion dollars? How does He know the bride loves his son and not just his son's possessions? A good father takes great joy in sharing everything he has with his son's wife as long as he knows she truly loves his son. If she is only interested in his son for personal benefit, a father will not share his wealth.

The Father is looking for a people He can give to His Son as an eternal companion.[9] However, the Father has a problem: *How does He find a people who love His Son for who He is and not just how they can benefit from Him?* In Jesus, we have the promise of tremendous rewards—rewards we cannot even fathom. He is worth far more than a billion dollars, and He is going to take great delight in bringing His people into His inheritance. However, He wants a people who truly love Him.

Though He is clothed with majesty, He is humble. Though He has all dominion, He is also a Servant who acts in the best interest of others. He passes through suffering before glory. Our path in this age is to follow His path. We do not receive our reward in this age. In this age, we learn to become like Him. By living like Him, we learn to love Him for who He truly is. We come to love the suffering Son of Man and not only the exalted Son of Man. The people who love Him will follow the path He followed, and He will take incredible delight in sharing His eternal inheritance with that people.

Far too many people follow Jesus for the rewards He can give. They are like a woman looking to marry a rich man's son for her own benefit. The Father wants to share His wealth with us, but He has a question for us: *"Do you truly love My Son?"*

Our Vision Is Too Low

Far too many of us are almost entirely focused on rewards in this age because we do not grasp the glory of the everlasting kingdom and the biblical hope of the saints. *Jesus motivated His disciples to embrace a path of suffering in this age in order to receive everlasting glory with Him.*

---

[9]John 3:29; 2 Corinthians 11:2; Ephesians 5:25–27; Revelation 19:6–7.

Paul pleaded with the Philippians to think like Jesus, who emptied Himself and took up human form (the Son of Man) and was obedient unto death (suffered under the beast):

Have this mind among yourselves, which is yours in Christ Jesus, who, though he was in the form of God, did not count equality with God a thing to be grasped, but emptied himself, by taking the form of a servant, being born in the likeness of men. And being found in human form, he humbled himself by becoming obedient to the point of death, even death on a cross. Therefore God has highly exalted him and bestowed on him the name that is above every name, so that at the name of Jesus every knee should bow, in heaven and on earth and under the earth. (2:5–10)

As a result of Jesus' obedience and suffering, He has been exalted above every other creature (received dominion over all dominions).[10] Paul invited the Philippians to embrace the same path in order to obtain the same outcome. If we think like Jesus and follow Him, even to the point of suffering, the Lord will highly exalt us as well. Obviously, we will not be exalted as divine, but He will share His dominion over the cosmos with us.

If you consider everything the New Testament says about the future condition of the saints, it is staggering.[11] The saints who endure will be so exalted they can be considered the "Bride of the Lamb"—a people joined to God in a relationship so close that marriage is its only human analogy. Marriage does not require two *equivalent* people (the saints will never be divine), but it does require two *compatible* people (the saints will be made like the Son of Man).

Jesus endured His suffering for a moment so He could receive everlasting glory. His example motivates us to persevere in this age to experience the same kind of glory:

Looking to Jesus, the founder and perfecter of our faith, who for the joy that was set before him endured the cross, despising the shame, and is seated at the right hand of the throne of God. Consider him who endured from sinners such

---

[10]Daniel 7:27.

[11]Romans 8:18, 29; 1 Corinthians 2:9; 15:49; 2 Corinthians 3:18; Philippians 3:21; 2 Peter 1:3–4; 1 John 3:2.

hostility against himself, so that you may not grow weary or fainthearted. (Hebrews 12:2–3)

The human heart naturally searches for beauty and majesty, and when biblical majesty is not proclaimed, the human heart begins to find fulfillment in lesser glory. Many Christians are focused on rewards in this age and enamored with the kingdoms (beasts) of this age because they have not heard the proclamation of the glory of the Son of Man, the invitation to participate in His kingdom, and the glory of His eternal inheritance.

If we truly grasped the glory of the Son of Man and the invitation to be exalted with Him in the age to come, every treasure in this age would fade. The most powerful empires of this age are dust, and all their achievements are trinkets compared to the kingdom of the Son of Man.

It is a tragedy when Christians seek success and glory according to the system of this age.

We are often seduced by the vision of financial success, popularity, nationalism, and a whole host of lesser "glories" when we lack a clear vision of the Son of Man and His kingdom. We must proclaim the beauty and majesty of the Son of Man, and our inheritance in Him. When we exalt Him, He is exalted, and He has the ability to capture the affection of the human heart.

We are not called to meaningless suffering. We are called to suffer to become like the Son of Man and inherit a kingdom with Him.

THE SON OF MAN AND HIS EXECUTION

As we have seen, while Jesus did not emphasize His messianic identity, He openly and publicly proclaimed His identity as the Son of Man. Jesus' audience understood this was a claim to divinity, and as we saw in an earlier chapter, they used it to accuse Jesus of blasphemy.[1]

Some people think Jesus was executed when He finally decided to reveal His identity, but He never hid His identity. Instead, Jesus was condemned, suffered, and was executed because of His claim to be the Son of Man. The disciples were confused by Jesus' prediction that the Son of Man would be rejected, suffer, and die. However, Jesus predicted He must suffer as the Son of Man at least twelve times, and that is exactly what happened.[2]

Matthew 26 gives a full account of Jesus' betrayal, arrest, and trial as Son of Man. It begins with Jesus' prediction that He would be "delivered up" to death as the Son of Man. We will see in a later chapter that the phrase *delivered up* is a direct quote from Daniel 7:

> *"You know that after two days the Passover is coming, and the Son of Man will be delivered up to be crucified." (Matthew 26:2)*

The Last Supper—The Son of Man Will Be Betrayed

Before He was arrested, Jesus gathered with His disciples for what is usually referred to as the *Last Supper*. During the supper, Jesus spoke very openly about His impending suffering. He even identified Judas as

---

[1] Matthew 26:64–65; Mark 14:62–64; Luke 5:21–24; John 10:24–25.

[2] Matthew 16:21; 17:12, 22–23; 26:2; Mark 8:31; 9:31; 10:33–34; Luke 9:22, 44; 17:24–25; 18:31–34; 24:7.

the betrayer while they ate. The conversation at the table was tense, awkward, and intimate.[3]

As they ate, Jesus predicted His betrayal as Son of Man:[4]

And as they were eating, he said, "Truly, I say to you, one of you will betray me." And they were very sorrowful and began to say to him one after another, "Is it I, Lord?" He answered, "He who has dipped his hand in the dish with me will betray me. The Son of Man goes as it is written of him, but woe to that man by whom the Son of Man is betrayed! It would have been better for that man if he had not been born." Judas, who would betray him, answered, "Is it I, Rabbi?" He said to him, "You have said so." (Matthew 26:21–25)

Jesus would not be betrayed as the Messiah—He would be betrayed as the Son of Man. He was not handed over for the claim He was Israel's political Deliverer—He was handed over to the Romans for the claim He was a divine Human—YHWH in the flesh.

After the meal, Jesus and His disciples went outside of Jerusalem to the Garden of Gethsemane where Jesus would be betrayed. Jesus was under incredible stress as He anticipated what was about to happen and asked His disciples to pray with Him:

Then he said to them, "My soul is very sorrowful, even to death; remain here, and watch with me." (Matthew 26:38)

Jesus prayed until the time came for the Son of Man to be betrayed:[5]

Then he came to the disciples and said to them, "Sleep and take your rest later on. See, the hour is at hand, and the Son of Man is betrayed into the hands of sinners." (Matthew 26:45)

Betrayed as the Son of Man

Jesus' last interaction with Judas was dramatic and chilling. Judas had been a member of Jesus' inner circle and even handled His money, but something had turned Judas's heart. In the dark of night, he betrayed

---

[3]Matthew 26:17–30; Mark 14:12–26; Luke 22:7–39; John 13:1–17:26.

[4]See also Mark 14:21; Luke 22:22.

[5]See also Mark 14:41; Luke 22:48; John 17:1.

Jesus into the hands of His enemies and set into motion Jesus' execution.

Judas approached Jesus with a greeting:

And he came up to Jesus at once and said, "Greetings, Rabbi!" And he kissed him. Jesus said to him, "Friend, do what you came to do." Then they came up and laid hands on Jesus and seized him. (Matthew 26:49–50)

Luke's account includes an extra comment in their conversation:

But Jesus said to him, "Judas, would you betray the Son of Man with a kiss?" (Luke 22:48)

This was a staggering question. When Jesus looked into Judas's eyes and asked this question, He communicated a simple message: *"Do you really know who I am?"*

These words must have brought to mind a previous conversation about Jesus' identity:

Now when Jesus came into the district of Caesarea Philippi, he asked his disciples, "Who do people say that the Son of Man is?" (Matthew 16:13)

Judas was not handing over a man who had claimed to be Messiah. He was handing over YHWH. Jesus set the terms of His betrayal. He would not be betrayed as a false messiah. He would be betrayed *as God*.

Arrested as the Son of Man

The disciples had put all their hope in Jesus, and their future was inseparably connected to who He was. They had seen Jesus exercise divine authority and do powerful miracles, but on this night Jesus suddenly seemed helpless. The Man they had put all their hope in was arrested like an ordinary criminal.

The atmosphere was filled with confusion, pain, despair, and hopelessness. One of Jesus' disciples quickly tried to save Him by pulling out a sword and assaulting the servant of the high priest. At that moment, Jesus spoke to their despair and hopelessness by reminding the disciples who He really was:

Do you think that I cannot appeal to my Father, and he will at once send me more than twelve legions of angels? (Matthew 26:53)

Jesus used a Roman analogy, but the reference to Daniel was clear:

"A stream of fire issued and came out from before him; a thousand thousands served him, and ten thousand times ten thousand stood before him; the court sat in judgment, and the books were opened." (Daniel 7:10)

These may be the last words Jesus' disciples heard Him speak before His arrest. Jesus communicated a simple message: "Do not be discouraged by My execution. I am the exalted Son of Man. I am the divine Son of the Ancient of Days, and He has given Me charge of His hosts. The only power the Romans and the high priest have over Me is the power I have allowed them to have."

Interestingly, Jesus used a Roman term *legion*, which was a unit of several thousand troops, to reference the thousands of heavenly hosts in Daniel 7:10. Jesus likely used Roman language so the Roman guards would understand the message: He was an exalted King. He had an army at His disposal, but it was not merely a human army like the Roman legions. Heavenly legions (the hosts of the heavens) were at His command and would come whenever He called.

Condemned as the Son of Man

Shortly after His arrest, Jesus was put on trial. He stood silently while accusations were made and His character maligned. The high priest, frustrated with Jesus' silence, challenged Jesus to identify Himself as Israel's Messiah:

But Jesus remained silent. And the high priest said to him, "I adjure you by the living God, tell us if you are the Christ, the Son of God." Jesus said to him, "You have said so. But I tell you, from now on you will see the Son of Man seated at the right hand of Power and coming on the clouds of heaven." (Matthew 26:63–64)[6]

The high priest's use of the phrase *Son of God* was not a reference to divinity because not everyone expected a divine Messiah. The high priest was pulling from the language of 2 Samuel 7:14 and Psalm 2:7. Everyone understood the Messiah would have an exalted position as a "son of god," but this was not necessarily a statement of divinity. As

---

[6]See also Luke 22:66–71.

we have seen, the Old Testament contained several references to sons of god.[7]

The high priest was trying to set a trap for Jesus. If Jesus claimed to be the Messiah, He could be accused of presenting Himself as the political Deliverer of Israel who would defeat the gentiles and liberate Israel. This claim would have given the high priest the ability to take Jesus to Pilate for execution as a political revolutionary who wanted to liberate Israel from Roman rule. The high priest, in turn, would likely benefit from seemingly helping Rome maintain the peace.

Jesus refused to be caught in the high priest's trap. His answer was short and direct, "From now on you will see the Son of Man seated at the right hand of Power and coming on the clouds of heaven." The high priest asked Jesus to confirm whether He was Israel's political leader, but Jesus made a *higher* claim by combining Psalm 110 with Daniel 7. He was not only Messiah—He was Israel's God.

Messiah is one of Jesus' titles, but He refused to die over that claim. He would not let the high priest hand Him over to the Romans as a political Savior instigating rebellion against Rome. Jesus' used His answer to set the terms of His execution.

As we have seen, there were many Jews who claimed to be messiah, and many gentile kings who claimed to be sons of God. Those titles were controversial, but not nearly as controversial as claiming to be the Son of Man. No one else dared claim that title. The high priest tried to have Jesus executed as another failed leader of a political rebellion against Rome, but Jesus refused.

The high priest's reaction demonstrates he knew exactly what Jesus was saying:

> *Then the high priest tore his robes and said, "He has uttered blasphemy. What further witnesses do we need? You have now heard his blasphemy. What is your judgment?" They answered, "He deserves death." (Matthew 26:65–66)*

---

[7]See Genesis 5:1; 6:2–4; Deuteronomy 14:1; 32:8; Job 1:6; 2:1; 38:7; Psalm 82:6; Isaiah 64:8; Daniel 3:25; Luke 3:38. James Hamilton addresses this conversation on page 90 of His Daniel commentary *With the Clouds of Heaven: The Book of Daniel in Biblical Theology.*

Jesus died over His claim to be the Daniel 7 Son of Man, not His claim to be Messiah or even Son of God. This is one of the strongest statements of the centrality of Daniel 7 to the gospel.

Jesus did not want to die as a political challenger to Rome—He wanted to die as Israel's God.

Jesus' trial followed a consistent pattern. The claim He died for was the claim He had made His entire life. He made the claim openly and publicly. His condemnation as the Son of Man set into motion the shocking mystery: The Son of Man would pass through death and suffering to become exalted.

The Divine High Priest

It was very significant that Jesus combined Psalm 110 with Daniel 7 in His answer to the high priest. It was common at that time to combine two Old Testament passages to reveal a greater meaning, and that is precisely what Jesus did. It was also understood at the time that, when a part of a passage was referenced, the entire passage was being referenced.

By combining Daniel 7 with Psalm 110, Jesus used Daniel to interpret David's prediction of an exalted ruler:

> The LORD says to my Lord: "Sit at my right hand, until I make your enemies your footstool." (Psalm 110:1)

The high priest understood Jesus was claiming to be both divine and the exalted human "lord" (ruler) David predicted. However, Psalm 110 also says this ruler is a priest:

> The LORD has sworn and will not change his mind, "You are a priest forever after the order of Melchizedek." (v. 4)

By combining these two passages Jesus claimed to be divine, a ruler, *and* an exalted priest. We tend to think of a king as the most important person, but when God established Israel, the high priest was the true leader of the nation.[8] Israel was a kingdom of priests[9] ruled by the high priest who presided over a worship sanctuary. As a result, the Torah barely mentions a king but gives significant instructions for the priesthood. Israel was designed

---

[8] Crispin Fletcher-Louis, *Jesus Monotheism* (Eugene: Cascade, 2015), 221.

[9] Exodus 19:6.

to be a picture of man's calling to be a priestly creature ruling God's creation through worship.[10]

Jesus was usurping the high priest by declaring He, as God, had become a superior Priest King to the current high priest. The high priest understood this was a direct challenge to his authority and legitimacy. Jesus was claiming to be God, King, and a priest superior to the Mosaic priesthood. For that reason, he was accused of blasphemy and condemned to death.

How Jesus Chose to Die

There has been tremendous debate over the centuries about precisely why Jesus was sentenced to death. Christians usually assume it was because Jesus brought a brand new message to Israel and Israel was not willing to receive it. However, this is simply not true. When you read the Gospels in context, Jesus does not present Himself as the leader of a new religion and does not attack Israel's institutions. He fiercely challenged corruption and injustice, but Israel had a long history of prophets doing similar things. If Jesus did not denigrate Israel's law nor mount a political challenge, why was He condemned to death?

Some scholars propose Jesus was executed because, though He honored Israel's law and Israel's story, He made the claim that Israel's story was fulfilled in Himself and not in Israel's institutions. This is close, but not the heart of the issue.

The answer to this question is simple, and it is found in Jesus' own words. The Gospel authors carefully recorded Jesus' trail so we would know exactly why Jesus was condemned to death: *He claimed to be God in the flesh.*

Jesus' claim was especially controversial because of the power in His ministry. He could heal, cast out demons, command nature, and even raise the dead. If He had claimed to be God but did not work miracles, He could have been written off as a crazy man. Because of Jesus' power, He was either precisely who He said He was or He was an extremely dangerous man with unequalled spiritual power.

Jesus was not condemned for claiming He would replace Israel's prized institutions though He is the fulfillment of them. Nor was He condemned for political reasons. As we are about to see, Pilate was

---

[10] N.T. Wright, *The Day the Revolution Began* (New York: HarperCollins, 2016), Kindle Edition, 76–7.

confused as to why Jesus was condemned. Jesus was condemned *as God.* God had come in a human form, and the people could not receive Him.

Christians throughout history have spoken much about the blindness and hardheartedness of the Pharisees. We need to consider our own arrogance, though. What makes us so confident we would not be offended by Jesus? The religious leaders knew the Bible well, and Jesus' teaching was not all that different from theirs. They also had great expectation that God would send a deliverer. They were simply unable to receive God as He is.

Beloved, this should terrify us.

We live in a time when most Christians do not know the Bible nearly as well as the Pharisees did. The Bible also tells us the return of Jesus and the events surrounding it are going to be far more dramatic than we can imagine. Even the prophets struggled for language. John summarized the incredible events coming as the "revelation" or unveiling of Jesus.[11]

If Israel's religious leaders could not handle the revelation of God in Jesus, why are we so confident we will not be offended when God fully unveils His Son?

When God unveiled Himself as Sinai, the people were terrified and could not handle the revelation of God.[12] When God sent His Son as the full manifestation of God,[13] again Israel could not receive the revelation of their God. This is a profound warning. Do we think we are better than them? Are we truly ready for the Son of Man to return with the clouds and fully reveal who He is? Will we love Him—or will we be offended? Will we receive God when He returns?

Pilate's Accusation

Jesus' trial demonstrates He did not try to hide His identity or avoid His own death. Jesus avoided a political conflict with Rome in order to establish Himself as Someone *greater* than other political challengers. He was Messiah, but He was also much more. His conversation with

---

[11] Revelation 1:1.

[12] Exodus 20:18–21.

[13] Hebrews 1:1–3.

Pilate reveals He was willing to challenge Rome's authority, but only on the basis of His exalted identity, not on the basis of a political claim.[14]

When Jesus stood before Pilate, Pilate was genuinely confused about why Jesus had been sent to him. Jesus had not claimed to be Messiah nor stirred up anti-Roman sentiment, but He had been handed over to Pilate as a revolutionary who had claimed to be King. Pilate's confusion caused him to ask Jesus a simple question, "Are you the King of the Jews?" Pilate was looking for some sort of messianic challenge.

John's Gospel gives the longest account of the conversation:

So Pilate entered his headquarters again and called Jesus and said to him, "Are you the King of the Jews?" Jesus answered, "Do you say this of your own accord, or did others say it to you about me?" Pilate answered, "Am I a Jew? Your own nation and the chief priests have delivered you over to me. What have you done?" Jesus answered, "My kingdom is not of this world. If my kingdom were of this world, my servants would have been fighting, that I might not be delivered over to the Jews. But my kingdom is not from the world." Then Pilate said to him, "So you are a king?" Jesus answered, "You say that I am a king. For this purpose I was born and for this purpose I have come into the world—to bear witness to the truth. Everyone who is of the truth listens to my voice." (John 18:33–37)

Pilate asked a political question expecting to get a political answer, so Jesus' answer seemed very strange to Pilate. Jesus' answer is frequently misinterpreted as a claim to His having an invisible, spiritual kingdom, but Jesus did not make a metaphysical statement, indicating His kingdom would be "heavenly" and not physical.

Jesus said His kingdom was "not of this world" because He had authority over Rome ("this world"). "This world" meant "this age." Jesus' kingdom belongs to the next age that will come when this age is judged. It was a reference to Daniel's prediction that the beasts will be removed and replaced with a superior kingdom that comes with heavenly authority.

Jesus' response was a reference to Daniel:

"And in the days of those kings the God of heaven will set up a kingdom that shall never be destroyed, nor shall the kingdom be left to another people. It shall

---

[14]John 19:11.

break in pieces all these kingdoms and bring them to an end, and it shall stand forever." (Daniel 2:44)[15]

Jesus refused to give Pilate a political reason to execute Him, but He also made it plain—Rome was under His authority. Because Jesus' authority did not come from this world, He did not need to challenge Rome to obtain His kingdom. Pilate misread the entire conversation. Pilate was confused because Jesus did not present Himself as the political Deliverer of Israel. Pilate missed the fact that Jesus was claiming He was *superior* to every other messiah who had tried to challenge Rome for control of Judea.

Jesus' message to Pilate was simple: *"I am not King because I have conquered other men. I am King because I descended from the heavens."* To ensure Pilate did not miss His message, Jesus addressed Pilate's claim to have authority over Him:

> *So Pilate said to him, "You will not speak to me? Do you not know that I have authority to release you and authority to crucify you?" Jesus answered him, "You would have no authority over me at all unless it had been given you from above." (John 19:10–11)*

Pilate thought He had authority over Jesus, but in reality his authority was subservient to One who was above him and, by implication, also above Rome. Jesus had already told Pilate His authority (kingdom) was not of this world because it came from heaven (above).

The implications of Jesus' statement were stunning: *Jesus was the One who came from the heavens (above); therefore, Jesus had given Pilate the authority to execute Him.*

Pilate's Declaration

Because Pilate was troubled and confused over Jesus' identity,[16] he tried to escape the situation by severely scourging Jesus rather than executing Him. After scourging Jesus, Pilate presented Him to the crowd with a remarkable declaration:

> *So Jesus came out, wearing the crown of thorns and the purple robe. Pilate said to them, "Behold the man!" (John 19:5)*

---

[15]See also Daniel 7:14, 27.

[16]Matthew 27:18–19; Mark 15:14; Luke 23:4, 14–16; John 18:38; 19:4, 8.

Pilate was a Roman pagan, but in light of everything Jesus said in the Gospels, John likely intended us to read this pronouncement in light of Jesus' identity as the Son of Man because "the man" was an abbreviation of Jesus' favorite title. In that moment, the beaten, bleeding Jesus was visible in all His humanity, and He was *the Man.*

Jesus stood before the crowd as the *ultimate Human* who will also return with the clouds of heaven. It was a holy moment, even though Pilate did not grasp what he was saying. The scene did not last long. The crowd's condemnation was swift, and the Son of Man was carried off to His execution.[17]

---

[17]John 19:6–15.

Enthroned as the Son of Man

The descriptions of Jesus' death in every Gospel clearly portray Jesus as a king and His death as the shocking and surprising way He is being enthroned. As a result, many commentators assume the cross was Jesus' enthronement as Messiah and, therefore, a radical redefinition of the messianic hope. It is often assumed Jesus took His throne through His suffering instead of the way the disciples expected Him and in the process completely redefined the Messiah, the kingdom, and the future of Israel. Therefore, many people see little need for Jesus to come as Messiah to establish His kingdom on the earth and release His judgments.

This view of the cross has contributed to an understanding of the gospel that is nearly entirely focused on Jesus' first coming and puts very little emphasis on His second coming. After all, if Jesus secured redemption and was enthroned as Messiah in His first coming, then the first coming is the most significant event. As a result, people forget Jesus' death did not *fulfill* all the promises of God; it *secured* them. Also, they overlook the fact that the second coming was the key hope of the apostles.

This view of Jesus' execution is partially correct, but it misses the way Jesus described His own execution. As we have seen, Jesus was not condemned to death by claiming to be Messiah. He was condemned for His claim to be the Son of Man. Furthermore, every time He predicted His death, He predicted He would die as the Son of Man, not as the Messiah. There is only one passage where Jesus connected His suffering with His title as Messiah. This occurred after the resurrection, and Jesus did this to give the disciples courage that He would still fulfill the messianic promises, not to explain the messianic promises already had been fulfilled.[1] On the contrary, Jesus clearly taught His disciples the messianic promises would be fulfilled in the future, not that the promises had already been fulfilled:

> They asked him, "Lord, will you at this time restore the kingdom to Israel?" He said to them, "It is not for you to know times or seasons that the Father has fixed by his own authority." (Acts 1:6–8)

> "Repent therefore, and turn back, that your sins may be blotted out, that times of refreshing may come from the presence of the Lord, and that he may send the Christ appointed for you, Jesus, whom heaven must receive until the time for restoring all the things about which God spoke by the mouth of his holy prophets long ago." (Acts 3:19–21)

Jesus' death was an enthronement. In context, it was not the enthronement of Jesus as Messiah, but the enthronement of Jesus as the Son of Man.

Consider Jesus' statement to the high priest:

> Jesus said to him, "You have said so. But I tell you, from now on you will see the Son of Man seated at the right hand of Power and coming on the clouds of heaven." (Matthew 26:64)

Notice Jesus did not predict His death would exalt Him as Messiah. He predicted His death was going to exalt Him as the Son of Man so He could become Messiah. As a result of Jesus' crucifixion, the high priest was going to see Jesus as the exalted Son of Man. Jesus did not die to become Messiah (though it is not entirely wrong to say this). He died to become the Son of Man as Daniel saw Him. As we have seen repeatedly, Jesus revealed that His death was a part of the Son of Man story. He did not predict His death using messianic prophecies.

Exalted to Become Messiah

While many scholars assume Jesus' death enthroned Him as Messiah, based on Jesus' own words, His death enthroned Him as the Son of Man. Even in His conversation with Pilate, Jesus claimed a kingdom not of this realm which was an allusion to Daniel 7:14. Jesus' en-

---

[1] Luke 24:26, 46.

thronement as the Son of Man positioned Him to fulfill the messianic promises when He returns, but they were not fulfilled in His death and resurrection. This may seem like a small detail, but it is very significant for two reasons.

First, it misses the full weight of the crucifixion event as a revelation of God. As we have seen, Son of Man was a divine title, so when Jesus chose to die as the Son of Man, He chose to die *as God* not as man. This means God chose to be enthroned as God through the cross. The uncreated, all-powerful Creator and Ruler of the cosmos chose to exalt Himself through suffering and death. When we say Jesus became Messiah through His suffering, we miss the full magnitude of the cross. The cross did not simply enthrone the Messiah—it enthroned the divine Human. The fact God chose to enthrone Himself as God through suffering is perhaps the most profound revelation God has given of Himself in all eternity. Human words cannot adequately describe what God chose to reveal through His suffering. I believe we have still not grasped the full implications of the way God chose to exalt Himself.

Second, the idea Jesus was established as Messiah in His death has led to a radical redefinition of the messianic hope and the assumption that Jesus fulfilled it by establishing a spiritual kingdom very different from what the prophets predicted. If the cross is the key fulfillment of the messianic hope, then the messianic hope has to be radically redefined because the saints were not exalted, Israel was not saved, the nations were not judged, and Jesus did not sit on a throne in Jerusalem. The church has mostly spiritualized the messianic promises based on the assumption that Jesus took His throne as Messiah in His execution. As a result, we have overlooked future aspects of the redemptive story.

Jesus did die under a messianic sign ("King of the Jews") as a statement that this divine Human exalted through suffering was God's chosen Messiah and King. Jesus was announced as the messianic king on the cross, but the narratives around His death emphasizes the event was enthroning the Son of Man who will completely fulfill the messianic promises when He returns.

Jesus now sits ready to fulfill the messianic promises when the Father determines it is time. These promises are principally fulfilled in His second coming. Because Jesus is going to fulfill the messianic promises as God, the fulfillment will go far beyond what the prophets anticipated, but the fulfillment will make sense when Jesus exalts His people, saves Israel, judges the nations, and sits on an actual throne in Jerusalem.

Jesus' death did not fulfill the messianic hope. It set the stage for the fulfillment of the messianic hope by the divine Human.

The Son of Man's Exaltation

THE SON OF MAN WILL RISE AGAIN

The Son of Man's suffering set the stage for His exaltation, and Daniel 7 as the primary Old Testament passage Jesus used to predict His resurrection, His return, and His exaltation.

Jesus repeatedly predicted He would die and rise on the third day as was prophesied:

> *Then he opened their minds to understand the Scriptures, and said to them, "Thus it is written, that the Christ should suffer and on the third day rise from the dead." (Luke 24:45–46)*

Paul also claimed Jesus rose on the third day according to the Scriptures:

> *He was raised on the third day in accordance with the Scriptures. (1 Corinthians 15:4)*

Jesus' resurrection in three days was obviously predicted in the Old Testament, but the question is where? Jesus compared His death to the story of Jonah, but He did not interpret Jonah's time in the fish as a prediction of His death:

> *For just as Jonah was three days and three nights in the belly of the great fish, so will the Son of Man be three days and three nights in the heart of the earth. (Matthew 12:40)*

As Nicholas Lunn wrote, there must be a text other than Jesus' reference to Jonah:

> *His use of the introductory formula "Thus it is written" strongly implies that there was a textual warrant, not only for Messiah's death, nor for his resurrection also, but even specifically for a resurrection on the third day.... Yet it is hard to*

believe that the creedal formula "raised on the third day according to the Scriptures" rests upon the figural interpretation of one sole passage.[1]

Jesus obviously had a biblical basis for His prediction, but the source of this prediction has eluded many theologians. Yet, Jesus gave us the most likely source of the prediction.

The Son of Man Will Rise on the Third Day

Each time Jesus predicted His resurrection in three days, He referred to Daniel. Even in His comparison with Jonah, Jesus predicted the *Son of Man* would be in the earth three days and three nights:

> *For just as Jonah was three days and three nights in the belly of the great fish, so will the Son of Man be three days and three nights in the heart of the earth. (Matthew 12:40)*

> *Now when Jesus came into the district of Caesarea Philippi, he asked his disciples, "Who do people say that the Son of Man is?" ...From that time Jesus began to show his disciples that he must go to Jerusalem and suffer many things from the elders and chief priests and scribes, and be killed, and on the third day be raised. (Matthew 16:13, 21)*

> *See, we are going up to Jerusalem. And the Son of Man will be delivered over to the chief priests and scribes, and they will condemn him to death and deliver him over to the Gentiles to be mocked and flogged and crucified, and he will be raised on the third day. (Matthew 20:18–19)*

> *See, we are going up to Jerusalem, and the Son of Man will be delivered over to the chief priests and the scribes, and they will condemn him to death and deliver him over to the Gentiles. And they will mock him and spit on him, and flog him and kill him. And after three days he will rise. (Mark 10:33–34)*

> *The Son of Man must suffer many things and be rejected by the elders and chief priests and scribes, and be killed, and on the third day be raised. (Luke 9:22)*

> *And taking the twelve, he said to them, "See, we are going up to Jerusalem, and everything that is written about the Son of Man by the prophets will be*

---

[1]Nicholas P. Lunn, "Raised on the Third Day According to the Scriptures: Resurrection Typology in the Genesis Creation Narrative." *Journal of the Evangelical Theological Society* 57.3 (2014). 524–25.

accomplished. For he will be delivered over to the Gentiles and will be mocked and shamefully treated and spit upon. And after flogging him, they will kill him, and on the third day he will rise." (Luke 18:31–33)

Jesus used Daniel to predict His resurrection, ascension, and exaltation, so it is plausible Daniel was also the source of the prediction that Jesus would be raised in three days.

There are three significant reasons Jesus most probably used Daniel 7:25 to predict His resurrection in three days:

"And they shall be given into his hand for a time, times, and half a time."

First, Jesus repeatedly used Daniel as the passage to predict His suffering and exaltation. Jesus could have used a number of passages, but He always pointed to Daniel by saying the Son of Man must suffer.

Second, Jesus embraced the pattern of exaltation through suffering found in Daniel. Because Jesus is the "firstborn of many" saints,[2] He must walk their path of suffering first in identification with His people. The Gospels reveal prophecies about the people of God that can also be prophecies about Jesus.

For example, Matthew quoted Hosea 11:2 as a prophecy of Jesus, but in context, it is a prophecy of Israel:

And remained there until the death of Herod. This was to fulfill what the Lord had spoken by the prophet, "Out of Egypt I called my son." (Matthew 2:15)

Because Jesus is deeply connected to His people, a prophecy about His people can also be a prophecy about Him. As the ultimate Israelite, Jesus lived Israel's story, and therefore, statements made about Israel— even statements that must be fulfilled in Israel—can also be applied to Him.

The Gospels present Jesus as the perfectly obedient Israelite as a prediction of a day when God will transform Israel into a saved and righteous people.[3] This imagery includes the flexible use of units of

---

[2]Romans 8:29; Colossians 1:8; Revelation 1:5.

[3]Deuteronomy 30:1–6; Isaiah 4:3; 45:17, 25; 54:13: 59:21; 60:4, 21; 61:8–9; 66:22; Jeremiah 31:31–34; 32:40; Ezekiel 20:40; 36:10, 27–36; 39:22, 28–29; Joel 2:26, 32; Zephaniah 3:9, 12; 12:13; Zechariah 12:10–13; Matthew 23:39; 24:30; Acts 1:6–7; 2:21; Romans 10:13; 11:26–27; Revelation 1:7.

time. For example, many commentators have noticed Israel was tested in the wilderness for forty years, and Jesus was tested in the wilderness for forty days. Israel's testing over forty years was a picture of Jesus' testing over forty days. The units of time were different, but the length of time was the same.

Jesus is not only the ultimate Israelite, He is also the firstborn of the saints. If He is the firstborn, we will follow the patterns He has established. Therefore, Daniel's prophecy of the saints being handed over to the beast for three and half units of time before they are resurrected to rule can be applied to Jesus just as Matthew applied Hosea's prophecy of Israel to Jesus.

Jesus confirmed this way of interpretation when He invited the disciples to *follow* His path of suffering to inherit the kingdom:

> *Then Jesus told his disciples, "If anyone would come after me, let him deny himself and take up his cross and follow me." (Matthew 16:24)*

The third reason is the unusual reference to time in Daniel 7:25. Daniel 7 predicts the beast prevails over the saints for *times, time, and half a time*, but we are not told if that is days, months, or years. This is the only prediction of a period of time without any units in Daniel's prophetic visions.[4]

The lack of units of time in Daniel 7 was intentional because it allowed the prophecy to serve as a prediction of Jesus' suffering *and* the end-time suffering of the saints. Jesus' suffering was three and half units of time measured in days, and the saints end-time suffering will be three and half units of time measured in years.[5] Jesus was resurrected to receive the authority of the kingdom after His suffering, and the same will be done for the saints. Like other prophecies, Daniel's prediction applies to the Son of Man and His people.

---

[4]The angel uses the same phrase *time, times, and half a time* in Daniel 12:7, but it is a reference back to the prediction in Daniel 7. Daniel 9 predicts seventy "weeks" (sevens), but in context, those are seventy sevens of years. Nebuchadnezzar's dream in Daniel 4 is the other instance of periods of time without units (Daniel 4:16, 23, 25, 32), but it was not one of Daniel's prophetic visions.

[5]Revelation 11:2–3; 12:6; 13:5. See also Daniel 9:27. End-time desolation will happen in the "middle of the seven" (week), which in context is seven years.

The fourth reason we know Jesus referenced Daniel for His three-day prophecy is the language He used. Jesus predicted He would be "delivered" into the hands of sinful men for suffering and then rise in three days:

The Son of Man must be delivered into the hands of sinful men and be crucified and on the third day rise. (Luke 24:7)

The Son of Man is about to be delivered into the hands of men. (Matthew 17:22)

The Son of Man will be delivered over to the chief priests and scribes, and they will condemn him to death and deliver him over to the Gentiles to be mocked and flogged and crucified, and he will be raised on the third day. (Matthew 20:18– 19)

The Son of Man is going to be delivered into the hands of men, and they will kill him. And when he is killed, after three days he will rise. (Mark 9:31)

The Son of Man will be delivered over to the chief priests and the scribes, and they will condemn him to death and deliver him over to the Gentiles. And they will mock him and spit on him, and flog him and kill him. And after three days he will rise. (Mark 10:33–34)

Jesus' prediction that He would be "delivered" into the hands of sinful men for execution came from Daniel who predicted the saints would be "given" into the hands of the beast for suffering for three and half units of suffering.[6]

Jesus used the word *paradídōmi* (παραδίδωμι) for "delivered," which is the same word used for "given into" in the Greek translation of Daniel.[7] Just as the saints will be "delivered into" the hands of the beast for three and half units of suffering before being raised up to inherit the kingdom, so also the Son of Man had to be "delivered into" the hands of the "beast" for three units of suffering before being raised up to inherit the kingdom. The similar language makes the connection to Daniel decisive.

---

[6]Daniel 7:25.

[7]LXX.

Based on Jesus' use of Daniel, we can confidently say Jesus died and was resurrected three and half days later *according to the Scriptures*.[8]

- Jesus' use of *Son of Man* points us to Daniel.
- Jesus' suffering before exaltation points to Daniel.
- Jesus' identification with His people points to Daniel.
- Jesus' being "delivered" over for suffering links to Daniel.
- The duration of Jesus' suffering points to Daniel.

---

[8]Jewish scholar Daniel Boyarin has made a similar argument for this interpretation of Daniel: "Ancient Jewish readers might well have reasoned, as the Church Father Aphrahat did, that since the theme of riding on the clouds indicates a divine being in every other instance in the Tanakh (the Jewish name for the Hebrew Bible), we should read this one too as the revelation of God, a second God, as it were. The implication is, of course, that there are two such divine figures in heaven, the old Ancient of Days and the young one like a son of man. Such Jews would have had to explain, then, what it means for this divine figure to be given into the power of the fourth beast for "a time, two times, and a half a time." A descent into hell—or at any rate to the realm of death—for three days would be one fine answer to that question." *The Jewish Gospels: The Story of the Jewish Christ,* Location 691.

The Son of Man Will Return in Glory

Jesus used Daniel 7 almost exclusively to describe His second coming. Jesus described His return at least 18 times.[1] He used imagery from Daniel 7 every time. In 17 of the 18 references, Jesus referred to Himself as the Son of Man.[2]

> *Then will appear in heaven the sign of the Son of Man ... and they will see the Son of Man coming on the clouds of heaven with power and great glory. (Matthew 24:30)*

Because Daniel saw the Son of Man coming in the glory of the second coming, Jesus' use of *Son of Man* was not only a statement of His divine identity, it was a reminder the gospel is a forward-looking, future-oriented message that proclaims the day Jesus returns in glory to judge and redeem the earth.

Why Use Daniel?

The prophets are filled with predictions that YHWH will come to judge the nations, liberate His people, and rule on the earth. Many passages predict the events that surround Jesus' return. However, Jesus focused pretty much exclusively on Daniel 7. There are likely several reasons He did this.

---

[1]Matthew 13:41–49; 16:27–28; 19:28; 23:39; 24:30, 36–44; 25:31; 26:64; Mark 8:38; 13:26–32; 14:62–64; Luke 9:26; 12:40; 17:24–30; 18:8; 21:27; 22:69; John 14:1–3.

[2]In Matthew 23:39, Jesus did not refer to Himself as *Son of Man*, but He expounded on His second coming in the following chapter frequently using the title *Son of Man*. In John 14:1–3, Jesus did not call Himself *Son of Man* but predicted He would prepare a place for the saints with His Father, which can be considered an allusion to Daniel 7.

First, Daniel is the only prophet who revealed precisely *how* YHWH will come. He will come as a man with the clouds of heaven. The other prophets described events that happen when YHWH comes to the earth, but Daniel was the only prophet who saw YHWH descend from the heavens as a man.

Second, Jesus used Daniel 7 far more than any other passage to define His identity. Jesus descended in His first coming, but He did not come with the clouds of heaven in the glory of His Father. Because Jesus staked His identity on Daniel 7, He needed to explain when and how He would come with the clouds. If He never comes with the clouds, He is not the true Son of Man. When Jesus identified Himself as the Son of Man coming with the clouds, He predicted He would ascend to heaven again so He could come with the clouds as a man, just as Daniel had predicted.

Third, Daniel 7 gave the best summary of the timeline of the kingdom. The kingdom would be established on earth *after* the most terrible beast in human history rules for a limited period of time. It will be established when the Son of Man comes with the clouds. Jesus' teaching removed any mystery or ambiguity about the timing of the kingdom. The saints should expect persecution until the beast and the Son of Man comes with the clouds to establish His kingdom. The saints will experience a present demonstration of the kingdom in the context of the church, but the kingdom will not be established on earth until the Son of Man returns.

Fourth, Daniel 7 presents the Son of Man enthroned with His Father as Judge over the beasts. The Old Testament repeatedly described YHWH coming to the earth to judge the nations. However, Daniel revealed YHWH is coming to the earth *as a man* to judge the nations. Because YHWH gave dominion over the earth to men, the earth must be judged by a man. Daniel 7 is the only Old Testament prophecy that clearly described YHWH descending to judge as a man. It reveals the other prophets' descriptions of YHWH's judgment are descriptions of the Son of Man.[3]

---

[3]For example, in Matthew 25:31, Jesus predicted He would judge the nations as the Son of Man, but He is expounding on Joel 3, which predicts YHWH will judge the nations.

Daniel's description of Jesus' return was so complete Jesus could use it nearly exclusively to describe His return. Obviously, this does not mean we should neglect other passages in the prophets. Jesus' audience was familiar with the other prophets, and His use of Daniel should provoke us to read everything else the prophets wrote. His affirmation of Daniel is an affirmation of everything spoken about Him.

He Will Return to Israel as the Son of Man
Because the church has a responsibility to speak to Israel about their God and their Messiah, we must learn to present the gospel to Israel the way Jesus did. Not only did Jesus present Himself as the Son of Man in His first coming, He also described Himself as the Son of Man in every description of His second coming:[4]

> *For the Son of Man is going to come with his angels in the glory of his Father. (Matthew 16:27)*

> *When the Son of Man comes in his glory.... (Matthew 25:31)*

> *Jesus said to him, "...you will see the Son of Man seated at the right hand of Power and coming on the clouds of heaven." (Matthew 26:64)*

> *And then they will see the Son of Man coming in a cloud with power and great glory. (Luke 21:27)*

Jesus' description of His second coming is significant because He will fulfill the messianic promises when He returns. As Peter said, Jesus has ascended into the heavens until the time for restoring all the things the prophets had spoken about. This includes the messianic predictions:

> *That he may send the Christ appointed for you, Jesus, whom heaven must receive until the time for restoring all the things about which God spoke by the mouth of his holy prophets long ago. (Acts 3:19–21)*

Jesus will fulfill the messianic promises in His second coming, but it is significant that He did not describe His second coming in terms of

---

[4]See also Matthew 23:37–39; 24:27, 30, 37, 44; 26:64; Mark 8:38; 13:26; 14:62; Luke 9:26; 12:40; 17:24; 18:8; 21:27; Acts 1:11.

His messianic identity. He never said, "The Christ will come"; instead, He always said, "The Son of Man will come."

We cannot overlook this detail because it means Israel will receive Jesus as the Son of Man in His second coming. Most Christians expect Israel to welcome Jesus as Messiah in His second coming—and that is certainly true—but Jesus put the emphasis on Israel's receiving Him as Son of Man.

Therefore, the primary message of the church to Israel should be about Jesus the Son of Man.

Jesus is coming as the Son of Man, and He wants us to proclaim Him this way. When most believers speak about Jesus' second coming, they speak about Him coming as Messiah. This is certainly not wrong —we should explain how Jesus will fulfill the Messianic promises in His second coming. Though Jesus is coming as Messiah, He did not summarize His coming that way, and that is significant. Particularly when speaking to Israel, we must learn to describe Jesus' return the way He did.

If you know who the Son of Man is, then you also know who the Messiah is. If God has become a man, He will be king as well. However, the inverse is not necessarily true. No one expected the Messiah to be divine, so Jesus could be received as Messiah without being received as fully divine.

Jesus predicted He will come *as the Son of Man.* This is the message He wants us to proclaim because it emphasizes His identity. He is not just coming as the political Deliverer. He is coming as God.

The Son of Man Will Be Messiah

In His longest teaching about His return, Jesus warned about the coming of false messiahs:

> *Then if anyone says to you, "Look, here is the Christ!" or "There he is!" do not believe it. For false christs and false prophets will arise and perform great signs and wonders, so as to lead astray, if possible, even the elect. (Matthew 24:23–24)*

Daniel's prophecy is so robust it keeps us from deception. We must ignore anyone who claims to be Messiah but does not come in the way Daniel predicted. Jesus' return sets Him apart from the false messiahs:

"So, if they say to you, 'Look, he is in the wilderness,' do not go out. If they say, 'Look, he is in the inner rooms,' do not believe it. For as the lightning comes from the east and shines as far as the west, so will be the coming of the Son of Man.... Then will appear in heaven the sign of the Son of Man." (Matthew 24:26–27, 30)

Furthermore, Jesus combined His prediction of His return as the Son of Man with Zechariah's prophecy of Israel's repentance and restoration:

"And I will pour out on the house of David and the inhabitants of Jerusalem a spirit of grace and pleas for mercy, so that, when they look on me, on him whom they have pierced, they shall mourn for him, as one mourns for an only child." (Zechariah 12:10)

"Then all the tribes of the earth will mourn, and they will see the Son of Man coming on the clouds of heaven with power and great glory." (Matthew 24:30)

Jesus combined these two passages to communicate a significant message: He has not forgotten the salvation of Israel. Israel's restoration will occur when they see and receive Jesus as the Son of Man. When He returns, He will fulfill every messianic promise, but first He wants to be received by Israel as the Son of Man.

Jesus wants to be received as the God of Israel before He is welcomed as the political Deliverer of Israel. He wants Israel to embrace Him as the One who made covenant with them on Mount Sinai. He wants to be truly and fully known by Israel and the nations. This is yet another reason for the mystery of the two comings. Israel and the nations have been looking for a political Deliverer for a long time. Jesus will be our King, but He has a deeper desire: *He wants to be our God.*[5]

It is not enough for Jesus to be known as Israel's greatest King and the Ruler of the earth. He wants to be loved and known as God in the flesh.

Jesus was warmly welcomed into Jerusalem in Matthew 21 as the *Son of David,* the messianic King. However, He refused to rule because Jerusalem was ready to receive Him as Messiah, but not as the Son of Man:

---

[5]Genesis 17:8; Exodus 6:7; 19:5; Leviticus 26:11–12; Ruth1:16; Song of Songs 2:16; 6:3; Jeremiah 7:23; 11:4; 30:22; 31:33; Ezekiel 36:28; 37:26–28; Zechariah 2:11; 8:8; Revelation 21:3.

"For I tell you, you will not see me again, until you say, 'Blessed is he who comes in the name of the Lord.'" (Matthew 23:39)

This same pattern was present in the Exodus. God delivered Israel from Egypt and brought Israel into the wilderness where He revealed Himself to Israel in fire on top of the mountain. God brought Israel into the wilderness to know Him *before* He brought Israel into the land to build a kingdom. God described that encounter in the wilderness as a betrothal[6] because He wanted Israel to know Him as God before Israel took possession of their inheritance in the land.

In the same way, Jesus wants Israel and the nations to receive Him as God before they receive their inheritance. Israel wanted a Messiah, and many Christians want a Savior who will deliver them and cause them to flourish. Jesus is more than a Deliverer who fulfills our destiny and our promises—He is God.

God wants to be more than our Savior or our King. He wants to be our God. He is not a means to an end—He is the end.

None of this minimizes Jesus' identity as Messiah. Speaking about Jesus as Messiah is important, but He will not function as Messiah until He is received as God. Therefore, our main message is *Jesus Son of Man,* the divine Human equal to the Ancient of Days, who will descend to rule and exalt a people to rule with Him as His eternal companion.

The Lord's Prayer

Jesus left us with a model prayer we frequently call *The Lord's Prayer.* The prayer opens with a cry for the kingdom of God:[7]

"Do not be like them, for your Father knows what you need before you ask him. Pray then like this: 'Our Father in heaven, hallowed be your name. Your kingdom come, your will be done, on earth as it is in heaven.'" (Matthew 6:8–10)

Many commentators have recognized this is an eschatological prayer—a prayer for God to finish His plan of redemption. We could refer to this prayer as *Jesus' prayer list for His church* because He gives specific requests that are important to Him.

---

[6]Jeremiah 2:2.

[7]See also Luke 11:2.

The prayer is full of allusions to Daniel 7, indicating Jesus taught His disciples to pray from a Daniel 7 paradigm:

- The prayer is addressed to "Our Father in heaven," which comes directly out of Daniel.

- The timing of the kingdom depends on the Father's will being done on the earth as it is in heaven, which is an allusion to the Ancient of Days sitting in judgment.

- Until He comes, the beasts rule in the earth, but He will bring His will to the earth, destroy the rule of the beasts, and establish His kingdom.

The prayer is according to Daniel's description of God's plan to resolve the age:

- The Father's will is going to be done on the earth when He sits in judgment and removes the beasts (Daniel 7:9–10).

- The beasts who presently rule this age will be destroyed (Daniel 7:11–12).

- The kingdom will come when God's will is done (Daniel 7:13–14, 21–22, 26–27).

There are times and seasons God has set over the beasts. They cannot extend their time, and we cannot reduce it. However, we have been commissioned by Jesus to pray for the kingdom to come because our intercession plays a role in His return.

Jesus used Daniel's prediction to undergird His model prayer and, in the process, gave us a profound revelation: The intercession of the church is connected to the coming of the kingdom.

The Lord's Prayer is a prayer for the Father to send the Son of Man in glory to liberate the earth from the rule of the beasts and to reward the saints. This connection reveals why the revelation of Daniel 7 was given to Daniel. Daniel was not a leader of Israel or a public figure like Jeremiah. *He was an intercessor.*

Daniel ordered his daily rhythm around prayer. He fasted and prayed. He prayed the Scripture. He prayed for his nation. He responded to the revelation he was given with intercession. Daniel's life and the vision that he was given in Daniel 7 make a profound connection: The coming of the kingdom is connected to the life of intercession.

Revelation 8 describes the moment when the accumulated intercession of the church through history will set into motion the events of Daniel 7:

> *And another angel came and stood at the altar with a golden censer, and he was given much incense to offer with the prayers of all the saints on the golden altar before the throne, and the smoke of the incense, with the prayers of the saints, rose before God from the hand of the angel. Then the angel took the censer and filled it with fire from the altar and threw it on the earth, and there were peals of thunder, rumblings, flashes of lightning, and an earthquake. (vv. 3–5)*

The Lord's Prayer is Jesus' invitation into the Daniel 7 storyline. *Through intercession, we become a part of the Lord's plan to overcome the beasts and establish the kingdom.*

Will the Son of Man Find Faith on the Earth?

Intercession is such an important part of the Daniel 7 storyline that Jesus also made reference to it in another key teaching on intercession in Luke. In Luke 17, Jesus spoke about His promise to come in power as the Son of Man:

> *And he said to the disciples, "The days are coming when you will desire to see one of the days of the Son of Man, and you will not see it. And they will say to you, 'Look, there!' or 'Look, here!' Do not go out or follow them. For as the lightning flashes and lights up the sky from one side to the other, so will the Son of Man be in his day…. Just as it was in the days of Noah, so will it be in the days of the Son of Man. … so will it be on the day when the Son of Man is revealed." (vv. 22–24, 26, 30)*

Jesus concluded His prediction with a parable found in Luke 18, which teaches us how to respond to the promise of His coming:

> *And he told them a parable to the effect that they ought always to pray and not lose heart. (v. 1)*

Jesus knew His followers were about to face an incredible test: The Son of Man would return to heaven for a long period of time. During His absence, the church would have to overcome the beasts through endurance and patiently waiting for the Son of Man to come in glory and liberate the earth.

Daniel 7 warns the test that the saints face is the test of endurance, and that is the issue Jesus addressed in Luke 18. In the parable, a widow keeps asking for justice:

"And there was a widow in that city who kept coming to him and saying, 'Give me justice against my adversary.'" (v. 3)

A widow in that culture was vulnerable because she did not have the protection of a husband. This is a description of how the church will feel under the reign of the beasts:

"As I looked, this horn made war with the saints and prevailed over them.... He shall speak words against the Most High, and shall wear out the saints of the Most High, and shall think to change the times and the law; and they shall be given into his hand for a time, times, and half a time." (Daniel 7:21, 25)

The absence of the Son of Man combined with the rule of the beasts and their apparent success will cause the saints to lose heart. In the parable, the widow kept asking for justice from an unjust judge. Jesus uses this analogy because the apparent delay in God's justice and deliverance combined with our vulnerability will test us severely. We will be tempted to think God is unjust because of His apparent delay—especially when it seems we have been handed over to the beasts.

The parable ends with two profound statements. The first statement is an affirmation of the Daniel 7 promise, and Jesus connected intercession with the Lord's judgment:

"'But the court shall sit in judgment, and his dominion shall be taken away, to be consumed and destroyed to the end. And the kingdom and the dominion and the greatness of the kingdoms under the whole heaven shall be given to the people of the saints of the Most High; his kingdom shall be an everlasting kingdom, and all dominions shall serve and obey him.'" (Daniel 7:26–27)

"And will not God give justice to his elect, who cry to him day and night? Will he delay long over them?" (Luke 18:7)

The second statement is a challenge to the church:

"I tell you, he will give justice to them speedily. Nevertheless, when the Son of Man comes, will he find faith on earth?" (Luke 18:8)

This is a challenge in light of Daniel 7. When the Son of Man comes, will He find faith? Will He find saints confident in His coming and His deliverance? Will the dominion of the beasts discourage us, or will we be eagerly looking for His deliverance?

Jesus' reference to His coming is more profound than it seems at first glance. Collins explains:

> *The parable of the unjust judge functions as a reassurance to the audience that God will vindicate the elect. The last saying of this unit ... implies either that the Son of Man will be an advocate in the heavenly court for those who have faith or, more likely, that the Son of Man will be God's agent in executing judgment. He is thus portrayed here implicitly as the eschatological judge.[8]*

In the parable, justice was given because the widow was persistent in her cry for justice, and Jesus described the cry for justice as faith. The application is simple: The people who have faith in the Son of Man should be like the widow consistently crying out for justice, even though it does not seem like they have an advocate and deliverance appears unlikely. Jesus will appear at the darkest moment of human history, just as the Son of Man appeared suddenly in Daniel 7 during the reign of the most terrible beast.

Jesus' message in Luke 18 is the same message He gave in the Lord's Prayer. Faith and endurance will be necessary, but the Son of Man will come in response to faith and persistent intercession. God will give justice to the saints who cry out day and night. He will destroy the beasts. He will give them the kingdom. He will fulfill all His promises. And all this is connected to the intercession of the saints.

---

[8]Collins and Collins, *Daniel: A Commentary on the Book of Daniel,* 100.

THE SON OF MAN MUST BE EXALTED

As we have seen, Jesus used Daniel 7 to present Himself and His kingdom. Because the Son of Man was supposed to come with the clouds to destroy the beasts, Jesus' suffering and death were incredibly confusing for His followers. Jesus used Daniel 7 to predict His suffering, but the disciples did not understand Jesus' exposition of Daniel and even resisted Jesus' message of suffering.[1]

When the women went to look for Jesus' body and found He had risen, the angels reminded them the Son of Man must suffer and rise.[2] Jesus died, but He was not subject to death, and His resurrection convinced the disciples that Jesus was who He said He was.[3] After the resurrection, the disciples had profound questions about the Son of Man and the kingdom. As a result, Jesus spent forty days teaching about the kingdom in order to answer the disciples' questions:

> *He presented himself alive to them after his suffering by many proofs, appearing to them during forty days and speaking about the kingdom of God. (Acts 1:3)*

Because Jesus used Daniel 7 as the primary basis for His teaching on the kingdom, His teaching over those forty days was likely an exposition of Daniel 7. His teaching was not limited to Daniel, but He definitely used Daniel to fully explain the kingdom.

Given the centrality of the kingdom in Jesus' teaching and the present confusion over the kingdom in many parts of the church, it is easy to read Acts 1 and wish Luke had recorded Jesus' teaching on the kingdom. However, in all likelihood, we *do* have what Jesus taught. We

---

[1]Matthew 16:22; Mark 8:32.

[2]Luke 24:4–7.

[3]John 20:28.

have Daniel 7, we have the prophets, and we have Jesus' exposition of Daniel in the Gospels.

Jesus probably reviewed everything He had said about the kingdom in the Gospels in light of His suffering, death, and resurrection, revealing the mystery of how He would fulfill everything Daniel had predicted. Considering the way Daniel was used by Jesus to unlock the prophets, He probably used Daniel to explain what the other prophets predicted about the kingdom. Jesus also explained the mystery of the prophecy.

Explaining Daniel's Prophecy

Daniel's prediction that the Son of Man would come with the clouds was the most challenging prediction Jesus had to explain. His miracles, transfiguration, and resurrection proved He was divine and not subject to human limitations. However, Daniel said the Son of Man would come in power with the clouds to destroy the beasts. The disciples overriding questions were likely *how* and *when* this would happen, and Jesus revealed the mystery:

- The Son of Man was a real man; therefore, He must descend to be born and become a man.

- The Son of Man must be given into the hands of the beast and pass through suffering to inherit the kingdom just like the saints.

- The Son of Man must ascend back to the heavens. When Jesus entered the heavens as a man, He set the stage for His coming with the clouds. Before the ascension, there wasn't a divine Man in the heavens who could come with the clouds.

- When the Father decides to sit in judgment, the Son of Man will descend from the heavens and come with the clouds as a real man just as Daniel predicted.

Jesus' interaction with His disciples at the conclusion of His teaching reveals the centrality of Daniel in Jesus' teaching on the kingdom. When Jesus finished, they had one summary question:

So when they had come together, they asked him, "Lord, will you at this time restore the kingdom to Israel?" He said to them, "It is not for you to know times or seasons that the Father has fixed by his own authority." (Acts 1:6–7)

This question reveals Jesus gave the apostles an expectation of some sort of restoration for Israel. While the coming of the kingdom would be much different from what anyone expected and would include a people from the nations, Jesus taught it would be a specific fulfillment of Israel's promises. We must notice Jesus did not rebuke this expectation—He only adjusted their understanding of the timing.

The massive influx of the gentiles would not replace Israel's role in the redemptive story. Israel's story had not yet been resolved, and when Jesus returned, Israel would not be discarded—Israel would be saved.[4]

Because Jesus always used Daniel 7 to predict His second coming, the disciples' question could be phrased in light of Daniel: *"Because You have demonstrated You are the Son of Man, will You now come with the clouds to take dominion from the beasts and establish the kingdom?"*

Jesus' answer also contains Daniel language. The coming of the Son of Man was connected to the Ancient of Days (Father) being seated in judgment. Therefore, the "times" and "seasons" are "fixed" by the Father's authority. This reference to the times and the seasons came directly from Daniel:[5]

"He changes times and seasons." (2:21)

"He ... shall think to change the times and the law; and they shall be given into his hand for a time, times, and half a time. But the court shall sit in judgment, and his dominion shall be taken away, to be consumed and destroyed to the end." *(7:25–26)*

The disciples now understood Jesus' first coming was not the end of the beasts. His resurrection enabled Him to ascend to the heavens in glory as the Son of Man, but He would come with the clouds and bring the kingdom just as Daniel saw.

Jesus' first coming had not replaced His second coming—it had set the stage for it.

Jesus' answer also included another reference to Daniel. The kingdom must include all peoples:

---

[4]Matthew 23:39; 24:30; Acts 1:6–7; Romans 11:12, 15, 24, 26; Revelation 1:7.

[5]See also Daniel 8:14; 12:7, 11.

"But you will receive power when the Holy Spirit has come upon you, and you will be my witnesses in Jerusalem and in all Judea and Samaria, and to the end of the earth." (Acts 1:8)

"And to him was given dominion and glory and a kingdom, that all peoples, nations, and languages should serve him." (Daniel 7:14)

The Son of Man will restore Israel, but His kingdom will consist of people from all nations. It was not enough to carry the gospel of the kingdom to Israel, so Jesus commissioned the disciples to become His witnesses to the nations. The Son of Man would not come until He could receive a people out of the nations.

The conversation in Acts 1 should bring to mind a similar conversation in Matthew 24 when the disciples asked Jesus when the kingdom would come.[6] In that passage, He also affirmed His commitment to save Israel when He would come with the clouds,[7] but instructed them to carry the gospel to all nations.[8]

Demonstrating Daniel's Prophecy

Jesus explained Daniel's prophecy and identified Himself as the Son of Man, but He had not fulfilled the most dramatic parts of the prophecy. The gospel message Jesus had given the apostles depended on Daniel 7, so there was just one more thing He had to do: emphatically demonstrate He was who He said He was and would do everything He said He would do.

Jesus' ascension was an emphatic statement to His disciples that He was the Son of Man and would fulfill every prediction Daniel made about Him.

The resurrection alone was not the final proof of Jesus' identity. Jesus' ascension demonstrated He had conquered death and sin, and had authority over all dominions. As the disciples watched, Jesus demonstrated He was the Son of Man:

And when he had said these things, as they were looking on, he was lifted up, and a cloud took him out of their sight. (Acts 1:9)

---

[6]Matthew 24:3.

[7]Matthew 24:30 contains a quote of Zechariah 12:10–12, which predicts Israel's salvation at Jesus' return.

[8]Matthew 24:14.

Jesus would fulfill Daniel's prophecy in an unexpected way, but Jesus' dramatic exit left the disciples completely convinced He was the Son of Man and gave them the courage to boldly declare everything Daniel had said about Him.

The story of Jesus' ascension has become so familiar that we forget how spectacular it was. When Jesus ascended into the heavens on His own and carried by a cloud, it was His final message: *"I am the man Daniel 7 saw."* If Jesus of Nazareth could *ascend* to the Ancient of Days on a cloud, then He can also *descend* with the clouds, judge the beasts, and take dominion over all kingdoms.

Jesus always quoted Daniel 7:13 in reference to His second coming, but His ascension revealed a mystery hidden in Daniel 7:

"I saw in the night visions, and behold, with the clouds of heaven there came one like a son of man, and he came to the Ancient of Days and was presented before him. And to him was given dominion and glory and a kingdom." (vv. 13–14)

The Son of Man will *descend* with the clouds in His second coming, but He also *ascended* with the clouds, presented Himself to the Ancient of Days, and sat down at His right hand. Jesus used Daniel 7 to describe His second coming, but it contained the mystery of the first *and* second comings.

Jesus' ascent to the Ancient of Day is just as miraculous as His descent in judgment. Because He ascended into the heavens as a man, He can do everything else He promised to do. Jesus revealed Daniel's vision of the Son of Man riding the clouds has *two* fulfillments. *The first guaranteed the second will happen exactly the way Daniel saw it.* The first coming followed the pattern of what Daniel saw, but it did not completely fulfill the prophecy.

The disciples stood watching the clouds after Jesus ascended. They were shocked because they had just seen a man coming to the Ancient of Days on the clouds just as Daniel had predicted. *Jesus' ascension meant everything that they had hoped for—everything that they had dared to believe—was true.*

As the disciples stood looking, two angels stood by them with a message:

And while they were gazing into heaven as he went, behold, two men stood by them in white robes, and said, "Men of Galilee, why do you stand looking into heaven? This Jesus, who was taken up from you into heaven, will come in the same way as you saw him go into heaven." (Acts 1:10–11)

The message was short and to the point: *He will come in the same way you saw Him go to heaven.* Jesus ascended with the clouds, and He will come with the clouds. This was Daniel 7 language. The ascension of the Son of Man has set the stage for His coming with the clouds. He will return the same way He left—with the clouds of heaven as man.

These angels were also a final statement. Daniel saw the Ancient of Days was surrounded by a host who ministered to Him, and Jesus predicted He would come with these angels.[9] He was accompanied by angels in His ascension as a statement that He will come with the angels just as He said. It was yet another reference to Daniel's vision.

Because Jesus ascended in a cloud, the prediction He is coming with the clouds must be taken literally.

There is no indication Jesus or the apostles believed His return in the clouds was metaphorical and not literal. It is difficult for us to imagine a man coming with the clouds, but it is not any more miraculous than God becoming a man. Jesus' coming may very well be very different than we imagine, but it will be a literal coming with the clouds of heaven just like His ascension.

When we carefully consider the ascension scene that followed Jesus' last teaching, it points once again to Daniel 7 as the gospel of the kingdom.

The resurrection and ascension of Jesus explained the mystery of the two comings and revealed how Daniel's vision worked:

- The Son of Man was divine, so He always existed as God.

- He was also human, so He had to descend and become a human being.

- To fulfill Daniel's prophecy, He had to ascend to the place He first came from to become a "heavenly Man" who could come from the heavens as YHWH to execute judgment and become Messiah.

The ascension was Jesus' final explanation and confirmation of who He truly was.

---

[9]Matthew 13:41; 16:27; 25:31; Mark 8:38; Luke 9:26.

Jesus' Stunning Demonstration of His Identity

The ascension may be the most neglected event in Jesus' life. A lot of attention is given to the miracle of the incarnation. A lot of attention is also given to the death and resurrection of Jesus. Of course, this is fitting. It was all part of a stage God carefully designed to display His glory. Furthermore, the atonement that results from Jesus' sacrifice is core to the gospel.

We need to recover the place of the ascension alongside the other key events in Jesus' life.

In the incarnation, God became a man, but in the ascension a man became God. *Both are equally miraculous.* When I say a "man became God," it does not mean Jesus was not always God. Jesus was always God before He became a man. What I mean is God become a human and, then, as a real human being ascended as God into the heavens to rule from the heavens. No man before or since has done that.

The ascension is the public proof of the incarnation. The incarnation was a hidden event. God quietly became a man in Mary's womb with no outward manifestation. When Jesus ascended into the heavens *as a man,* it was a bold, public demonstration that Mary really had given birth to God as a man.

The ascension was also a public proof of the power of the resurrection. Jesus was not the first person in the Bible who was resurrected, but no other person rose from the dead and then ascended on his own into the heavens to be exalted. We tend to speak most about the resurrection as a proof of Jesus' identity—which is true—but the ascension demonstrated Jesus' resurrection was completely different from every other resurrection in Scripture.

The gospel is the message of Jesus' suffering (atonement), *and* it is a message of His exaltation, because Jesus' divine identity is what made His suffering unique and salvific. Therefore, the ascension was the ultimate demonstration that He was who He said He was.

The ascension in Acts 1 is a fundamental pivot point in the New Testament. Luke intentionally introduced the book of Acts with the ascension so we would read everything that followed in light of that event.[10] It is the grand conclusion of the Gospels, and it set the stage for the outpouring of the Spirit and the ministry of the apostles.[11]

The church is the people who follow the divine Man in the heavens and who will be glorified and become like Him. While we wait for Jesus' return, we proclaim Him as the divine Man in the heavens who suffered, died, rose, and will return.

---

[10]We will explore this more in Volume 2.

[11]John 7:39; 16:7.

The Gospel of Daniel 7

THE TURNING POINT

Once you view Jesus' teaching through the lens of Daniel 7, you will never read the Gospels the same way. The way that Jesus used one small Old Testament passage is stunning, and when we begin to hear His teaching the way His first-century audience did, the gospel becomes much simpler to grasp and more majestic at the same time. Daniel 7 not only makes Jesus' teaching easy to understand, it answers many of the issues and questions people raise about Jesus and His gospel. Jesus was not mysterious about His identity nor His gospel. It only seems mysterious to us because we have lost sight of the straightforward way Jesus revealed Himself.[1] The key of Daniel 7 removes much of the confusion and debate around Jesus' teaching.

Before Acts 1, Jesus' disciples were portrayed as genuine, but somewhat confused and out of sync with Jesus. They loved Him and made great sacrifices but could not make sense of His suffering. The events surrounding Jesus' crucifixion were so traumatic that they went into hiding before the resurrection, and even after the resurrection, at least one key disciple contemplated returning to fishing.[2]

When the apostles saw Jesus ascend into the heavens as a result of His suffering, they were firmly and fully convinced His message was true.

After Acts 1, everything begins to change in the New Testament. The disciples preached Jesus' message with power and conviction. They deeply embraced His message, and they were fearless even in the face of suffering and persecution.

---

[1] Of course, this does not mean everyone understood everything Jesus said. There were points in the parables people found it difficult to grasp, but the main message was understood better than we have assumed. Jesus did not *add* mystery to the gospel, He began to *reveal* the mystery.

[2] John 21:1–3.

When Jesus baptized the church with His Spirit, everything changed, and Jesus' followers began to live the way He did. However, Acts begins with Acts 1 and not Acts 2, because chapter 1 sets the stage for everything that follows.

Discipleship

In Daniel 7, the exaltation of the Son of Man is directly connected to the exaltation of a people. Therefore, if Jesus could ascend to the heavens through suffering, it meant His people would do the same. As a result, this event radically transformed the disciples' attitude toward suffering.

Men who had hidden in fear a few days before suddenly rejoiced in suffering.[3] Their rejoicing did not come through some morbid love of suffering. It was also something more than identification with Jesus. The ascension had changed their thinking, and the Holy Spirit subsequently gave them the power to live according to this new paradigm.

Paul reminded Timothy why the early church deeply embraced suffering:

> *Therefore I endure everything for the sake of the elect, that they also may obtain the salvation that is in Christ Jesus with eternal glory. The saying is trustworthy, for: If we have died with him, we will also live with him; if we endure, we will also reign with him. (2 Timothy 2:10–12)*

Jesus lives and reigns in the heavens, and if we are going to live and reign with Him, we will be exalted to the heavens as well. The disciples embraced suffering because they wanted to ascend and rule with the Son of Man. His suffering elevated Him into the heavens, and they were fully convinced it would do the same for them.

The New Testament process of maturity is typically referred to as *discipleship*. Christians are to be disciples (followers) of Jesus. We are to live the way that He lived to be transformed into His image. That transformation is more than a moral transformation—it includes sharing in His heavenly exaltation. Jesus became like us in His incarnation, and we are called to become like Him in His exaltation.

---

[3]Acts 5:41.

Jesus' ascension is more than a statement of glory—it is also a divine invitation. In the ascension, we should hear the phrase John heard in Revelation 4: "'Come up here.'"[4]

Jesus wants us with Him where He is.[5] This means the process of discipleship is designed to result in our exaltation. We embrace discipleship—the path Jesus walked—so we can ascend into the heavens with Him to rule alongside Him. The disciples understood this, so when they saw Jesus ascend, they knew it was more than a statement of His dominion. It was a prediction that His people would be exalted as well. This hope energized them. They were willing to lose everything, including their own freedom and even their own lives, for the hope of ascending into the heavens with the Son of Man.

The message in Acts 1 summarizes the witness of the church: *On the basis of Jesus' ascension into the heavens, we can confidently proclaim the promise of exaltation into the heavens for those who embrace the path of Jesus.*

The outpouring of the Spirit empowers the church to proclaim this message, enables the church to embrace the difficulty of discipleship, and transforms the church so we become living witnesses—testimonies—of the transformation to come when we are exalted into the heavens as Jesus was.

We will not be made divine as the Son of Man is, but in every other way we will become like Him and exercise dominion with Him. This message is often overlooked, but it is foundational in the New Testament. The hope of becoming like Jesus in His exalted hope is the great hope of the New Testament. It is the motivation for suffering and holy living in this life. *If this promise is not true—we are of all men most to be pitied.*[6]

This future exaltation is the reason for what is commonly known as the rapture of the saints. Paul predicted, when Jesus comes, His people will be caught up with Him in the clouds:

For the Lord himself will descend from heaven with a cry of command, with the voice of an archangel, and with the sound of the trumpet of God. And the dead in Christ will rise first. Then we who are alive, who are left, will be caught up

---

[4]Revelation 4:1.

[5]John 17:24.

[6]1 Corinthians 15:19.

together with them in the clouds to meet the Lord in the air, and so we will always be with the Lord. Therefore encourage one another with these words. (1 Thessalonians 4:16–18)

At first this prediction seems strange. If Jesus is returning to the earth, why not gather His people on the earth? The reason is embedded in Acts 1. The people of the Son of Man must be exalted to the heavens with Him. When He comes, He will raise us up to meet Him in the clouds. Those who die before Jesus returns and those who are alive when He returns will all be exalted and meet Him in the clouds. We have missed how profound this prediction is. God is the only One who rides the clouds, but He is preparing a company of humans to ride the clouds with Him.

Acts 1 is not just history, it is *prophecy.* Jesus was the first man to ride the heavens, but He was the first among many to come. As a result, we can confidently say Acts 1 summarizes the hope of the New Testament.

THE GOSPELS RISE AND FALL ON DANIEL

When we carefully consider Jesus' teaching in the Gospels, it leads us to an incredible conclusion: *The Gospels, as they are written, rise and fall on Daniel 7 because Jesus used this one chapter to undergird His identity and every primary theme He taught.* While Jesus quoted a number of Old Testament passages, no other chapter comes close to being referenced as many times as Jesus referenced Daniel 7.

The *gospel* itself does not rise and fall on Daniel. The main aspects of the gospel can be found in a number of Old Testament passages, and because we now have the witness of the New Testament, the gospel can certainly be preached without Daniel 7.

However, the *Gospels* we have in the New Testament do rise and fall on Daniel. This does not mean Daniel is superior or more important than other Old Testament prophets, but Daniel 7 was used as a unique key to unlock the mystery of Jesus' identity and reveal the full meaning of many other passages.

Jesus could have taught differently, and the Gospel authors could have recorded His teaching differently, but Jesus intentionally decided to make His message dependent on Daniel. The Gospel authors carefully composed their books to communicate the way Daniel taught the gospel, and this is not unique to a Gospel—all four Gospels are dependent on Daniel 7.

Why were the Gospels written this way? Why did Jesus make His message dependent on one small chapter in a small prophetic book?

Jesus' Jewish Gospel

Jesus' gospel was much more Jewish than many Christian commentators throughout history have imagined. His teaching was based on the Jewish prophets. Jesus brought tremendous revelation to *how* the Old

Testament would be fulfilled, but He built it upon those prophecies. He was not trying to create a brand new religion.

Jesus used Daniel 7 as a key to unlock other important Old Testament prophecies. Daniel's paradigm changes the way other passages are read and interpreted. It removes the ambiguity in some interpretations, and this is what make makes it so essential. Jesus used Daniel 7 because it was the most efficient and conclusive way to support His teaching. Daniel had been given a unique revelation of a divine Human within a summary of the redemptive story.

As we've seen, when Jesus quoted Daniel 7, He often combined it with other messianic passages. He combined Daniel 7 with Psalm 110:1:

Jesus said to him, "You have said so. But I tell you, from now on you will see the Son of Man seated at the right hand of Power and coming on the clouds of heaven." (Matthew 26:64)

He also combined Daniel with Zechariah 12:10–12:

"Then will appear in heaven the sign of the Son of Man, and then all the tribes of the earth will mourn, and they will see the Son of Man coming on the clouds of heaven with power and great glory." (Matthew 24:30)

Combining two Old Testament passages to bring a new insight to both passages was a very Jewish way of teaching typically referred to as a *midrash*.[1] Jesus also quoted Daniel 7 with other passages to demonstrate the *kingdom of heaven* was not a new idea. It was part of Israel's story, and Jesus would fulfill Israel's story not replace it.

Jesus combined His claim to divinity with other predictions about Messiah, so His audience understood He was enlarging the understanding of Messiah, not dismissing Israel's promises and expectations. Jesus wanted to be received as the Son of Man, but He did not abandon His

---

[1]The subject of *midrash* is a broad subject. I am only speaking of *midrash* in the limited sense of combining two passages to convey a message not always immediately apparent when the passages are interpreted in isolation. I am not suggesting Jesus used the *midrash* style which creates entirely new interpretations not supported by the original texts. A *midrash* can be unbiblical, and I am not suggesting Jesus or the apostles used *midrash* to create new ideas not already supported by Scripture.

messianic calling. He was still Messiah and would do everything the prophets predicted Messiah would do.

The gospel remains first of all a message to Israel about their God.

Jesus demonstrated this priority in His own ministry.[2] Paul was sent to the gentiles, but he maintained the same priority. When he entered a city, he went to the synagogue first. Paul's practice of beginning at the synagogue was not just a pragmatic approach. He understood the gospel of the kingdom was first of all a message to Israel.[3] Sadly, the church has not maintained this same priority nor spoken the gospel to Israel the way Jesus and Paul did.

Misreading Jesus

The gospel of the kingdom is a Jewish gospel that bases Jesus' identity in the Jewish Scriptures.

While there are notable exceptions, over the last two thousand years the vast majority of Christianity has struggled to connect the gospel to the Old Testament in a robust way. As a result, the gospel is almost never preached from the Old Testament. It is only quoted from the New Testament. It is certainly not wrong to preach from the New Testament, but our avoidance of the Old indicates we do not grasp the foundations of the gospel message. Consequently, there is much confusion about what the gospel of the kingdom actually is.

This remains a profound problem even though we have more biblical information available than at any other time in history. In spite of all the resources we have, the Old Testament remains neglected or often interpreted as mostly ancient history and allegorical language predicting the church. If the church is going to return the gospel to Israel, we must understand the origins of our gospel. Jewish believers in Jesus can be an incredible resource for gentile believers in this area. Their natural grasp of Jewish history enables them to read the Bible differently and connect the New Testament with its Old Testament roots.

Because most Christian interpreters have missed the Jewish nature of the Gospels, they have reinterpreted them. This combined with a zeal to prove Jesus is Messiah has caused most Christian theologians to

---

[2]Matthew 10:5–6; 15:24.

[3]Romans 1:16.

radically redefine the concept of Messiah to the point it would hardly be recognizable to a Jewish audience.

Some have gone even further and tried to force Jews to convert from being Jewish to Christian as if receiving Jesus required an abandonment of Jewish identity. This is not what Jesus did. He presented Himself in a very Jewish way. His message was shocking, but it was not foreign.

Jesus did not reject His messianic identity, but His messianic identity is more fulfilled in His second coming than His first coming. In a sense, we can say Jesus is the Son of Man who will function as Messiah in His second coming. As a result, it was not the main emphasis in Jesus' first coming, and Peter's preaching demonstrates the apostles understood Jesus' message this way:

> *Repent therefore, and turn back, that your sins may be blotted out, that times of refreshing may come from the presence of the Lord, and that he may send the Christ appointed for you, Jesus, whom heaven must receive until the time for restoring all the things about which God spoke by the mouth of his holy prophets long ago. (Acts 3:19–21)*

When we do not understand how Jesus used Daniel's prophecy, we can easily misrepresent Jesus to His Jewish brethren and create unnecessary confusion. We tend to emphasize His messianic identity, but because Jesus did not fulfill most messianic expectations in His first coming, we come up with new definitions for Messiah in our zeal to prove Jesus is Israel's Messiah. The result is a witness of Jesus that sounds and feels very foreign to a Jewish audience.

The answer is to preach Jesus the way He preached Himself: as the divine Son of Man whom Daniel saw.

This will not reduce the controversy of the gospel, and it will not make it any easier to preach the gospel. The message that Jesus came first and foremost as Israel's God is more extraordinary than the message Jesus is Messiah. However, it will reduce the unnecessary confusion that results when we present Jesus as Messiah in a way Jesus Himself did not. This is not a peripheral issue, nor is it just a tool for more productive religious discussions. God wants the gentiles to return the message of the good news to the Jewish people. Therefore, learning how to deliver that message the way Jesus did is profoundly important.

At best, the church has given the Jewish people a witness of Jesus as a divine Savior, but the church has not yet given the Jewish people a biblical witness of Jesus the Son of Man. The age will not end until this witness is given, so we will look at an example of how Jesus gave this witness in the next section.

"Who Do You Say That I Am?"

FOUNDATIONS OF JESUS' GOSPEL

We have looked at how Jesus used Daniel in the key themes of His teaching, and we have covered a lot of material. By now, I hope you are reading the Gospels differently and discovering new facets of Jesus' beauty. Our ultimate goal is to know Jesus better and to proclaim His gospel in a clear way. With that in mind, in this last section we will examine a specific example of how Jesus communicated the gospel of the kingdom and used Daniel to undergird His message. Matthew 16–17 gives us an excellent example of how Jesus summarized the main themes of the gospel of the kingdom.

Matthew 16:13 marks a turning point in Matthew's Gospel.[1] At this point in Matthew's Gospel, Jesus began setting into motion the final events of His ministry. He traveled to the farthest point north He ever went, and then He moved back south through Galilee and continued south to Judea, and ultimately to His own execution in Jerusalem.

Because this was the turning point in Jesus' ministry and His execution was near, Jesus summarized His message, emphasized things that were essential, and prepared His disciples for what was coming. After Jesus' resurrection and ascension, the disciples remembered these events, and they became foundational to their understanding of who Jesus was. As a result, the preaching of the apostles in the New Testament reflects the themes found in this section of Matthew.

Five Key Foundations

In Matthew 16–17, Jesus established five foundations of the Gospel:

- His identity (Matthew 16:13–20)
- His suffering (Matthew 16:21–23)

---

[1]France, *The Gospel of Matthew*, 612.

- His people and His kingdom (Matthew 16:24–28)
- His judgments (Matthew 16:27)
- His glory (Matthew 17:1–9)

There is much more to each of these foundations than what is found in Daniel, but Jesus used Daniel as the starting point for each one.

HIS IDENTITY: THE HEART OF THE GOSPEL

A. W. Tozer identified the most important thing about a man:

> *What comes into our minds when we think about God is the most important thing about us.*[1]

What Tozer said is also true of the gospel: *The most important thing about the gospel is what we think about Jesus because the identity of Jesus is the foundation of the gospel.* As we have seen, this explains why Jesus emphasized Son of Man over Messiah. God reveals Himself in what He does, but He wants to be known for who He is.

The gospel begins with the proclamation of who Jesus is. God has commissioned humans to carry the most precious message in all of creation—the revelation of His one and only Son. This is far more serious than most of us realize. God has entrusted *us* with the assignment to present *Him* correctly. As a result, we must carefully study how Jesus revealed Himself from the Scriptures.

We carry a message that brings salvation and judgment, life and death, light and darkness. It is light to those who receive it, and it brings darkness to those who refuse it.[2] We have been commissioned to speak the revelation of who God is into the darkness of a sin-saturated age.

Preachers are not the only ones who carry this message. Every believer is commissioned by God to carry this message. Daniel is a perfect example. He was given the most profound summary of the gospel of the kingdom in the Bible, and he was an official in a pagan king's

---

[1]A.W. Tozer, *The Knowledge of the Holy* (New York: HarperCollins, 1961), 1.

[2]Romans 2:8; 1 Corinthians 1:18; 2 Thessalonians 2:10.

government, who likely spent much of his time in administration. As far as we know, Daniel was not a teacher or a speaker. Nothing about Daniel fits our paradigm of "messengers" of the gospel, and yet he was given some of the most profound revelations in the entire Bible.

The gospel is ultimately made known by divine revelation and not by human interpretation,[3] so we must know how God has revealed it. Far too many times, we carry a gospel formed on our own understanding and our own preferences, but because of the preciousness of the gospel, we do not have the luxury of interpreting it ourselves.

God is gracious with our limited understanding, but He is not concerned with our preferences or opinions. He wants us to proclaim His Son *as He is,* not as we imagine Him to be nor as we want Him to be. Every detail of how Jesus revealed Himself is important because He is the very center of the gospel. We must recover the gospel of the kingdom as Jesus delivered it to the apostles.

The better we know Jesus, the better we know the gospel, and the best place to begin is by studying how Jesus revealed Himself.

On This Rock I Will Build My Church
Jesus began a conversation with His disciples with a question about His identity because He is the central issue of the gospel.

> Now when Jesus came into the district of Caesarea Philippi, he asked his disciples, "Who do people say that the Son of Man is?" And they said, "Some say John the Baptist, others say Elijah, and others Jeremiah or one of the prophets." He said to them, "But who do you say that I am?" Simon Peter replied, "You are the Christ, the Son of the living God." And Jesus answered him, "Blessed are you, Simon Bar-Jonah! For flesh and blood has not revealed this to you, but my Father who is in heaven. And I tell you, you are Peter, and on this rock I will build my church, and the gates of hell shall not prevail against it." (Matthew 16:13–18)

The knowledge of Jesus is the foundation of the church. He is the "Cornerstone,"[4] the most important part of the foundation. Everything is built on Him. If you look at every cult of Christianity, they all

---

[3] 1 Corinthians 2:1–10; Galatians 1:12; 2 Peter 1:19–21.

[4] Ephesians 2:20.

share one thing in common: They do not hold to a true knowledge of who Jesus is.

When we misinterpret the identity of Jesus, we misrepresent the gospel, so Jesus began with a simple question:

Who do people say that the Son of Man is? (Matthew 16:13)

Jesus did not ask, "Who do people say the Son of God is?" Nor did He ask, "Who do people say the Messiah is?" If we assume the title *Messiah* best described Jesus' identity, we have lost sight of the way Jesus revealed Himself from the Scriptures, and we do not proclaim the gospel of the kingdom with the clarity Jesus wants us to have.

Jesus' question was very simple: *Have you properly understood who the Son of Man is?*

Peter identified Jesus as the "Christ, the Son of the living God," which seems to indicate the disciples still did not fully grasp Jesus' identity. However, the second half of Peter's answer was significant: "You are ... the Son of the living God." When Peter added, "Son of the living God," to the title *Christ*, he was beginning to grasp who Jesus was. He was not only the Christ—He was the divine Son of the Ancient of Days—and this is what provoked Jesus' response. Peter had received revelation.

Jesus described Peter's revelation as a "rock," which was likely a reference to Daniel. In Daniel 2, a stone cut "by no human hand"[5] broke all the kingdoms of this age into pieces and became the foundation of a kingdom that will never be destroyed:

"And in the days of those kings the God of heaven will set up a kingdom that shall never be destroyed, nor shall the kingdom be left to another people. It shall break in pieces all these kingdoms and bring them to an end, and it shall stand forever, just as you saw that a stone was cut from a mountain by no human hand, and that it broke in pieces the iron, the bronze, the clay, the silver, and the gold. A great God has made known to the king what shall be after this. The dream is certain, and its interpretation sure." (vv. 44–45)

Daniel 7 expanded on the Daniel 2 vision by introducing the Son of Man as the One who is given the right to judge and inherit the ever-

---

[5]Daniel 2:34.

lasting kingdom. The Son of Man is the stone of Daniel 2. The kingdom will be established by a "rock," and that rock is the Son of Man. He is the Daniel 2 stone that brings an end to the kingdoms of this age and establishes the everlasting kingdom.[6]

Jesus' response to Peter connected the stone of Daniel 2 with the Son of Man in Daniel 7. Peter would become a rock (foundation stone) in the church because he would proclaim the revelation of who Jesus is. However, the rock that the church is established on is the Son of Man. In context, Jesus' response to Peter was relatively straightforward: *The Son of Man is the Rock upon which the kingdom (church) is built.*

Later passages in the New Testament view the kingdom the same way:

> *According to the grace of God given to me, like a skilled master builder I laid a foundation, and someone else is building upon it. Let each one take care how he builds upon it. For no one can lay a foundation other than that which is laid, which is Jesus Christ. (1 Corinthians 3:10–11)*

> *So then you are no longer strangers and aliens, but you are fellow citizens with the saints and members of the household of God, built on the foundation of the apostles and prophets, Christ Jesus himself being the cornerstone, in whom the whole structure, being joined together, grows into a holy temple in the Lord. In him you also are being built together into a dwelling place for God by the Spirit. (Ephesians 2:19–22)*

The church is established on the foundation of the Son of Man.

The apostles were foundational because they were given the privilege of making Jesus known when the mystery of His identity was unveiled in His first coming. They proclaimed and wrote down the revelation of the mystery of Jesus so the world could know who He is. The prophets are foundational because their prophecies were not ultimately about events. Their prophecies were recorded to give a witness (testimony) to Jesus:

> *For the testimony of Jesus is the spirit of prophecy. (Revelation 19:10)*

Those who testify to the true identity of Jesus are foundation stones in the church, and the entire foundation rests on one "chief

---

[6]Luke 1:33.

Cornerstone," the Son of Man. Therefore, Peter was a rock, but the whole structure is built upon another Rock—the Daniel 2 Stone.

The Gates of Hell Will Not Prevail

Because Jesus is the indestructible Rock, He made a profound prom-ise—the gates of hell would not prevail:

> *And I tell you, you are Peter, and on this rock I will build my church, and the gates of hell shall not prevail against it. (Matthew 16:18)*

This statement was very significant because of where Matthew 16 took place. Jesus had chosen an interesting location to ask His disciples if they truly understood His identity:

> *Now when Jesus came into the district of Caesarea Philippi, he asked his disciples, "Who do people say that the Son of Man is?" (Matthew 16:13)*

Caesarea Philippi was at the base of Mount Hermon, and the mountain had a long, dark history. According to an ancient story found in 1 Enoch 6:1–6, the "sons of god" swore on Mount Hermon and descended on that mount to join themselves with the daughters of men. The result was the "mighty men" (*nephilim*) who led the earth into such wickedness that God was grieved He had created man.[7] While the true identity of the *nephilim* and the accuracy of Enoch remain a matter of debate, Mount Hermon was associated with darkness.

The mountain had become a center of pagan worship:

> *More than twenty temples have been surveyed on Mt. Hermon and its environs. This is an unprecedented number in comparison with other regions of the Phoenician coast. They appear to be the ancient cult sites of the Mt. Hermon population and represent the Canaanite/Phoenician concept of open-air cult centers dedicated, evidently, to the celestial gods. During the 2d century B.C.E., chapels carved out of rock were incorporated within the enclosures. In the 1st century C.E., temples built in Classical style were added to the complex.[8]*

Where Mount Hermon and Caesarea Philippi were located, there was a long and dark association with false gods. In Jesus' time, it was

---

[7]Genesis 6:1–6.

[8]Rami Arav, "Hermon, Mount (Place)," *The Anchor Yale Bible Dictionary*, ed. David Noel Freedman, (New York: Doubleday, 1992), 159.

associated with the worship of Greek gods, particularly the Greek god Pan, and the worship of Caesar Augustus. At the bottom of the mountain was a large cave from which water flowed. Its large opening was considered to be a gateway to the spiritual world because the depth of the opening could not be measured. It was referred to as the *Cave of Pan* because it was used for the worship of Pan. There were also idols to the Roman emperors.

When Jesus stood in Caesarea Philippi, He referred to this large, dark opening at the base of the mountain by another of its names: *the gates of hell.* Why did Jesus take His disciples to a center of pagan worship to ask them if they knew who He was? He wanted to make a vivid statement: *He was the Son of Man who would destroy all the beasts.*

The beasts of Daniel 7 represent more than kings. They represent the spiritual powers behind the wicked rulers of this age. Mount Hermon was the largest mountain in the region, and it was a stronghold of darkness. At the foot of the mountain were temples to both the "spiritual" beasts (Greek gods) and "human" beasts (the king Caesar Augustus). Jesus stood in that location as the "Stone" of Daniel 2 who would crush every "beast" kingdom of this age. The powers of darkness—including evil spirits (the "sons of god" in Genesis 6), pagan gods (like Pan), and wicked emperors (like Caesar Augustus)—would ultimately be deposed by the Son of Man.

Caesarea Philippi was the perfect place for Jesus to make His statement because it was impressive and majestic. It was a statement to the power of Rome (political might) and the influence of the Greek gods (spiritual seduction). The city was a monument to the "beasts" of this age, so the Son of Man came to the city to predict their end.

Nothing can stand against the Stone not cut with hands (the "Son of God") and the exalted ruler (the "Son of Man."). Not even the most terrible ruler in human history, the ruler mentioned in Daniel 7. In a moment, the Son of Man will destroy the most wicked man in human history. *The gates of hell will not prevail.* The outcome is guaranteed because the church was established on the Rock that will shatter every other kingdom.

As Jesus stood in front of the impressive temples to the emperor and the gods of this age, He only had one question: *Do you know who I am?*

Mark's and Luke's Accounts

Mark's and Luke's version of this story are much shorter than Matthew's. They are virtually identical, so we can use Luke's account to examine the differences:[9]

> *Then he said to them, "But who do you say that I am?" And Peter answered, "The Christ of God." And he strictly charged and commanded them to tell this to no one. (Luke 9:20–21)*

The first obvious difference is Jesus' question. Mark and Luke omitted the phrase *Son of Man*. Jesus asked, "Who do you say that I am?" This seems like a critical difference, but if we consider the differences, we find Mark and Luke agree with Matthew; they simply wrote a much shorter account of the event.

Not only did they shorten Jesus' question, they also shortened Peter's response to Jesus' question. Peter simply said Jesus is the "Christ of God." They did not include "Son of the living God." At first, it appears Mark and Luke prioritized Jesus' messianic identity, but we have to look carefully at what follows.

Mark and Luke not only shortened Peter's answer, they also did not include Jesus' affirmation of Peter. The implication is clear. Peter's answer is true, but incomplete—the disciples still do not know who Jesus is. Jesus will not build His church on His messianic identity. It is important, but not the foundation of the church. Jesus' response to Peter confirms the answer is incomplete:[10]

> *And he strictly charged and commanded them to tell this to no one. (Luke 9:21)*

People assume Jesus was hiding His identity, but as we have seen, He did not hide His identity. Furthermore, this passage marks a profound turning point in Jesus' ministry. From this point, Jesus begins to head directly to the cross. Jesus is not trying to hide His identity; on the contrary, He is moving quickly toward His execution, which will result from Jesus' claim to be the Son of Man.

Peter and the rest of the disciples still saw Jesus as Messiah, and they had specific expectations of what that meant. Therefore, Jesus did

---

[9]See also Mark 8:27–30.

[10]See Mark 8:30.

not want them speaking about Him as Messiah yet. To emphasize His point, in the next verse, Jesus reminded them of His identity,[11]

saying, "The Son of Man must suffer many things." (Luke 9:22)

When we summarize Mark's and Luke's accounts, they communicate the same message as Matthew's:

- Jesus asked the disciples if they knew who He was.

- Peter answered Jesus was Messiah—a true but incomplete answer—which revealed the disciples still did not fully know who He was.

- Mark and Luke did not include Jesus' affirmation of Peter to emphasize Peter's answer was incomplete.

- Jesus told the disciples not to speak about His identity. This was not an attempt to hide His identity but to prevent His disciples from stirring incorrect expectations about Jesus.

- Jesus then identified Himself as the Son of Man, not as the Christ, to emphasize to the disciples His primary identity is not Messiah; it is Son of Man.

Jesus' interaction with Peter in Mark and Luke is similar to His interaction with the high priest when He was arrested. The high priest wanted to know if Jesus was the Christ, and Jesus answered He was the Son of Man:

And the high priest said to him, "I adjure you by the living God, tell us if you are the Christ..." Jesus said to him, "... you will see the Son of Man...." (Matthew 26:63–64)

Matthew's account is likely longer because he wrote for a Jewish audience more familiar with the promise of Messiah and the prediction of the Son of Man. Matthew expected his audience to understand the nuances of Jesus' response to Peter.

In Matthew's account, after Peter refers to Jesus as Christ, Jesus continues to use Son of Man and instructs the disciples not to tell anyone He is the Christ.[12] Since Jesus was not trying to hide His identity,

---

[11]See also Mark 8:31.

[12]Matthew 16:20.

this clearly reveals Peter's answer showed some revelation but was still incomplete. Mark and Luke recorded a shorter, simpler interaction that communicates the same thing.

HIS SUFFERING: THE PATH TO VICTORY

After Jesus used Caesarea Philippi to make a bold statement about His identity, He reiterated another foundation of His gospel. He shocked the disciples with the prediction the exalted Son of Man would suffer:

> *From that time Jesus began to show his disciples that he must go to Jerusalem and suffer many things from the elders and chief priests and scribes, and be killed, and on the third day be raised. (Matthew 16:21)*

Jesus reminded the disciples of a profound mystery contained in Daniel 7: *The Son of Man would triumph through suffering.*[1] When Daniel is combined with the other prophets, we discover the Son of Man's suffering would be for Himself *and* His people.[2]

Jesus revealed the Son of Man's suffering would secure His inheritance, defeat the beasts, and be an atonement (payment) for sin:

> *even as the Son of Man came not to be served but to serve, and to give his life as a ransom for many. (Matthew 20:28)*

Daniel 7 contained hints of the atonement, but not a complete theology of atonement. Because the atonement is a central part of the gospel, Daniel must be combined with the other prophets to develop the full theology of atonement that undergirds the gospel.

---

[1]See also Mark 8:31–38; Luke 9:22–26.

[2]See also Mark 10:45.

Get Behind Me Satan

At this point, the disciples still did not grasp the idea that the Son of Man would be exalted through suffering. This set the stage for one of the most awkward interactions between Jesus and one of His disciples:[3]

> *Then he strictly charged the disciples to tell no one that he was the Christ. From that time Jesus began to show his disciples that he must go to Jerusalem and suffer many things from the elders and chief priests and scribes, and be killed, and on the third day be raised. And Peter took him aside and began to rebuke him, saying, "Far be it from you, Lord! This shall never happen to you." But he turned and said to Peter, "Get behind me, Satan! You are a hindrance to me. For you are not setting your mind on the things of God, but on the things of man." (Matthew 16:20–23)*

This rebuke is well known, but must be understood in its full context. The conversation was not only about suffering, it was also about Jesus' identity. The disciples still saw Him primarily as a political Deliverer. Jesus' command to the disciples to not tell anyone about Him (v. 20) was a response to their expectation, and it was a rebuke. Jesus did not want His disciples to speak about Him because they could not yet be trusted to accurately convey the message of who He truly was.

After Jesus' rebuke in verse 20, Jesus defined His identity—and His future—very differently from what the disciples expected about Messiah. Mark's and Luke's accounts demonstrate Jesus explicitly described Himself as the Son of Man who must suffer:

> *And he began to teach them that the Son of Man must suffer many things and be rejected by the elders and the chief priests and the scribes and be killed, and after three days rise again. (Mark 8:31)*

> *"The Son of Man must suffer many things and be rejected by the elders and chief priests and scribes, and be killed, and on the third day be raised." (Luke 9:22)*

When Peter heard this, he took Jesus aside and rebuked Him. Peter's rebuke parallels the rebuke of verse 20. In verse 20, Jesus corrected the disciples by telling them not to speak about His identity because they did not know who He was. Peter responded in verse 22 by correct-

---

[3]See also Mark 8:29–31; Luke 9:21–22.

ing Jesus about His identity, which ironically confirmed Jesus' assessment: The disciples did not yet completely understand who He was.

When Peter pulled Jesus aside to rebuke Him, he in essence treated Jesus as *his* disciple.[4] Jesus turned around and looked at His disciples. This was essentially a mutiny. The disciples—with Peter as the spokesman—wanted to define Jesus according to their expectations. What made this so difficult was that their expectations were biblical, but not according to the way Jesus had revealed Himself.

This was a critical moment. Jesus' response to Peter was not subtle. It was blunt and direct:

> *But turning and seeing his disciples, he rebuked Peter and said, "Get behind me, Satan! For you are not setting your mind on the things of God, but on the things of man." (Mark 8:33)*

Peter had pulled Jesus aside to instruct Him, but Jesus put Peter back in His place. Peter needed to get behind Jesus—return to following Him. Peter was Jesus' disciple. Jesus was not Peter's. Jesus referred to Peter as *Satan* to indicate the seriousness of Peter's rebuke. Jesus' application of the term *Satan* to Peter was a severe way to refer to Peter as Jesus' opponent in that moment.[5]

Jesus' rebuke addressed the big issue: Peter had set his mind on the things of man. He had chosen his evaluation of Jesus' identity and his expectation of Jesus' future over what God had revealed. Peter was confident in his evaluation of Jesus because he could have quoted Bible verses for why Jesus was the Christ and why Jesus would do the things Peter wanted Jesus to do.

Jesus identified Peter's thinking—his human reasoning—with Satan's opposition.

Interpretation and Revelation

This interaction reveals the fundamental human issue: *Peter acted according to his own thinking rather than according to what God had revealed.*

---

[4]Adela Yarbro Collins and Harold W. Attridge, *Mark: A Commentary on the Gospel of Mark*, Hermeneia—a Critical and Historical Commentary on the Bible (Minneapolis, MN: Fortress Press, 2007), 407.

[5]Craig A. Evans, *Mark 8:27–16:20*, vol. 34B, Word Biblical Commentary (Dallas: Word, Incorporated, 2001), 19.

This is the ultimate human test: Do we submit to God's revelation or our *evaluation* of His revelation? This was the same test Eve faced in the garden. The fruit she saw on the tree of the knowledge of good and evil looked good, but God had forbidden it.[6] Eve had two options: She could trust her own perception or trust what God had revealed. She put her confidence in her own perception, and it set the rebellion into motion.

The gospel requires us to put more confidence in what God has revealed than what we can comprehend.

This is one of the biggest challenges of the gospel message. Jesus revealed He was the Son of Man and must suffer. However, Peter also knew He was the Christ, so he rebuked Jesus according to how he understood the Messiah. Peter could have quoted verses to support his rebuke, but he was acting according to human thinking.

Like Peter, we often use Bible passages to define Jesus' identity according to our own desires and our own understanding, and we are extremely confident in our own evaluation even when God plainly challenges it. This happens any time we make theological and sentimental arguments for why Jesus should be who we want Him to be rather than allowing Him to confront us with who He truly is.

Sometimes, we quote the promises of God but resist the process God has determined will bring about those promises. Furthermore, when our humanistic ideas of Jesus are challenged, we often find ways to explain away what the Bible clearly says and, instead, find ways to make it say what we want it to say.

Peter's rebuke was a bold move, and it revealed how difficult the prediction of Jesus' suffering was for the apostles. At this point, they were still unable to consider it. Peter's rebuke was not only an indication of *his* presumption but of *our* presumption. Peter's rebuke demonstrates how tightly we hold on to our own opinions and expectations of who we want God to be. When God does not match our expectations, we are prone to rebuke Him rather than wrestle with the fact that we have adopted a view of God according to our own wisdom.

We often have more confidence in our opinions about God and our interpretations of Bible verses than what God has revealed. Peter had seen Jesus demonstrate His power and authority. By this point, Pe-

---

[6]Genesis 3:6.

ter realized Jesus was divine—or at least the Son of God in a unique way.[7] However, Peter was still more willing to rebuke Jesus than to accept that his expectations and preconceived notions of who God was were incorrect.

According to Mark, Jesus rebuked Peter after He turned and looked at His disciples.[8] Jesus rebuked Peter publicly because He knew Peter was a spokesman who said what the disciples all thought. If we read this story as a statement of Peter's arrogance, we will miss the point. The story is a warning about how far we will go to cling to our own expectations.

Whenever we define Jesus according to our own understanding, we make Jesus our disciple rather than act as His.

The church is filled with opinions of who Jesus is and what He should do that are not in line with everything the Scripture says about Jesus. This story is a warning to us. We need to allow God to fully confront our expectations of who He is through the Scripture. We cannot avoid what God has revealed by hiding behind our personal interpretations—even if we can find verses to support them.

God is a Person, and He must be related to as a Person. We cannot divide up His identity and only engage the attributes we are most comfortable with. To truly relate to God, we must relate to Him as He is and not as we want Him to be. We must engage the totality of who He is. He is Servant *and* Lord. He is gentle *and* strong. He is Savior, *and* He is Judge.

As Jesus approached the climax of His first coming, the disciples could not agree with what Jesus predicted must happen. In the same way, the church is going to struggle with the things the Bible predicts must happen for the age to come. The closer we get to the end of the age, the more Jesus will challenge our conceptions of who He is through the unusual way in which He will redeem the earth.

According to Scripture, God is sovereign over the antichrist, end-time suffering, and end-time judgments. All of this is incredibly confusing and even offensive to human thinking. Even the prophets struggled to understand the intensity of what must happen for the age to end. Like the disciples, the end-time church will be tempted to choose another plan of redemption that makes more sense to us. The disci-

---

[7]Matthew 16:16.

[8]Mark 8:33.

ples' response just before Jesus' suffering is a sober warning for us—particularly if we live in the days before the church's final suffering.

Now is the time to choose what Scripture says about God and His leadership of history over and above our own understanding. Jesus faced this test the night before His crucifixion:

> *saying, "Father, if you are willing, remove this cup from me. Nevertheless, not my will, but yours, be done." (Luke 22:42)*

As Jesus considered the crucifixion and what would happen, He asked the Father if He could avoid the "cup." As He considered what was coming, the "cup" didn't seem like a good idea, but Jesus was willing to trust His Father's leadership more than His own perception. *Jesus faced the same test the disciples faced in Matthew 16, but He passed it.* The endtime church will face this test as well, and we must pass it. Human expectations—even when they are applied to Bible verses—are dangerous.

Christianity is a revealed religion, not a discovered or developed one. It is built on the foundation of the prophets because it is built on what God has spoken and revealed about Himself. When God liberated the people of Israel in the Exodus, He gathered them around Mount Sinai in the desert to make covenant. However, they longed for the promise of a land and a nation, and did not understand the strange process God was leading them through. They wanted an immediate inheritance.

Because Israel could not endure the process that God had determined, they created a golden calf, named it YHWH, and began worshipping it according to their own desires. Though God had spoken audibly on Mount Sinai, Israel chose their own desires which were based on biblical promises rather than on what God was speaking. We have the same tendency.

The good news is Jesus rebuked His disciples; He did not reject them. Jesus' suffering disillusioned the disciples, but after He suffered Jesus explained His suffering and commissioned His disciples to become witnesses of a message that they had previously rejected. Jesus' response to the disciples indicates His deep kindness. Rather than discarding the disciples, He brought them through a process of transformation.

Jesus will not compromise His leadership. He must rebuke our confidence in our own wisdom, but He will also patiently bring us into agreement with Him.

Genesis 3 revealed the fundamental human test: *Will we trust God's evaluation of our situation and His wisdom over our own evaluation?* The only way to pass the test is to carefully study how Jesus has revealed Himself in Scripture, limit ourselves to what He has revealed, and then submit to that revelation.

Who Do You Say That I Am?

The question "Who is Jesus?" is the most important question we can ask.

Matthew, Mark, and Luke emphasized different elements of Jesus' interaction with His disciples at Caesarea Philippi, but they all emphasized a single problem: The disciples had difficulty grasping who Jesus was because of their predetermined expectations.

Jesus is Messiah, but He is much more. He is the exalted Son of Man who will triumph over all the beasts. The seduction of the pagan gods of sexuality like Pan cannot corrupt Him. The might of Caesar cannot overcome Him. Jesus' path to victory was much different than anyone expected. He would not triumph over the beasts by leading a political revolt against Rome. He would triumph as a Suffering Servant.[9] *The Son of Man would suffer many things.*

The fact most Christians think Jesus predominantly revealed Himself as Messiah should concern us. *Peter thought the same thing, and Jesus rebuked him as an opponent.* We tend to adopt an arrogant posture toward the ancient Israelites and accuse them of being blind to Jesus' true identity, but this is our issue as well.

Any time we prioritize our own understanding and expectation over biblical revelation, we become like Peter. We pull Jesus aside and act as if He is our disciple—a God who exists mostly to meet our needs—rather than following Him as His disciple.

In order to keep the gospel pure, we must learn to declare the identity of Jesus the way He did. We simply do not have the luxury of deciding how to present Him.

---

[9]Isaiah 52:13–53:12.

HIS PEOPLE AND HIS KINGDOM: TAKE UP YOUR CROSS AND FOLLOW HIM

The saints who inherit the kingdom with the Son of Man are one of the main themes of Daniel. Because Jesus would be exalted through suffering, He asked His followers to adopt His attitude toward suffering so they could share in His exaltation:[1]

> *Then Jesus told his disciples, "If anyone would come after me, let him deny himself and take up his cross and follow me." (Matthew 16:24)*

Jesus gave five specific exhortations to His disciples to take up their cross and follow Him.[2] In four of the five, Jesus referred to Himself as the Son of Man to make sure His message was clear. They were to *follow* Him because His suffering was their suffering. He was taking on the suffering of the saints. Furthermore, as Daniel predicted, suffering would lead to an inheritance in the kingdom, dominion, and immortality.

The invitation to suffer alongside the Son of Man is an invitation to rule with Him because the gospel of the kingdom includes the message of a people who will pass through suffering like the Son of Man and inherit the kingdom with Him.

The Saints Who Follow the Son of Man
Peter's response to Jesus' prediction of suffering[3] revealed what Jesus already knew: His suffering could completely disillusion His disciples

---

[1]See also Matthew 10:17–22; 23:34; 24:9; Mark 13:9–13; Luke 21:12, 16, 17; John 15:19–20; 16:2.

[2]Matthew 10:38; 16:24; Mark 8:34; Luke 9:23; 14:27.

[3]Matthew 16:22–23.

who still expected an immediate political triumph. With this in mind, Jesus used Daniel's prophecy to motivate them to endure:

> *Then Jesus told his disciples, "If anyone would come after me, let him deny himself and take up his cross and follow me. For whoever would save his life will lose it, but whoever loses his life for my sake will find it. For what will it profit a man if he gains the whole world and forfeits his soul? Or what shall a man give in return for his soul? For the Son of Man is going to come with his angels in the glory of his Father, and then he will repay each person according to what he has done." (Matthew 16:24–27)*

The path of suffering was not just Jesus' path; it is the path the saints must embrace as well. If you are willing to lose your life in this age for the sake of identifying with the Son of Man, you will gain an everlasting inheritance. Those who follow the Son of Man will lose their lives in this age because it remains under the influence of the beasts who violently oppose the Son of Man. This does not always mean death, but it means a loss of acceptance, fulfillment, and inheritance in this age.

The path of the Son of Man is everlasting life, but the end of the beasts is destruction in the lake of fire. If you follow the beasts, you will gain nothing. Even if you gain the "whole world" (the power and influence of this age), you lose everything in the end.

This path of suffering offers the potential of incredible gain or incredible loss.

No matter what it costs, we are called to embrace Jesus' path of suffering so we can participate with Him in the kingdom when He comes as the Son of Man to repay the wicked and give the kingdom to the saints.

His Judgments: The Son of Man Will Come as a Judge

As we have seen, the gospel is the good news of Jesus' salvation *through* judgment, so Jesus reminded His disciples that He was coming as Judge. His prediction was loaded with allusions to Daniel 7:

> *"For the Son of Man is going to come with his angels in the glory of his Father, and then he will repay each person according to what he has done." (Matthew 16:27)*

The Son of Man is going to come. Jesus will appear in the clouds and destroy the beasts. His first coming was not the only coming. The second coming is certain. The vision of Jesus' coming with the clouds was part of a judgment scene which is why Jesus included the next significant detail.

The Son of Man will come with His angels in the glory of His Father. The Son of Man and His Father was a reference to Daniel's vision of the Ancient of Days being seated in judgment. When He sat in judgment, His appearance was terrifying. A river of fire flowed from Him, and He was surrounded by a great host.

Jesus predicted He would come in that same glory accompanied by those angels. This was a summary of Jesus' statement that the Father had given over all judgment to Him. Because Jesus will execute YHWH's judgment, the angels and glory that accompany the Ancient of Days when He is seated in judgment will accompany the Son of Man when He executes the decreed judgment.

Jesus is not only coming to save, He is also coming to repay. He will repay every man, and He will repay every spiritual power. The deeds done in this age have not gone unnoticed. Though God seems to overlook sin and delay His judgment, it is only temporary. The Son of Man is coming, and *He will repay.*

Jesus' return as Judge is both a warning and a promise. It is a warning to the nations that things will not always continue as they are. Though the rebellion has continued for thousands of years, a day is coming when God will put a sudden and complete end to it. This warning is designed by God to provoke men to repent of their sin and turn to Him before the day of judgment.

It is a promise to the saints that the suffering and oppression of this age will end. Those who submit to Jesus, face a number of tests and trials in this age. They face rejection from the system of this age. However, this is not the end. If we endure suffering in this age, we will reign with Him in the age to come. His judgment is certain and sure. This age will end.

The Gospel of Judgment

Because Jesus was revealed to Daniel in judgment, it means His identity as Judge and the certainty of His coming as Judge are a core part of the message of the gospel of the kingdom.

Jesus' return as Judge is so central to the gospel that Jesus *commanded* the disciples to proclaim Him as Judge:

> *"And he commanded us to preach to the people and to testify that he is the one appointed by God to be judge of the living and the dead." (Acts 10:42)*

Paul did the same. When he had the opportunity to speak in Athens to philosophers who did not know the Bible, he proclaimed Jesus as Judge:

> *"The times of ignorance God overlooked, but now he commands all people everywhere to repent, because he has fixed a day on which he will judge the world in righteousness by a man whom he has appointed; and of this he has given assurance to all by raising him from the dead." (Acts 17:30–31)*

Jesus is glorified in salvation that comes through judgment. He will be beautiful in His mercy and in His wrath. We tend to emphasize the glory of Jesus in His ability to redeem, but His judgments are part of the "good news" we carry.[1] We need to fill the earth with Jesus' generous offer of salvation, but His judgments are part of His plan of salvation.

His judgments liberate the cosmos from darkness and bring about the restoration of creation. In judgment, He demonstrates His nature and His commitment to His creation. Furthermore, Jesus' offer of mercy only makes sense in light of His judgments.

Jesus' work of salvation is incomplete without His judgments, and if we neglect that message, we preach an incomplete gospel.

The gospel is more than the redemption of individuals; it is a promise that the cosmos will be redeemed through the rule of the Son of Man and His kingdom. This promise cannot be fully realized until Jesus comes in His judgments to break the power and influence of darkness, and punish those who embrace this darkness. As a result, creation is groaning for the day of His judgments.[2]

God is a good Judge, and He will not stay silent forever.[3] Those who contribute to the corruption of His creation will be judged, and that judgment will bring about salvation for creation *and* those who are in Jesus.

Judgment is only controversial because most humans do not agree they should be judged. We all know a good judge punishes criminals for their crimes and removes them from society so others can flourish. We know judgment is good, but we are so self-centered we are not convinced *our evil* deserves punishment, nor do we grasp the way *our sin* corrupts God's good creation.

---

[1] For example, Paul declared Jesus as Judge when he spoke in Athens (Acts 17:31).

[2] Romans 8:22–23; 2 Corinthians 5:2, 4; Revelation 6:9–11.

[3] Isaiah 42:14–15.

HIS GLORY: THE DEMONSTRATION

Paul predicted a day will come when every creature must bow to Jesus, and they will be unable to resist because He is the exalted Son of Man. Even Jesus' fiercest enemies will be unable to resist His majesty when the Father demands they submit to His divine Son:

> *Therefore God has highly exalted him and bestowed on him the name that is above every name, so that at the name of Jesus every knee should bow, in heaven and on earth and under the earth, and every tongue confess that Jesus Christ is Lord, to the glory of God the Father. (Philippians 2:9–11)*

Jesus used Daniel 7 because it forced the issue of His divinity. The Person Daniel saw was divine. He could not be explained away as some sort of anointed human king. Everyone who heard Jesus' teaching then and who hears His teaching now must decide: *Is He the Son of Man or not?*

Daniel 7 was the key to unlocking Jesus' identity and other prophecies about Him. If you understood Jesus was the Daniel 7 Son of Man, you interpreted Psalm 2 and Psalm 110 correctly. If you rejected Jesus as the Son of Man, then you missed the true identity of the exalted Man in Psalm 2 and Psalm 110.

The human heart can endure tremendous delay and incredible pressure for the sake of love when the reward is clear. The revelation of Jesus in His glory gives the human heart strength to endure suffering and delay in this age. Perhaps we lack endurance in suffering because we have no biblical vision of the beauty of Jesus and have never seriously considered the reward we have been promised.

Jesus knew the revelation of His glory would give the disciples the courage necessary to receive the difficult message about suffering, so He concluded His message with a trip up a mountain and gave the disciples a glimpse of His glory.

Clarifying His Identity

From this point forward, Jesus set His face toward Jerusalem where He would be executed. He was moving into the final stage of His ministry, and His time with His disciples was running out. Because Jesus knew what was coming, every action He took was deliberate. He wanted to make sure the disciples understood His identity as He finished this stage of His ministry and began the journey to the cross.

Jesus knew what He was saying, but the disciples did not. He revealed His paradigm of suffering *before* He suffered to demonstrate His suffering was not accidental but a part of the plan for His exaltation. After Jesus' suffering, death, and ascension, the disciples could look back on Jesus' words, truly understand what He had said, and gain deep confidence in Jesus' message.

The disciples did not invent an explanation for the cross after Jesus died unexpectedly, nor did they fabricate the story of the ascension to make Jesus some sort of exalted Person. *Jesus had taught these things all along.* The shocking events of Jesus' crucifixion disturbed His disciples, but the events confirmed everything Jesus had said about Himself was true.

Jesus was Messiah, but if they saw Him only as Messiah—or even primarily as Messiah—they would misunderstand what was about to happen and become disillusioned. They needed to grasp He was the Son of Man and would suffer that way.

The Son of Man Revealed

The chapter breaks in our Bibles are a helpful tool for navigation, but they are not part of the original text. At times, they separate passages that should be read together. The chapter break at Matthew 17:1 is unfortunate because Matthew 16:13–17:13 should be treated as one unit.[1]

The Gospel authors carefully arranged the stories and teaching of Jesus to reveal who He was. Even though Matthew 17 occurred six days later than Matthew 16, it was put directly after Matthew 16 because Matthew 17 is the stunning conclusion to the message of Matthew 16.

Jesus' message in Matthew 16 ended with the prediction that He will come in glory as the Son of Man (v. 27). Jesus' words and Daniel's

---

[1]The same is true of Mark 8–9.

prophecy were enough, but Jesus wanted to give the disciples something more. He wanted to give them a demonstration.

Jesus took three of His closest disciples, climbed a mountain, and demonstrated He was the Son of Man, capable of fulfilling everything Daniel prophesied:

> *And after six days Jesus took with him Peter and James, and John his brother, and led them up a high mountain by themselves. And he was transfigured before them, and his face shone like the sun, and his clothes became white as light. (Matthew 17:1–2)*

The disciples had repeatedly *heard* Jesus' claim to be the Son of Man, but they suddenly *saw* Jesus as the exalted Son of Man. In an instant, His appearance was transformed, and He was visibly glorious and divine. It was a scene directly out of Daniel. *They were given a glimpse of the exalted Son of Man.*

No one ever doubted Jesus was a human—they doubted He was divine. Therefore, when He claimed to be the Son of Man, He was accused of blasphemy.[2] The ultimate point of the encounter in Matthew 17 was to prove Jesus was not only fully human, but also divine. To emphasize the point, Jesus' glory in His transfiguration was described in language Daniel had applied to the Ancient of Days:

> *"As I looked, thrones were placed, and the Ancient of Days took his seat; his clothing was white as snow, and the hair of his head like pure wool; his throne was fiery flames; its wheels were burning fire." (Daniel 7:9)*

When the Son of Man—Jesus of Nazareth—appears in glory, He looks like the Ancient of Days. In Daniel's vision, the Ancient of Days had brilliant white garments and was surrounded by fire. In the transfiguration, Jesus wore brilliant white garments, and His face shone like the fiery sun. It was a profound demonstration of His divinity.

This vision of Jesus was so significant that Peter used it years later to give the church courage to endure suffering:

> *For we did not follow cleverly devised myths when we made known to you the power and coming of our Lord Jesus Christ, but we were eyewitnesses of his majesty. For when he received honor and glory from God the Father, and the voice*

---

[2]Matthew 26:64–65; Mark 14:62–64; Luke 5:21–24.

was borne to him by the Majestic Glory, "This is my beloved Son, with whom I am well pleased," we ourselves heard this very voice borne from heaven, for we were with him on the holy mountain. (2 Peter 1:16–18)

Peter's description of Jesus in glory "on the holy mountain" likely reminded his readers of Israel's encounter with God around Mount Sinai because Peter described seeing God's glory visibly and hearing His audible voice on a mountain.[3] When Jesus appeared to the disciples the way YHWH appeared to Israel in the transfiguration, it was a revelation of YHWH.

Jesus was showing Himself to be YHWH.

The disciples were stunned. They knew Jesus was not an ordinary human, but they had not encountered His glory. What came next was surprising but also right out of Daniel 7:

And behold, there appeared to them Moses and Elijah, talking with him. And Peter said to Jesus, "Lord, it is good that we are here. If you wish, I will make three tents here, one for you and one for Moses and one for Elijah." (Matthew 17:3–4)

Jesus was not alone in His glory. He was accompanied by the saints. Moses' and Elijah's appearances were not described, but they were so majestic, and the disciples were tempted to honor them with structures.[4] The glory resting on the two saints with Jesus was a demonstration that Jesus was capable of fulfilling Daniel's prophecy of a glorified people who will inherit the kingdom with the Son of Man.

Peter's response to the sight revealed how profound that glory will be because he was tempted to build "shelters" for all three, implying the desire to worship. Mark's account explains why Peter gave such a strange answer:

For he did not know what to say, for they were terrified. (Mark 9:6)

The disciples were terrified by the glory of the Son of Man and the glory of the saints.

---

[3]Mount Sinai is not called the *holy mountain* in the Old Testament, but the revelation of God in glory and speaking audibly would have brought Sinai to mind (Exodus 19–20).

[4]See Luke 9:31.

To eliminate all confusion, the Father quickly addressed the situation:

> *He was still speaking when, behold, a bright cloud overshadowed them, and a voice from the cloud said, "This is my beloved Son, with whom I am well pleased; listen to him." When the disciples heard this, they fell on their faces and were terrified. (Matthew 17:5–6)*

The message of the encounter was simple and straightforward: Jesus is the divine Human, and He is forming an exalted, immortal humanity who will rule forever. When the saints are glorified, their glory will resemble the glory of the Son of Man. The saints are going to be so much like the Son of Man that, when Peter saw the future glory of the saints, he was tempted to worship them.[5] The scene was a profound commitment to the promise that Jesus reiterated in Matthew 16:27: When He comes in the glory of His Father, He will transform a people to share His glory.

Though the future glory of the saints can tempt a mortal to worship, there is One who stands alone. Jesus was the only One described like the Ancient of Days. *Jesus, Moses, and Elijah were all majestic, but Jesus alone shared the glory of the Ancient of Days.* He is part of the exalted humanity, but He also stands alone as the beloved, divine Son of the Ancient of Days. He alone is to be worshipped.

The transfiguration was the exclamation point on Jesus' teaching about His identity. No human could appear like the Ancient of Days unless He was divine. On the mountain, Jesus settled the issue—He was the Son of Man.

The disciples had seen a glimpse of what Daniel saw, but Jesus reminded them that His glory was connected to His suffering:

> *And as they were coming down the mountain, Jesus commanded them, "Tell no one the vision, until the Son of Man is raised from the dead." "... So also the Son of Man will certainly suffer at their hands." (Matthew 17:9, 12)*

He would be the suffering Son of Man. The disciples were still struggling to grasp Jesus' full identity, so He gave them an unusual re-

---

[5]Romans 8:18, 29; 1 Corinthians 2:9; 15:49; 2 Corinthians 3:18; Philippians 3:21; 2 Peter 1:3–4; 1 John 3:2.

quest: They were not to tell the vision until He had risen from the dead.

This request was unusual because Jesus never hid His identity as the Son of Man. However, Jesus had a reason for this request. Because the disciples had seen Jesus' glory, they were eager to call people to follow Him. However, the glory of the Son of Man had to be revealed through His suffering before the mission could begin.

The entire event confirmed everything Jesus had spoken:

- He was the exalted Son of Man.

- His exaltation was connected to His suffering.

- He would rise from the dead in His glory as the Son of Man.

- The saints who followed His path of exaltation through suffering would rise in glory as well.

On a High Mountain

The purpose of the spectacular transfiguration scene was to demonstrate everything Jesus had said about His identity as the Son of Man was true. Jesus' choice of a "high mountain" for His transfiguration was very strategic.

Jesus … led them up a high mountain. (Matthew 17:1)

The description of a high mountain is designed to remind us of an earlier moment on a "high mountain":

Again, the devil took him to a very high mountain and showed him all the kingdoms of the world and their glory. And he said to him, "All these I will give you, if you will fall down and worship me." (Matthew 4:8–9)

These are the only two events Matthew recorded on a high mountain. In the first event (Matthew 4), the devil offered Jesus all the kingdoms of this world in return for worship. In other words, he offered Jesus dominion over all the beasts of Daniel 7. Jesus could have become the most powerful of all the beasts if He had simply worshiped the one who led the beasts.

Jesus was destined for dominion over the beasts, but He had to take dominion over the beasts through suffering.

In the second event (Matthew 17), Jesus ascended a mountain to demonstrate His superiority over the beasts as the exalted Son of Man who will destroy all the beasts. The message was straightforward: *Jesus will not inherit the kingdoms of this world. He will replace them and bring an everlasting kingdom.*

Matthew did not name the mountain that Jesus ascended with His disciples, so we cannot be completely certain which mountain Jesus ascended. However, the last location named in the story was Caesarea Philippi which was at the base of Mount Hermon, which is by far the highest mountain in the region. We have already seen that mountain had a long association with evil power from the Enoch tradition to the pagan worship in Jesus' day.

Mount Hermon symbolized the rule of the spiritual beasts, and Jesus' transfiguration was a statement of superiority over the beasts. He would triumph over them and destroy their power. After declaring His identity in Caesarea Philippi, it is very possible Jesus ascended Mount Hermon to make a statement and demonstrate His supremacy over the beasts on the very mountain associated with their rule.

Even if Jesus ascended another mountain, an ancient reader would have made the connection. Jesus' ascent of a high mountain after He declared supremacy over the beasts at Caesarea Philippi would have brought to mind Mount Hermon because the point of the transfiguration was to demonstrate His superiority over the beasts associated with "high places" like Hermon.

The Son of Man Coming in His Kingdom

All three accounts of the transfiguration are preceded by the same prediction:[6]

> *"Truly, I say to you, there are some standing here who will not taste death until they see the Son of Man coming in his kingdom." (Matthew 16:28)*

This passage has been a source of debate and confusion because people assume Jesus was speaking about His rule as the messianic king. Because Jesus obviously did not begin to rule as a king on the earth in His first coming, Christians have been struggling to interpret this for nearly two thousand years. However, the interpretation is clear when it is read in context.

---

[6] See also Mark 9:1; Luke 9:27.

As we saw in a previous chapter, Jesus' suffering and resurrection were part of His exaltation as the *Son of Man*. These events did not not begin the messianic rule on the earth the prophets predicted; it set the stage for it.[7] Right now, God is offering mercy to the nations before Jesus comes to rule as King and replace every other kingdom:[8]

> *I charge you in the presence of God and of Christ Jesus, who is to judge the living and the dead, and by his appearing and by his kingdom.... (2 Timothy 4:1)*

This has been misunderstood throughout history because people have assumed Jesus began to rule the kingdom as Messiah in His first coming. In order to reconcile this assumption with the fact that Jesus did not begin to rule on the earth, many have attempted to redefine the role of Messiah to better fit the events of the first century. This is well meaning but unhelpful because it adds confusion. The New Testament makes it plain that Jesus will rule as the messianic king in the future. He first had to be enthroned as the Son of Man.

The Gospel authors arranged their material very intentionally and in all three gospels Jesus' prediction that people would see the Son of Man and His kingdom coming in power was followed by the story of the transfiguration. This means each author expected us to read this statement in light of the transfiguration.

The transfiguration was a demonstration of Jesus' identity as Son of Man, so we should read Matthew 16:28 as a prediction of Jesus' exaltation as the Son of Man which is precisely what occurred after Jesus' suffering. Jesus' ascension in Acts 1 enthroned Him as the king Daniel saw coming from the heavens, and in that sense those who saw the ascension saw the heavenly ruler (divine Human) set into place.

Jesus now rules in the heavens as a divine Man who will descend as King. Because the kingdom of God is a kingdom that descends from heaven, Jesus' ascension set the stage for everything Daniel saw and every messianic promise to be fulfilled. However, His ascension did not replace His future exaltation on the earth as Messiah. The messianic kingdom on the earth still must come.

---

[7] Acts 1:6–7; 3:19–21.

[8] Acts 17:30–31.

JESUS' IDENTITY IS CENTRAL TO THE GOSPEL

Jesus asked, "Who do people say that the Son of Man is?"[1] because His identity is central to the gospel. He is the ultimate revelation of God *and* man.

The knowledge of God comes through Jesus because He reveals to us what God is like:

> Long ago, at many times and in many ways, God spoke to our fathers by the prophets, but in these last days he has spoken to us by his Son, whom he appointed the heir of all things, through whom also he created the world. He is the radiance of the glory of God and the exact imprint of his nature, and he upholds the universe by the word of his power. (Hebrews 1:1–3)

Because Jesus is fully man, He also reveals to us who man was always meant to be. Through the knowledge of Jesus, we find out what man was meant to be and what is required to redeem and restore man to fellowship with God.

When we do not perceive Jesus correctly, we begin to lose clarity on the gospel, and Matthew 16 provides one of the best examples of this. Peter was both commended *and* rebuked as Satan within a few verses because He perceived aspects of Jesus' identity while not perceiving other aspects.

---

[1]Matthew 16:13.

There are many things the church needs, but perhaps most of all we need clear, biblical, passionate preaching[2] of the Person of Jesus. The message of salvation is deeply rooted in the beauty and majesty of Jesus. The beauty of God is what makes God desirable and sin so hideous. His beauty and majesty reveal our desperate need for redemption and transformation.

That salvation only occurs through the Person of Jesus, the Son of Man.

The Gospel Begins with God

The gospel does not begin with man—it begins with God. What God has done through Jesus offers tremendous benefits for humanity, but that does not mean the message revolves around man. It benefits us, and God enjoys us, but we are not the center. The gospel revolves around what God has revealed about Himself by becoming a man in the Person of Jesus and suffering and dying to redeem, restore, and resurrect His creation.

The biblical gospel of the kingdom is not a message just about how Jesus can serve man's calling. It is a message about the majesty of Jesus, His calling, and the incredible lengths He has taken so that we can know Him and participate in His rule and His reign.

Jesus consistently confronted the disciples with His identity as the Son of Man because they understood His identity through their own expectations. They were looking for a Messiah who would deliver them from their political oppression. Their expectation was correct, but it needed to be put in the right context. The disciples were captured with their own national aspirations, but they needed to be captured by Jesus' identity.

Some Christians look down on the disciples for their nationalistic hopes, but the same kind of thinking exists in the church today. Jesus is often presented as Savior who primarily exists so we can be successful and happy. He is often presented as a means to our end. As a result, the hope of the gospel is often portrayed as immortality, health, peace, and comfort when in reality the hope of the gospel is intimate and relational knowledge of God without experiencing His wrath.

---

[2]When I use the word *preaching*, I mean the function of proclamation. This is not limited to a pastor's Sunday morning service. Every believer can "preach" or proclaim the beauty of Jesus in the sphere they have been given. Jesus can be proclaimed in a simple conversation with a business colleague, family member, or friend.

The disciples longed for the hope of Israel, and modern man longs for the hope of his own prosperity. While Jesus will take great delight in fulfilling Israel's promises[3] and in bringing His people into glory, the gospel can never fundamentally be about our own benefits. Whenever Jesus becomes a means to our own end, He becomes "Messiah" when He must be "Son of Man" first.

He will take great delight in being "Messiah" to us, but only when He is first received as "Son of Man."

Our gospel is the gospel of the kingdom because a kingdom is defined by its king. It is a message about Jesus' glory ruling and reigning before it is a message about our rewards. Too many are enamored with things that are secondary. Ancient Israel was enamored with Israel. We are enamored with our own prosperity and our own inheritance in the kingdom.

As long as anything captivates us more than the beauty of Jesus, we are using Jesus as a means to an end and using Him as a method to obtain the things we find truly valuable and truly beautiful. The biblical gospel revolves around the glory of the Son of Man, and we need to become captivated by His majesty.

Who do we say the Son of Man is? Is He truly the most beautiful and majestic Person? Is He truly the ultimate Prize?

The Beauty of the Divine Man
In Isaiah, we find an outrageous statement about Jesus:

> *He had no form or majesty that we should look at him, and no beauty that we should desire him. (53:2)*

Isaiah predicted Jesus would not have any natural beauty. Because Isaiah's words are familiar, we can easily overlook just how surprising these words are. The Messiah of God, the ultimate human King—God in the flesh—has no natural majesty or beauty that is appealing to humans.

Isaiah's prophecy was demonstrated in the Gospels. People were not in awe of Jesus' appearance. If anything, it was the opposite. He appeared very ordinary to them.[4] People did not show Jesus any unusu-

---

[3]Acts 1:6–8; 3:19–21.

[4]Matthew 13:46, 55–58; Mark 6:4–5; Luke 4:22–24; John 12:34.

al respect or attention on the basis of human appearance. Even John the Baptist, who prepared the way for Jesus, did not recognize Jesus until the Holy Spirit rested on Jesus.[5]

The subject of Jesus' beauty is a paradox. He possesses beauty beyond any other human and yet does not possess what humans consider to be beautiful. The reason for this paradox is simple: *Jesus' beauty does not flow from His humanity; it flows from His divinity.*

When we see Jesus, we are seeing a divine Human, and His divinity is what makes Him beautiful. He is not beautiful because He is the "ultimate Man" by a human standard. His beauty is not a natural beauty—it is a transcendent beauty. It is a revelation of the beauty no man could see before God became human.

Moses could not see God's beauty, but we can see it in the face of Jesus.[6] If we look at Jesus as a human and look for beauty, we will not see it. If we see Him as God in a human body, we will be staggered by the beauty of who He is.

Most pictures of Jesus are evidence that we do not perceive the true nature of His beauty. We continue to create pictures of Jesus that present Him as a handsome, attractive man according to our cultural definitions of His beauty. For example, in the West, Jesus is often presented as an attractive white man with blue eyes and soft features. Nearly all pictures of Jesus look nothing like a middle eastern man from the first century who has "no beauty we should desire him."

We are still captivated by human thinking, and therefore, we tend to make Jesus in our own image, according to our own definition of beauty, rather than allowing what Scripture has revealed about Him to redefine our understanding of true beauty.

Until we grasp the fact that Jesus' beauty flows from His divinity, we will not see Him correctly, and we will continue to view Jesus as a more perfect human, and we will continue to have a humanistic gospel. Jesus did not come to improve our humanity and make us more perfect versions of man. Jesus came to make us in the image of God.

The New Testament warns us not to pursue beauty according to human terms because our beauty flows from the image of God in us,

---

[5]John 1:31–34.

[6]Exodus 3:6; 33:18–20; 2 Corinthians 3:18; 4:6.

not because of our human form.[7] Many Christians are hoping to become ultimate humans through the gospel, but that is not the hope of the gospel. The saints are not going to become "beautiful" humans. The gospel promises the saints will become transformed humans by demonstrating the beauty of God.

The people of the Son of Man will be beautiful in the way He is beautiful. While He alone is divine, the saints are like Him because they have God dwelling inside of them through the Holy Spirit. Like Jesus, the beauty of the saints flows from the demonstration of God's nature in us. The saints will never be beautiful the way "beautiful people" are in this age. The splendor of the saints will flow from the degree to which God is expressed in their human form.

As long as we view Jesus as a beautiful human, we do not fully grasp the gospel. His beauty flows from His divinity. In His human frame, we would not find Him attractive according to human definitions of beauty. As a result, people continue to reject Him. If the Holy Spirit does not release revelation, human rejection of Jesus is perfectly normal because He is not beautiful according to human definition. He is beautiful as God.

If God is beautiful to us, Jesus will be beautiful. If God is not attractive to us, Jesus will be repulsive to us.

Preaching the Kingdom

Paul consistently reminded the saints of their inheritance in the kingdom,[8] but anytime the kingdom becomes more preeminent than the Son of Man, we have lost sight of the biblical gospel of the kingdom.

If we honestly evaluate the songs and sermons that fill our churches, can we truthfully say we primarily preach Jesus, or do we primarily preach our personal reward in the kingdom?

Do our songs, our conversations, our books, and our sermons reveal a deep fascination with the Son of Man, or are we more fascinated by our own assignments, callings, destinies, and imagined futures? Does the gospel we preach truly revolve around the Son of Man both in our words and in our practice, or does it revolve around us?

---

[7]1 Timothy 2:9–10; 1 Peter 3:3–4.

[8]Romans 14:17; 1 Corinthians 6:9–10; 15:50; Galatians 5:21; Ephesians 5:5; Colossians 1:13; 1 Thessalonians 2:12; 2 Thessalonians 1:5; 2 Timothy 4:1, 18.

The gospel of the kingdom must start with the King.

The Revelation of Jesus

The revelation of the identity of Jesus has profound power to transform the human heart:

- Moses was commissioned by his vision of Jesus.[9]
- Isaiah was completely undone by his majestic vision of Jesus.[10]
- Ezekiel's ministry flowed from a stunning vision of Jesus.[11]
- All of Daniel's visions revolved around his vision of Jesus.[12]
- The disciples saw Jesus transfigured in His glory.
- The apostle Paul's life was revolutionized by his vision of Jesus.[13]
- John the apostle could not stand up when he saw Jesus in glory.[14]

Each of these stories carries a profound message: *The revelation of Jesus brings profound transformation.* Paul reminded the church in Corinth that the transformation of the human heart begins with beholding the majesty of Jesus:

> *And we all, with unveiled face, beholding the glory of the Lord, are being transformed into the same image from one degree of glory to another. For this comes from the Lord who is the Spirit. (2 Corinthians 3:18)*

How many churches have made beholding the beauty of God corporately part of their discipleship strategy? According to Paul, this is where discipleship begins.[15]

Even the disciples were tempted to worship two glorified saints on the Mount of Transfiguration. Beholding the glory of the Son of Man

---

[9]Exodus 3.

[10]Isaiah 6; John 12:41.

[11]Ezekiel 1.

[12]Daniel 7.

[13]Acts 9.

[14]Revelation 1.

[15]See also 1 John 3:2.

keeps us from being enamored with human glory and our future inheritance. We need to know the weight of our inheritance, but we need to behold the majesty of the Son of Man so we do not become enamored with ourselves. Any real glory we ever possess is really *His* glory shared with us. Like Paul, we must decide to *know* Christ and Him crucified:

> For I decided to know nothing among you except Jesus Christ and him crucified. (1 Corinthians 2:2)

We need to ask ourselves if Paul's priority is our priority. Have we allowed our desires, dreams, hopes, and emotions to be shaped by this same thinking? Paul's message and his focus were not accidental. Paul *decided* to make Jesus and Him crucified his central focus.

The revelation of Jesus is not only for a few privileged individuals who had an encounter for a specific purpose.

Because Jesus is alive and the Bible is a divinely inspired book, the Holy Spirit can take the revelation of Jesus recorded in Scripture and make it real to our inner man. The Spirit loves to do this, and when He reveals Jesus to us through the Scripture, that revelation can be just as profound, true, and life-altering as it was for the ones who wrote it down.

The apostle Paul had a profound experience with Jesus on the road to Damascus that transformed him and changed world history.[16] He apparently also had another mystical experience he could not even speak about.[17] Paul had a profound encounter with Jesus, but he did not believe the revelation of Jesus depended on an experience like his.

Paul knew the Holy Spirit reveals the beauty of Jesus to the human heart, just as Jesus promised He would.[18] Paul's prayer for the church in Ephesus revealed His desire and expectation for the church to be full of the knowledge of Jesus:

> I do not cease to give thanks for you, remembering you in my prayers, that the God of our Lord Jesus Christ, the Father of glory, may give you the Spirit of wisdom and of revelation in the knowledge of him. (Ephesians 1:16–17)

---

[16]Acts 9.

[17]2 Corinthians 12:2–4.

[18]John 16:12–15.

JESUS' IDENTITY REVOLVED AROUND SON OF MAN

Jesus' identity in the Gospels revolved around *Son of Man* because it was the best summary of who He truly was: *YHWH in human form.*

Most Christians assume Jesus' identity revolved around Messiah, and as a result, we have misunderstood how Jesus presented Himself and, in some cases, redefined Messiah to the point He bears little resemblance to what the prophets predicted. In order to proclaim the gospel of the kingdom with clarity, we must grasp how Messiah relates to Jesus' identity as the Son of Man.

Most prophecies about Messiah in the Old Testament do not seem to describe Jesus' first coming. The prophets presented the Messiah as a political leader who judges wickedness, liberates Israel, brings peace to the nations, and rules the cosmos. Jesus, on the other hand, came relatively quietly, refused political power, suffered, died, and ascended into the heavens.

This was a profound mystery hidden in the prophets. In light of the messianic prophecies, it was incredibly confusing—particularly for Israel. When we carefully consider the way Jesus presented Himself, we can better understand the mystery. This mystery is the reason Jesus did not primarily present Himself as Messiah. Once we grasp Son of Man, not Messiah, was the central description of Jesus' identity, things become much easier to understand.

Son of Man—The Central Description of Jesus' Identity

Son of Man was the most complete description of Jesus' identity because His other titles all fall under that central identity. For example, let's consider two of Jesus' other prominent titles: *Suffering Servant* and *Messiah.*

Isaiah described Jesus as a Suffering Servant,[1] and this aspect of who Jesus is was profoundly demonstrated in His first coming through His voluntary embrace of suffering and death. It will always be part of His identity. For example, John saw Jesus exalted in heaven as a slain Lamb.[2]

Messiah is another one of Jesus' titles. It describes His rule over Israel and the nations as King. Jesus will rule as Messiah as a result of His second coming. When He returns, He will judge the wicked, liberate Israel, rule the nations, and bring about the restoration of the earth.

These titles are important, but they cannot fully define Jesus' identity. Jesus' suffering was completely unique, but there have been others in history who have suffered on behalf of a people. There is also no king like Jesus, but there have been other great kings throughout history.

Jesus is not unique because He suffered or because He will rule. He is completely unique because He is God in the flesh.

The Suffering Servant and Messiah are not descriptions of a great human. They are titles that describe what God looks like when He becomes a man. When God becomes a man, He is the ultimate Suffering Servant because God is ultimately self-sacrificing. When God becomes man, He is the ultimate King (Messiah), because God is the majestic Ruler of the cosmos.

The Suffering Servant is unique from every other suffering man because it is God suffering as a man. The Messiah is greater than any other leader because it is God as King. Again, Jesus' divine identity is what makes His suffering and His rule completely unique. These titles are expressions of divinity in human form, and they belong to Jesus because He is the revelation of God in human flesh.

Jesus suffered as God, and He will rule as God. This is what sets Him apart from every other man in history.

Son of Man is Jesus' fundamental identity in the Gospels because it defines Him as the divine Human—the uncreated God who descends from the heavens as a man. Some see Jesus as a martyr, but He is greater than His suffering. Ancient Israel wanted Jesus to become King, but He is more than a King. Jesus did not come to reveal suffering or

---

[1] Isaiah 42:1–9; 49:1–6; 50:2–9; 53.

[2] Revelation 5:6.

kingship. He came to reveal God. In His suffering and His rule, we discover what God is like—therefore, He must primarily be identified as God.

Taken independently, Suffering Servant and Messiah seem to be at odds with one another, but when these are understood as expressions of the divine nature, they become unified. As a result, Jesus consistently unified His identity around Son of Man.

Because Jesus' suffering flowed from His divine identity, when Jesus alluded to Isaiah 53:10, He predicted He was a Servant who would give His life as a ransom, but He identified Himself as the Son of Man:

> *"For even the Son of Man came not to be served but to serve, and to give his life as a ransom for many." (Mark 10:45)*

We would expect Jesus to predict His death as the Suffering Servant or the suffering Messiah,[3] but He did not in order to clearly communicate He was going to suffer *as God*.

Likewise, we would expect Jesus to describe Himself as Messiah when He predicted His judgments and dominion over the nations, but He did not. He always predicted the Son of Man would execute judgment and sit on a glorious throne. Even when Jesus was put on trial and commanded to identify if He was Messiah, He affirmed His messianic identity by stating He was the Son of Man.[4] Son of Man is so central to His function as Messiah that He warned us not to pay attention to any messiah (christ) who does not come with the clouds of heaven as Daniel predicted. He will descend as God to rule.

Jesus' use of language was very intentional. He wanted to make sure we understood *who* He was. *God* would suffer. *God* will rule. *God* will judge the nations. And He will do it as a man.

Jesus emphasized this in Luke 18:

---

[3]Jesus said the "Christ must suffer" one time in Luke 24:26. This was said after His resurrection in order to re-orient the disciples' thinking about Messiah. Before Jesus died, He only described His suffering as the Son of Man. This is the only time Jesus connected Messiah and suffering, so in light of the Gospel witness, Jesus overwhelmingly presented Himself as Son of Man in His suffering. Jesus likely shifted His language because He was about to ascend, and the ascension set the stage for Jesus to come as Messiah.

[4]Matthew 26:64; Mark 14:62; Luke 22:69.

Everything that is written about the Son of Man by the prophets will be accomplished. (v. 31)

The prophets spoke about the Messiah, the Suffering Servant, and the Judge, but Jesus did not use those titles in Luke 18. He said everything written about the Son of Man must be accomplished. Jesus organized His identity this way for a very simple reason: He wants us to know Him as He truly is. While it's certainly not incorrect to say the Messiah is divine or the Messiah had to suffer, it's not precisely how Jesus presented Himself. These titles all flow from His divinity expressing itself through His humanity.

He primarily presented Himself as the Son of Man instead of Messiah, Suffering Servant, or any other title because His chief goal was to reveal Himself as the full demonstration of who God is when He becomes a man.[5]

The Son of Man Is the Bridegroom

There's one other important title in the Gospels we should mention: *Bridegroom.* John the Baptist referred to Jesus as the Bridegroom:

> *The one who has the bride is the bridegroom. The friend of the bridegroom, who stands and hears him, rejoices greatly at the bridegroom's voice. Therefore this joy of mine is now complete. (John 3:29)*

The title *Bridegroom* was significant because YHWH was the Bridegroom of Israel. When that title was applied to Jesus, it emphasized His divinity. Though YHWH presented Himself as a Bridegroom on Mount Sinai, Jesus' humanity enables Him to be a much greater revelation of God as a Bridegroom. John spoke of Jesus as the Bridegroom, but Jesus will fully reveal God as a Bridegroom in the second coming.

God Revealed in Human Form

Jesus is not just a Messiah who happens to be divine. The Romans thought their kings were divine. Nor is He a suffering figure who happens to be divine. He is first and foremost the uncreated God, and when the uncreated God takes on human flesh, He suffers and He rules—not simply because there is a need for either of these, but because it is who God is.

---

[5]John 1:14; 10:30; Colossians 2:9; Hebrews 1:1–3.

Ancient Israel was willing to receive Jesus as King, but not God. Plenty of people have been willing to see Jesus as some sort of noble, suffering martyr, but not divine. However, the question is not whether Jesus can rule or whether His suffering was noble.

The gospel confronts us with one ultimate question: Is Jesus is the one true God in human form? If He is, then everything else falls into place. If He is not, then the rest is meaningless, so Jesus emphasized one title to confront us with who He is.

Jesus is the ultimate revelation of who God is, and everything that He is flows from His divinity; therefore, His primary identity had to be one which presented Him as YHWH in human form.

The prophets all saw in part[6] and, as a result, saw different aspects of what Jesus would do. Jesus used Daniel to unlock and unify the prophecies made about Him.

The idea Jesus came as the Messiah is so embedded in Christian thinking that we tend to interpret His entire message and life through that lens. Of course, Jesus is Messiah. We do not want to overcorrect and dismiss His messianic assignment. However, when we make Messiah Jesus' dominant identity, we add an element of confusion to the gospel by trying to put everything onto that assignment when Jesus did not. It is possible to explain the gospel that way, but it is not the way Jesus chose to do it.

When Jesus is received as the Son of Man, He is received as the Messiah as well. However, the inverse is not necessarily true—in Matthew 21, people were ready to receive Jesus as Messiah, but not as YHWH.

Though it is a beautiful—and important—part of His identity, Jesus did not publicly announce the Davidic Messiah—the King of Israel—had arrived. Instead, He declared, *"I am the One like a Son of Man —the ruler of the everlasting kingdom."* That is our message to the nations. God has appeared. He has suffered for our sake, and He is going to rule over us.

The Gospels emphasize Jesus' identity is at the heart of the gospel, and we must learn to present the gospel the way Jesus did—especially when speaking to Israel. Speaking the gospel to Israel the way Jesus did does not make the gospel less controversial, but it does make it clearer.

---

[6]1 Corinthians 13:9, 12.

Jesus is not just Messiah; He is the *Son of Man*—YHWH in human form.

THE CORE ELEMENTS OF JESUS' GOSPEL

Matthew 16–17 gives us a summary of the core elements Jesus included in the gospel of the kingdom. Jesus used Daniel 7 as the foundation of each element, demonstrating He used Daniel's prophecy as a framework to proclaim the gospel of the kingdom.

The events recorded in these two chapters emphasize the core elements of the gospel of the kingdom. When we list the core elements we can easily see they are a basic summary of the main themes of Daniel 7.

The identity of Jesus is at the heart of the gospel. God has become a man, and He is the main message of the gospel. He must be received as the preeminent and divine Son of Man. He is the divine Human *first,* and then He is Messiah, Savior, and Suffering Servant.

The cross is at the center of His identity. He is the suffering Son of Man. Any view of Jesus that denies His suffering is in direct opposition to who He is. The cross is central to who God is, and therefore, Jesus' exaltation came through His suffering. His suffering reveals His nature. The necessity of His suffering also reveals the nature of man and of sin because the death and suffering of God were required for man to be reconciled to God and become part of Jesus' people.

He is gathering a people. Jesus is looking for a people whom He will transform into His own image. He calls this people to embrace His path of exaltation through suffering, and those who follow Him will be greatly rewarded and exalted in the age to come. They will inherit the kingdom and all dominion with the Son of Man. Jesus used the promise of reward at His second coming in glory as motivation to embrace self-denial in this age and become like Him.

Jesus will be given a kingdom. Jesus will be given a kingdom, and this kingdom will be the context for the fulfillment of what the prophets predicted. This kingdom is the kingdom of Israel. It is not a redefinition of Israel, but it is a radical expansion of Israel. It will be much greater than any of Israel's historical kingdoms. The kingdom will come to the earth when the Son of Man comes with the clouds. The kingdom will be the ultimate salvation of Israel, but it will not be limited to the people of Israel. People from all nations will be brought into the kingdom.

Jesus will come as Judge. Jesus is coming to execute the judgment of God. The Son of Man appeared to Daniel in a judgment scene, and the Son of Man will appear in the sight of the nations in judgment because salvation will come through judgment. His judgment is part of His glory, and it sets the stage for His redemption of the cosmos. He will judge the beasts and bring an end to their rule, and an end to the powers of this age. He will set up an everlasting kingdom and reward the saints.

A day is coming when the full majesty and glory of Jesus will be revealed. What is currently hidden will be revealed. Jesus will be transfigured and unveiled in the sight of the world; however, it will not happen until He comes with the clouds. At the time of His second coming, His majesty will be made known.[1]

Jesus only made a few key points in Matthew 16–17, but these key points summarize a robust gospel and reveal Daniel was shown a concise summary of the gospel of the kingdom.

The gospel message in the New Testament basically follows along these lines. The apostles proclaimed the Person of Jesus, attested to the suffering of Jesus, issued an invitation to become part of His people, and warned Jesus will come as the Judge who has all authority in heaven and on the earth.

Proclaiming the Kingdom

The New Testament describes the church as a people in the nations who are ambassadors of another kingdom.[2] We live in the kingdoms of this world, but we represent another kingdom. Using this analogy, the church can be described as an embassy of the kingdom. In the same way that a country's embassy is not the fullness of that country but a

---

[1]Revelation 1:1.

[2]2 Corinthians 5:20; Ephesians 6:20; Philippians 3:20.

representation of it, so also the church in this age is not the fullness of the kingdom, but it points to the kingdom that is coming.

The church in this age is not the fullness of the kingdom, but each church is a valid expression of the kingdom. Churches are a present expression of a future reality, and when people come into the church, they experience the values and the power of the kingdom to which the church points. Our assignment in this age is to build as many "embassies" of the coming kingdom as we can.

The assignment of the church is relatively straightforward:

- Proclaim the gospel of the kingdom—the good news of the coming kingdom.
- Invite people to submit to the King to obtain citizenship in the coming kingdom.
- Warn the nations that the coming kingdom will replace and judge the beast kingdoms of this age.
- Train people to live in the kingdom according to the values of the King.
- Build as many "embassies" of the kingdom (churches) as possible.

Conclusion

Daniel is far more central to the Gospels than most people realize. Jesus referenced Daniel 7 far more than any other passage. He used it to summarize His identity and lay the foundations of the New Testament gospel. According to the apostle John, it would be impossible to record everything Jesus taught and did,[3] and this makes the use of Daniel in the Gospels even more significant.

The authors of the Gospels could not capture everything about Jesus, so they wrote down the things that presented the best portrait of who Jesus was and provided the best summary of His message. Everything they wrote down was part of a very intentional portrait of Jesus, and they wrote the gospels so we would look at Jesus and His gospel through the lens of Daniel 7.

It would take a much bigger volume than this to consider every use of Daniel and every possible allusion to Daniel in the Gospels. Howev-

---

[3]John 21:25.

er, we have examined enough passages to demonstrate Jesus consistently used Daniel in a way He did not use other passages of Scripture.

The reason is simple: There is no other text that brings together as many key gospel themes in a concise and yet remarkably complete prophetic message. As a result, Jesus referenced Daniel 7 far more than any other Old Testament passage.

THE IMPLICATIONS OF DANIEL 7

For nearly two thousand years, the church typically has tried to grasp who Jesus is through a Messiah-centric lens. Of course this is not entirely wrong because the apostles frequently applied the title *Christ* to Jesus. (In the second volume, we will examine how this relates to Jesus' preference for Son of Man.) While Jesus is certainly Messiah, we must understand and interpret His messianic identity through the lens of Daniel 7. The fact most Christians are unaware Daniel 7 is the passage Jesus referenced more than any other passage is evidence we do not fully grasp how Jesus revealed Himself.

Jesus' messianic identity is a core part of who He is, but it must be understood through the lens of Daniel 7. Messiah is not the starting point for understanding who He is. To understand Jesus, you must begin with His divine identity. He is God who has become a man. His identity as Messiah is an outworking of His identity as the divine Human—the Son of Man. When you begin with Messiah, you seek to understand how a man is also God. When you begin with Son of Man, you understand God has become a man and as that man is a great king among many other things.

Rethinking Christology, Missiology, and Eschatology

This book cannot consider all the implications of Jesus' use of Daniel 7, but there are at least three things that are profoundly affected by a proper understanding of how Jesus presented Himself. It is important we give careful attention to each of these so we can fill the earth with a bold and clear witness of who Jesus is before He returns.

The first is Christology. Christology is the word generally used to describe how we understand the Person, message, and work of Jesus. By now, it should be clear that Christology must begin by examining Jesus, His words, and His work through the lens of Daniel 7. Throughout history the church has traditionally developed Christology through the lens of Jesus as Messiah, and much effort has been spent to demonstrate how Jesus presented Himself as the divine Messiah. That work is valuable, but it must be re-examined through the lens of Daniel 7.

The church needs a strong Christology based on Jesus' identity as Son of Man. As Crispin Fletcher-Louis has noted:[1]

> *When Peter and Caiaphas think in terms of Jesus as the "Messiah" or the "Son of God" (Mark 8:29; 14:61 and pars.), Jesus talks instead about the Son of Man (Mark 8:30; 14:62 and pars.). And it is the title that, for Jesus, fully expresses the heart of his own Christological self-claim."*

Son of Man is "the title that, for Jesus, fully expresses the heart of His own Christological self-claim." Jesus did not primarily present Himself as a messiah who was also divine, but as God who had become a human and subsequently was the promised Messiah. The difference may seem subtle, but it is significant. While the church has largely come to the correct conclusions about Jesus' identity, Jesus' identity and majesty are much clearer when we follow the way Jesus revealed Himself.

The second is missiology. Missiology is a word used to describe the message the church carries, how that message is communicated, and how churches should be discipled to obey that message.[2] Based on Jesus' pattern, we are called to present Him to the world as the Son of Man and proclaim the kingdom according to the message of Daniel 7. While every presentation of the gospel has been valuable and powerful for nearly two thousand years, we need to sharpen our gospel message with this in mind. (In the second volume, *Son of Man: The Apostles' Gospel,* we examine how the apostles used Daniel 7 as a framework for their gospel.) This is especially important for the church's witness to Israel because the Gospels make it clear Jesus wants to be presented to Israel as the Son of Man. We need to ask whether or not our gospel of the kingdom conforms to the main messages of Daniel 7 and whether we are discipling people according to the framework found in Daniel 7.

---

[1] Crispin Fletcher-Louis, *Jesus Monotheism* (Eugene: Cascade, 2015), 104.

[2] Matthew 28:19–20.

The third is eschatology. Eschatology refers to the study of the "last things" or the things typically referred to as the "end times." A lot of Christian eschatology is based on the premise that Jesus fulfilled most of the messianic promises in His first coming. In a well-meaning attempt to present Jesus as Messiah, scholars have wrestled for centuries with the predictions of the prophets and frequently ended up proposing Jesus fulfilled most of the messianic promises in His first coming in surprising, shocking, and almost completely unforeseen ways. Jesus' use of Son of Man makes it clear this is not the way Jesus saw His mission. He came the first time to secure atonement and be exalted as Son of Man so that He could fulfill most of the messianic promises in His second coming.

It is true Jesus certainly spoke and acted in symbolic ways in His first coming to demonstrate He was the true Messiah. Furthermore, the way Jesus fulfills the messianic promises will certainly be shocking and surprising. The final fulfillment of the promises will go far beyond what the prophets anticipated, but it will also be true to what the prophets spoke.

In many ways, the church has reinterpreted the prophets' expectations to the point that their oracles no longer make sense by claiming nearly all the messianic promises were fulfilled in the first coming. In order to make this interpretation work, many of Jesus' teachings and sayings have to be interpreted in excessively figurative ways, and many of His statements become overly vague and mysterious. When we view Jesus' eschatology through the lens of Daniel 7, we find He was not vague or mysterious about how His redemptive plan would be fulfilled.

This was driven by the noble desire to demonstrate Jesus is the true Messiah, but it has nearly always resulted in an eschatology that is confusing in light of the overarching arch of the Bible and does not make sense of what the prophets and the apostles expected. We need to reevaluate many of our eschatological conclusions according to what Jesus spoke and what the apostles understood would be fulfilled in the future. They fully expected Jesus to be enthroned as Judge and Messiah when He returned.

Honoring Those Who Have Gone Before
We must carefully reconsider our gospel in light of Daniel 7, but as we do we must honor the historical church. While many things need to be examined and

our gospel has not been as clear as it needs to be, the fact is the church has largely preserved an accurate summary of Jesus' identity and His message for the last two thousand years. We must value that faithful witness and the tireless work of Bible teachers. Though we have overlooked things that are important in Jesus' teaching, the church has by and large taught the correct conclusions.

We live in an unusual moment in time. There is now more access to the Scripture and information about the Scripture than any generation in history has had. Previous generations would be shocked by what we have access to. In the last hundred years or so, information about the Bible has grown exponentially, and the access we currently have to the Scripture is unprecedented. We must take advantage of this great privilege to better understand the Bible while also valuing the faithful labor of previous generations who did not have many of the benefits we now have.

SPEAKING WITH CLARITY

Jesus commissioned the church to proclaim the gospel of the kingdom. To fulfill this task, we must understand how Jesus preached the gospel, and we should present Him the way He presented Himself.

When Jesus was challenged, He did not usually appeal to miracles or unusual signs. He appealed to the fact that He was the Son of Man. When He did appeal to miracles, He used miracles as evidence He was the Son of Man.[1] He had full authority because He was the Man from the heavens, and He was going to return as the Man from heaven.

There is a significant amount of confusion and debate over the gospel in our generation. A lot of the confusion comes from not understanding how Jesus presented Himself and, more specifically, how Jesus used Daniel to unlock all the Scriptures said about Him. Most Christians know information about the gospel but do not know the gospel of the kingdom in the way Jesus proclaimed it.

The gospel carries power to transform the heart and cause the hearer to love Jesus, so we should not overly criticize the faithful proclamation of the gospel through church history. Every preaching of the gospel that exalts Jesus is valuable. The Father enjoys it, and it carries power for salvation.[2]

In every generation, there have been many in the church who faithfully and sacrificially carried the message of the gospel as they understood it. We should not despise, minimize, or overly criticize their labor.

---

[1]Matthew 9:5–6; Mark 2:9–12; Luke 5:23–25.

[2]Romans 1:16; Philippians 1:12–18.

A Significant Moment

While we must honor the faithful witness of the church throughout history, we need also to recognize we stand in a significant moment in history.

We live in the first generation in history where the gospel could possibly be proclaimed to all people, and Jesus predicted the age would not end until the *gospel of the kingdom* is proclaimed to all people.[3] There is still a lot of work to do because nearly two billion people have yet to hear the gospel according to some estimates. However, it is possible for the first time in history that all peoples could hear the gospel within a generation. It would take significant effort on the part of the global church, but it is possible. Because we live in a such a significant moment, we must recover the simplicity and accuracy of the gospel proclaimed by Jesus.

If we are going to proclaim the gospel of the kingdom to all nations, we must understand it.

Furthermore, the church is rediscovering the biblical priority of speaking the gospel to Israel[4] because the age will also not end until God brings salvation to Israel. For the last two thousand years, the church has almost exclusively focused on the gentiles, but that focus must shift to Israel before the age ends.

In order to give a biblical witness to Israel, we need to learn how Jesus presented Himself to Israel. As gentiles, we first heard the gospel proclaimed after the suffering, death, resurrection, and ascension of Jesus. Jesus was introduced to the gentiles as the divine, suffering Messiah because we first heard the message *after* the mystery was revealed.

However, Israel has a very different story. Israel was given the covenants and the prophets[5] long before God revealed the mystery that He would become fully human, be executed for our sakes, rise from the dead, and ascend into the heavens to come again in glory. Gentiles tend to think about the coming of Jesus as the beginning of the story, but Jesus came in the middle of an unfolding story. He used the Old Testament to describe who He was and how the story would unfold.

---

[3]Matthew 24:14.

[4]Romans 1:16.

[5]Romans 9:4.

It is easy to see how the New Testament message can be incredibly challenging for Israel to grasp in light of Israel's understanding of the prophets and reasonable expectations regarding the Messiah. *Therefore, it is especially critical we follow Jesus' example when speaking to Israel.*

This will not remove all mystery or all the controversy over the Person of Jesus, but it will present a clearer presentation of who Jesus is. Jesus carefully presented Himself to His Jewish brethren, and we must do the same.

Daniel 7 is one of the most important keys to grasping the gospel of the kingdom that must be preached to all nations and the message Jesus wants carried back to His Jewish brethren.

Defending the Gospel

Understanding Jesus' presentation of the gospel not only helps us proclaim the gospel with clarity, it also answers many of the challenges raised against the gospel. Over the last hundred to two hundred years, the gospel has been under assault from critical scholars who have analyzed and questioned virtually every aspect of the Gospels. As we have repeatedly said, this debate essentially boils down to one question: *Did Jesus believe He was divine?*

As we have seen, Jesus did not present Himself the way most Christians assume. Critics have used this to claim Jesus did not think He was divine, did not present Himself as the Son of God, and did not necessarily even see Himself as Messiah. They based this critique on a combination of doubt in the reliability of the Gospels and a challenge to the way the church has interpreted Jesus' words.

These objections are answered easily with Jesus' use of Daniel.

When we grasp the way Jesus used Daniel to present His identity, there is no question Jesus boldly presented Himself as God in the flesh. This understanding combined with Jesus' historical context also helps us grasp why Jesus did not primarily present Himself as Messiah or Son of God.

In context, Jesus' use of Daniel clearly demonstrates everything about Him the church has traditionally claimed to be completely true:

- He is divine.
- He is Messiah.
- He is the Suffering Servant.

- He is the Judge.

- He has all dominion.

- He is coming with the clouds to rule and exalt a people.

While some critics refuse to accept the plain witness of Scripture, the fact remains: When Jesus is carefully examined within the context of Scripture, there is simply no question about who Jesus is. Paul and the apostles did not transform Jesus into Someone He never claimed to be; they merely expounded on what Jesus revealed about Himself through His use of Daniel.

While the apostles did not frequently use the title *Son of Man*, we will see in Volume 2 that they also used Daniel 7 as the foundation of their gospel. Once you recognize how they used Daniel, you can see it everywhere in the New Testament letters.

Recovering a Biblical Witness

It is time for a new generation of messengers to emerge who declare Jesus with exceptional clarity to Israel and the nations.

I pray everything we have examined will stir a deeper affection for the Son of Man, and that affection will overflow in a passionate proclamation of the beauty and majesty of the Son of Man. It's time for the church to recover the fullness of the gospel of the kingdom to present Jesus the way He presented Himself.

There are many more passages in the Gospels we could examine, but I sincerely hope what we have examined to this part will radically change the way you read the Bible and will help you continue to discover the majesty and mystery of the Person of Jesus.

Daniel's description of Jesus was filled with majesty, mystery, and awe. We need to recover a sense of all three. Jesus is not just our brother; He is our God. He is a not just a man; He is YHWH. He shares His divinity with His Father, and He shares His humanity with us. The most intimate thing you can do for a person is to share your life with them. Jesus shares the divine life of His Father *and* shares our human life.

In Him, we have been given a profound invitation to intimacy, relationship, communion, and awe. The only reasonable response is our worship *and* our loyalty. While God is just to demand this response, when we see Jesus for who He truly is, this should be the natural reaction to His beauty. We desperately need preachers (which include every human who proclaims Jesus to one or a thousand) who provoke this kind of response when they speak, write, or sing about the Son of Man.

While much more could be said about Daniel and the Gospels, we also need to turn our attention to the rest of the New Testament to see how the apostles used Daniel to proclaim the gospel of the kingdom. We will do that in the next volume.

Appendix

SON OF MAN COMBINED WITH DANIEL THEMES IN THE GOSPELS

When Jesus referred to Himself as the *Son of Man,* He also usually included references or allusions to Daniel. Some were more direct than others. This appendix classifies each use of *Son of Man* in the Gospels according to whether it also directly references or alludes to Daniel. For more on why some of these verses can be considered allusions to Daniel, see the chapter "The Undeniable Link to Daniel" in the first section of this book.

Direct Reference (24 Verses)

These verses contain very clear references to Daniel alongside Son of Man in a single verse.

- Matthew 9:6; Mark 2:10; Luke 5:24; John 5:27—The Son of Man has divine authority to judge (forgive sins).
- Matthew 12:8; Mark 2:28; Luke 6:5—The Son of Man has divine authority over the Sabbath
- Matthew 13:41—The Son of Man comes with His angels to render judgment and purge His kingdom.
- Matthew 16:27; Mark 8:38; Luke 9:26—The Son of Man comes with the glory of His Father and His Father's angels to render judgment.
- Matthew 19:28—The Son of Man will sit on His glorious throne and judge. The kingdom of heaven (v. 14) and treasure in heaven (v. 21) are also mentioned in the passage.
- Matthew 24:30; 26:64; Mark 13:26; 14:62; Luke 21:27— These contain a direct quote of Daniel 7.

- Matthew 25:31—The Son of Man in glory with His angels sits on a throne in judgment.

- Luke 12:8—The Son of Man acts in judgment before the angels of God.

- Luke 17:30—The coming of the Son of Man is like fire raining from heaven.

- Luke 21:36—The Son of Man is describe as a Judge. Verse 27 also contains a quote of Daniel 7.

- John 1:51—The Son of Man is in the heavens, and angels ascend and descend on Him.

- John 3:13—The Son of Man has descended from heaven.

- John 6:62—People will be shocked if they saw the Son of Man ascending to where He was before.

Direct References to Daniel in the Surrounding Chapter (29 Verses)

These verses are found in a chapter containing other references to Son of Man using direct references to Daniel.

Very clear references to Daniel occur in another verse in the chapter where these references occur.

- Matthew 12:40—Jesus predicted the Son of Man will rise in three days and, in verse 8, claims divine authority.

- Matthew 13:37—Verse 41 contains an explicit reference to the Son of Man, His angels, and His kingdom.

- Matthew 16:13—In verse 27, Jesus predicts the Son of Man will come in judgment, in the glory of His Father, and with His Father's angels.

- Matthew 16:28—The Son of Man will come in His kingdom. The previous verse predicts this will happen when He comes in His Father's glory and with His Father's angels to render judgment.

- Matthew 17:9; Mark 9:9—Jesus commented on the transfiguration, which is a scene from Daniel. Jesus also predicts His resurrection.

- Matthew 26:2—Jesus explicitly quoted Daniel 7 in verse 64 and predicted His own suffering.
- Matthew 26:24, 45—Jesus explicitly quoted Daniel 7 in verse 64.
- Matthew 24:27, 37, 39, 44—Jesus predicts the coming of the Son of Man and directly quoted Daniel 7 in verse 30.
- Mark 14:21—Jesus explicitly quoted Daniel 7 in verse 62.
- Mark 14:41—Jesus explicitly quoted Daniel 7 in verse 62.
- Luke 6:22—Jesus described a reward in heaven for those who suffer on account of the Son of Man.
- Luke 9:22, 44—Jesus predicted the Son of Man's suffering, and verse 26 describes the Son of Man coming in His Father's glory with His angels. The passage also includes the transfiguration, which is a Daniel 7 scene.
- Luke 9:58—Jesus described coming as the Son of Man in His Father's glory with His angels in verse 26. The transfiguration is also in the chapter.
- Luke 12:10—Verse 8 describes the Son of Man as Judge in the presence of the angels. Verse 33 describes treasure in heaven, and verse 40 predicts the coming of the Son of Man.
- Luke 12:40—The coming of the Son of Man is predicted. Verse 8 describes the Son of Man as Judge in the presence of the angels, and verse 33 describes treasure in heaven.
- Luke 17:22, 26—The coming of the Son of Man is described. Verse 30 contains a comparison to Daniel, and verse 24 uses dramatic language to describe the coming of the Son of Man.
- Luke 17:24—Verse 30 compares the coming of the Son of Man to fire raining from heaven, which alludes to Daniel 7.
- Luke 22:22, 48—Jesus explicitly quoted Daniel 7 in verse 69.
- John 3:14—The Son of Man must be lifted up. Jesus described Himself in verse 13 as the Son of Man who descended from heaven.

- John 6:27, 53—The Son of Man is the living Bread which came from heaven and can give eternal life (verses 33, 38, 50–51). People would be shocked if they saw the Son of Man ascend to where He came from in verse 62.

Allusions to Daniel (7 Verses)

These verses include ideas that are allusions to main themes in Daniel. The allusions either appear in the verse or in surrounding verses as indicated below.

- Matthew 10:23—The verse describes the coming of the Son of Man in vague terms. However, in verse 32, Jesus is described as sitting in judgment with the Father, who is referenced as the Father in heaven in verses 32–33.

- Matthew 12:32—In verse 40, Jesus' suffering and resurrection in three days are predicted, and in verse 50, Jesus refers to the Father in heaven.

- Luke 18:8—The Son of Man is coming as Judge to bring justice.

- Luke 22:69—The Son of Man is seated at the right hand of the power of God.

- John 12:23, 34—The Son of Man must be lifted up and glorified.

- John 9:35—In verse 39, Jesus predicted He came into the world for judgment.

References to Suffering (13 Verses)

These verses describe the suffering of the Son of Man, including the prediction He will die and rise in three days. In light of Jesus' use of Daniel, references to suffering should viewed as allusions to Daniel when Son of Man language is present. See the section "The Son of Man's Suffering" for more reasons why these are significant references.

- Matthew 20:28; Mark 10:45—This verse describes the Son of Man's death as a ransom, but in Matthew 20:18 (and also Mark 10:33), the suffering of the Son of Man is predicted.

- Matthew 17:12; Mark 9:12—The Son of Man will suffer.

- Matthew 17:22; 20:18; Mark 10:33—The Son of Man will be delivered over for suffering (*delivered* is language drawn from

Daniel 7:25). Mark also contains a reference to treasure in heaven in Mark 10:21.

- Mark 8:31; 9:31; 11:30—The Son of Man will suffer and rise after three days.

- Luke 18:31—Jesus also predicts the Son of Man will rise on the third day in verse 33.

- Luke 24:7—Angels speak about the suffering of the Son of Man.

- John 8:28—Jesus references the Father and predicts His suffering.

No Apparent Reference to Daniel (6 Verses)
These are verses that use the title Son of Man but do not include any references or allusions to Daniel other than the phrase Son of Man.

- Matthew 8:20; 11:19; Luke 7:34; 11:30; 19:10; John 13:31.

AUTHOR BIO

Samuel Whitefield's primary labor is as an intercessor in the context of night-and-day prayer. He is also an author and speaker. He is the director of OneKing, a ministry that helps connect the global church to God's purposes for Israel and the nations. He also serves on the leadership team of the International House of Prayer of Kansas City and as faculty at the International House of Prayer University. His passion is to declare the beauty of Jesus until He is loved and adored on earth as He is in heaven (Matthew 6:10; Revelation 5:13).

For additional resources, please visit samuelwhitefield.com.

ACKNOWLEDGMENTS

Thank you to my wife whose labor and sacrifice make it possible for us to engage in the task the Lord has given us.

Thank you to the entire family for enduring the process that produces books like this.

Thank you to Jason Chua and the entire Burning Hearts family for calling a twenty-one-day fast and setting aside that time to study Daniel. I could never have imagined what that fast would produce, and I will be forever grateful for what the Lord gave us during that fast.

Thank you to Jeffrey Jackson for your encouragement and your investment in this project. You played a key role in my decision to prioritize this project and in getting this in print.

Thank you to Edie Mourey for your work on this manuscript. You really went above and beyond on this one. Without you, this book would be very different.

Thank you to the prayer team who faithfully prayed for months over this book. This finished product is a result of your prayers and would not be possible without your labor. Specific thanks to Grant G, Reggie K, Sarah T, Rob G, Penny R, Judy D, Corey R, Alan S, Rui P, Covey M, Salli M, Rick C, Jason P, Wayne H, Julie H, Thomas L, Jian A, Josh J, Benji N, Caleb D, Chris R, Marvin L, Dori L, Renato C, Stephanie J, Sarah C, Chris T, Ian R, Suzanne C, Janee H, Edie M, and Tat S.

Thank you to all those who read early drafts of portions of the book and gave input. Your input was helpful in refining the book.

Thank you to Ed Hackett for your encouragement that the Lord would release wisdom to understand Daniel. You predicted this book five years ago.

Made in the USA
Middletown, DE
05 June 2021